KEN
DODD

KEN DODD

Laughter and Tears

Gus Smith

VIRGIN

First published in Great Britain 1989
by Virgin Books a division of
W H Allen & Co PLC, Sekforde House,
175/9 St John Street, London EC1V 4LL

Copyright © Gus Smith 1989

Set in Palatino by Input Typesetting Ltd, London
Printed and bound in Great Britain by
Biddles Ltd, Guildford and King's Lynn

ISBN 0 491 03504 7

I've always been a salesman, so when I came into the business I decided I was a laughter salesman, and in my little Knotty Ash way I looked into humour to see what it was I was selling.

Ken Dodd

Page 103, 157

CONTENTS

Author's Acknowledgements

I should like to thank a number of people who contributed their time and conversation during the research period for this book. Among them were theatre staffs and managements, impresarios, radio and television production teams; a few people, for reasons I can only respect, wished not to be identified, though their contributions were extremely important to the story.

I am particularly grateful to the following: Dr Anthony Clare, Bobby Jaye, Barney Colehan, Jim Casey, Josef Locke, Dick Condon, Joe Riley, Cyril Critchlow, Ron Harris, Harry Bailey, Dave Grimley, Frank Carson, Terry Warrick, Antony Tuckey, Bill Platt, Michael McClain, Peter Harvey. To Philip Key, show business editor *Liverpool Daily Post* for permission to draw from his personal account of Ken Dodd's early life in Liverpool.

Useful agencies consulted in the course of my research included BBC's Transcript and Tape Unit, *Woman's Own, The Listener, Stage, Radio Times, TV Post, Observer* Colour Magazine, *The Guardian, Yorkshire Post, Daily Express, Manchester Evening News, The Financial Times, The Sunday People, Daily Telegraph, Halifax Evening Courier.*

I am grateful to the BBC and Thames Television library staffs for their valuable assistance, as well as the publishers of the following books: *Make 'em Laugh* by Eric Midwinter (George Allen & Unwin, 1979), *The Best of Parkinson* (Pavilion Books Ltd., 1982), *Funny Way to be a Hero* by John Fisher (Frederick Muller Ltd., 1973), *How Tickled I Am* by Michael Billington (Elm Tree Books, 1977), *It's*

Hello from Me by Ronnie Barker (New English Library, 1988), *The Modern Actor* by Michael Billington (Hamish Hamilton, 1973), *Book of Liverpool Humour* by Tom O'Connor (Headline Publications, 1987), *Tarbuck on Showbiz* (Willow Books, 1985), *And This Is Me* by Mike Yarwood (Jupiter Books, 1974), *Eric & Ernie: The autobiography of Morecambe & Wise* (W,. H. Allen, 1973), *McCartney* by Chris Salewicz (MacDonald & Co., 1986), *Bob Hope: The Road from Eltham* by Charles Thompson (Thames Methuen, 1981).

Introduction

More than once in this book the words 'comic genius' are used to describe Ken Dodd. Anyone lucky enough to have seen his stage act will undoubtedly find them apt and by no means an exaggeration. In fact, after one has described him as clown and jester, myth-maker and balladeer, there is an irresistible urge to sum up with the word 'genius'.

As theatre critic for two decades I was more attuned to the drama of O'Casey, Wilde, Pinter and Shakespeare than the subtle art of the stand-up comedian, yet the gulf is not as wide as some people imagine. Ken Dodd has after all played a Shakespearean role convincingly and performed his own one-man show to critical acclaim.

I was tickled therefore to be asked to do this book about Doddy, as he is affectionately known, mainly on two counts: first, it afforded me a unique opportunity to compare his present-day performance with his London Palladium triumphs in the middle 1960s (where I first encountered his comic genius) and, secondly, to find out how he was coping with the private trauma in his life, i.e. his tax problems and the subsequent court charges. Unsurprisingly, this news rocked the show business world. Furthermore, the case posed a powerful challenge to the comedian's own character. Could he in the best showbiz tradition ensure that the show went on? Or, at the age of sixty, would the strain prove too much even for this resilient Liverpudlian who has never spared himself?

Everyone is familiar with stories of comedians bravely going on stage in spite of personal troubles, even family bereavements. The great Jimmy James, an undeniable influence on Ken Dodd's career, near the end of his glittering career, occasionally entertained his audience although in physical pain. However, the main thrust of *Ken Dodd: Laughter and Tears* is not about his tax dilemma: it is essentially about a man who has been making people laugh for thirty-five years, an instinctively funny man who· can count among his titles the Sage of Knotty Ash. Above all, he is in that noble tradition of genuinely great stage comedians.

CHAPTER 1

'I could never let my audience down'

Grand Theatre, Blackpool, Sunday 16, October, 1988. Exactly at 8.40 the second house curtain was scheduled to rise, but so far there was no visible sign of movement in the long queue extending, snake-like, up the street towards the Opera House and around the theatre in the direction of the stage door. No one complained. For anyone who was even vaguely familiar with a Ken Dodd show knew what to expect. To the constant delight of his loyal audiences, if not his musicians who complained of missing late-night drinks, his stage show invariably overran.

This night's variety show was billed as 'An Evening of Happiness with Ken Dodd & Friends'. From somewhere inside the theatre at that moment laughter erupted – an indication that the first house audience was being entertained merrily. Doddy, as he is affectionately known to his fans and friends in his native Liverpool, was back in Blackpool giving a series of Sunday night shows.

At 8.30, a burly dinner-jacketed man stood on the steps of the theatre and announced in a loud voice that ticketholders would soon be admitted. By now it was noticeable that the first house was beginning to empty and as men, women and children filed into the street some of the children clutched tickling sticks they had purchased in the

Grand Theatre foyer; a few of the parents were holding Ken Dodd records and cassettes of his songs.

At last the people in the queue began to move forward towards the main door in orderly fashion. On this fine night their faces looked cheerful under the street lighting. Facing them were large posters of Ken Dodd, easily recognisable by his protruding front teeth that had long threatened to become a national landmark, bulging eyes, and dark bushy hair that covered his angular head like an umbrella. It was the unmistakable face of a funny-man, at once smiling and mischievous; a face not easy to forget.

In the space of a few minutes the Grand Theatre was filled to capacity. It is a large, though cosy theatre, and from every corner there is a good view of the stage. Small wonder that it is one of the Liverpool comedian's favourite theatres in Britain. At 9.05 the picturesquely named Knotty Ash Philharmonic Orchestra under its musical director, Stanley Clarke, consisting of an organist and a drummer, began to play the opening bars of music, which was a cue for the buzz of conversation in the auditorium to cease.

Suddenly, from the wings bounded Doddy to announce in an excited voice: 'Hello folks, how tickled I h'am to welcome you to our laughter show.' His words were greeted with rapturous applause. Sporting a neat, well-fitting white suit, maroon shirt and red tie and wearing suede shoes and armed inevitably with a small tickling stick, he quickly warmed up his audience with a string of crackling jokes. He managed, almost miraculously, to sustain the patter for minutes on end and scarcely allowed his audience time to draw their breath. Doddy was in exuberant mood and warmth radiated from the stage. There was a 'restive excitement of the circus' about his performance and he quickly confirmed to all and sundry he was a 'celebratory comic'.

From the dress circle he looked taller than his photographs suggested, and although bulky about the waist he could not be described as fat. He moved with the ease of a dancer and his hands, when he used them, were compelling. Despite his years, there was not a tint of grey in his hair and occasionally as he spun gags with bewildering speed, he exposed his teeth, as though they were sparkling pearls. It is no secret that his teeth are insured for £10,000. His voice, soft and cheery, did not grate on the sensitive ear, yet his accent was not particularly Liverpudlian.

Tonight he exuded confidence and employed the accepted technique of the stand-up comic to make his snappy one-liners make their mark. In Doddy's case, his tickling stick is a useful asset. Sometimes he reached out into the stalls in seductive fashion and pointed the stick at an unsuspecting lady, uttering at the same time, 'Would you like a tickle, Missus?' To the more discerning the tickling stick is an obvious phallic symbol, as in the tradition of the jester's slapstick or Mr Punch's truncheon. To children it is nothing more than something they want in their Christmas stockings and the sight of it merely makes them chuckle.

Opening up his audience is a key part of Doddy's act. He himself has described it as like making a flower blossom. 'You go on first of all and you're just a professional idiot. You go on there and make 'em laugh and you promise 'em all sorts of wild things, but gradually, as you gain their confidence, you can see they trust you. They trust you with their minds and personalities.'

Friendly relations were quickly established. He carried on a conversation with his audience and they responded with applause and cheers. He did not spare himself. Tonight, as a promoter of happiness, he made it clear that he was a Liverpool football supporter, but this bold assertion brought jeers from Everton and Manchester United fans. He queried and cajoled. 'All the ladies look tickled tonight,' he cried as he furiously waved his tickling stick. 'Well done, lads.' And: 'Me grandad stood all winter with his back to the fire . . . We had to have him swept . . . I wonder if he can hear us now' . . . (a pause from the audience as the comic stared upwards) . . . 'He's on the roof picking lead.'

Alone on stage he looked eccentric, like a clown in the circus ring. He ran his hand through his hair making it shoot upwards and he stared at the audience as though he had seen a ghost. His performance was all action and he seemed determined not to give poor grandad any respite. 'He's in the Darby and Joan club. I don't know what he does but he's got three notches on his walking-stick.' Next it was men's legs: 'Men's legs have a lonely life. Standing in the dark in your trousers all day.' By now it was obvious that some of the audience did not know which joke they were laughing at, or whether they were laughing at several jokes at the same time. It was a heady tonic that Doddy was dispensing.

As he fired gag after gag at his audience, it was noticeable that he seldom ceased to laugh himself, as if he was intoxicated by the exercise. The heavy make-up on his face, combined with his lunatic expressions created, as one critic aptly put it, 'a fine madness in the spectators'. Undoubtedly Doddy's appearance is half his success. Tonight, there was something strangely frenetic about his performance, as though he dared not stop until he had finished his twenty-minute spot.

Was he using the stage solely as a desperate form of escapism? Perhaps. Gag followed gag but some of the sexual innuendoes were lost on the audience as they failed to keep up with him.

Not all the jokes were exactly new. The one about Widnes had been trotted out before, but it seemed worth repeating: 'That's the place to go for your holidays. The only place where they grow brown daffodils . . . The air there is so strong they pay a man to go round the graveyards saying, "Lie down, lads".'

As the laughter in the auditorium subsided, Doddy

4

announced the next act on the programme: 'For your pleasure . . . It is Sybie Jones . . . our delightful Country and Folk entertainer.' He vanished, leaving the stage to Miss Jones, a smiling, confident woman in her early forties who proceeded to entertain the audience with a lively medley of popular songs. A former Bluebell Girl, it was known by now that she was Doddy's girlfriend. There was no talk of marriage. After fifteen minutes she walked off the stage to gentle applause. It was the cue for Doddy to bounce back, waving his tickling stick and shooting, in machine-gun fashion, a score of gags at the audience.

He introduced the Diddymen, a group of children in bizarre costumes who sang along with him and showed they possessed lots of individual talent. When the comedian created them he added a new word to every household. Diddy is a Dodd family word; his great-uncle was very diminutive. The family nicknamed him 'Diddy' so anything that was cute or lovable was called Diddy from then on by Ken. In time, the Diddymen became a sensation with their own television and radio series. Children loved them.

At 10.15 the interval curtain came down on an audience obviously grateful for a brief respite from laughter. In a way it was a remarkable performance by Doddy. He had managed to conceal any hint of his own private stress, and even if he vaguely touched on his plight it was in a funny fashion. He wanted their laughs and not their sympathy. Avoiding sentiment like the plague, he ensured that the show was like any other Ken Dodd show, a pure celebration of laughter.

As he retired to his dressing-room, where he was joined by Sybie Jones, Doddy was able to relax. The show so far had gone with a swing. With Sybie, who knew the business, he felt no strain. It was she who urged him to keep working in order to forget his personal problems. It had not been easy. Once, at an airport, when he was surrounded by photographers, she tried to protect him. It was one of the very few occasions when the comedian vented his anger publicly. Sensing the torment he was going through, Sybie admired his courage. At least, she told herself, he had no pressures on stage. He could forget those events that otherwise tended to haunt him.

Early in that June of 1988 the show business world, as well as Doddy's friends and fans, had been taken utterly by surprise when the newspapers disclosed that comic Ken Dodd would be appearing in court in connection with tax returns. He would face eighteen charges. That week he was appearing at the Arcadia Theatre in Llandudno and on arrival at the theatre he was met by the press. It was an embarrassing moment for a man who usually basked in a different kind of limelight. Looking upset, he told reporters: 'The matter is in the hands of my solicitors. I can't say any more.'

For three years tax investigators had combed his bank accounts in England and the Channel Islands and the companies, Ken Dodd Enterprises, Diddy Scripts, and Happiness Music. It was stated that the Inland Revenue 'only prosecuted cases where they believed tax returns were less than frank'. In showbiz circles it was claimed that Ken Dodd had been earning an estimated £10,000 a week for many years. That same June day the papers highlighted the story of Lester Piggott, the jailed racing idol, who was reported to have wept in his cell when told that the Queen had stripped him of his OBE. At this time Piggott was serving a three-year sentence for a £3 million tax fraud.

It was inevitable that the sensational Piggott case would focus intense interest on the Ken Dodd affair. He had been awarded the OBE on Mrs Thatcher's recommendation in 1982 for his services to charitable causes. The possibility, however remote, of the popular comic's being stripped of that honour made many of his fans shudder. Similarly, any talk of a prison sentence was too appalling to contemplate. A few of the Fleet Street tabloids took a far less sympathetic view. One was downright hostile and accused him of being 'one of the meanest men in show business'. It seemed a curious label to pin on a man who made millions laugh.

Ken Dodd was not in court in Liverpool for the preliminary hearing; he had flown to Gatwick to attend the funeral of his former friend and agent, Dave Forrester. More than anyone else, he had been the man who helped launch Doddy on the road to stardom. Now, wearing a dark suit, the comedian looked pale and drawn as he joined mourners at the Jewish cemetery in Hove, East Sussex. He was shielded by six acquaintances and refused to talk to the media.

Later that August, the comedian's personal trauma continued when he appeared at Liverpool Stipendiary Magistrates Court and was ordered to surrender his passport. The court was told that Mr Dodd may flee the country to avoid facing trial on tax evasion charges.' The claim was strenuously denied by Ken Dodd's lawyer who said he had no intention of leaving Britain. The number of tax accusations against him amounted to twenty-seven, and he was committed for trial at Liverpool Crown Court. Bail was fixed with two sureties of £25,000 each. They were lodged by Ken Dodd's brother, William, and his girlfriend Sybil Jones.

Mr Peter Cockin, prosecuting, said the case was causing the Inland Revenue 'grave concern' and he added, 'The case has become much more serious simply because of the potential sentence.' No figure of the alleged amount of tax owed was disclosed during the 25-minute hearing, but sums of £350,000 and £475,000 were mentioned relating to a period up to April that year. Mr David Hartnett, who led the Inland Revenue investigation, told the court that in the last few days he had received information from a professional person, and he added, 'This suggests that Mr Dodd may not be at the trial which is to take place.'

The lawyer for the comedian, Miss Susan Klonin, told

the court, 'Mr Dodd is anxious that his protestations of innocence are given as wide a coverage as the fact that the allegations have been made against him. He proposes to stand trial and he has been co-operating fully with the Inland Revenue.'

It came as a surprise to some to learn that the comic was not in the best of health. Miss Klonin explained that doctors had advised her client to take a summer break and he needed a holiday because he suffered from bronchitis and emphysema. Mr Hartnett disclosed that an offer of payment had been made. As he sat in court, Doddy looked a solitary figure. He was seen to shake his head as the Stipendiary Magistrate ordered that his passport be surrendered, although he was told that he could apply for its return for a specific period.

Although obviously shaken by the court events and the wide publicity, the popular comedian was encouraged by his friends in Liverpool to battle on. Many messages poured into his home and soon he was able to declare, 'Nothing will stop the laughter.' It was the old Doddy talking, and he added bravely, 'I would never let my audience down. My business problems count for nothing when I'm on stage. I've made my life out there making millions of other people laugh. They expect that from me and I'm determined not to let this court case get in the way.'

He promised to fulfil every engagement in his diary. One of the first was at the Floral Hall in the Northern seaside resort of Southport, where as usual he planned to give two shows nightly. A capacity second house awaited him. He had lost nothing of his familiar vibrancy, though afterwards he admitted to a close newspaper friend, 'I can't deny I'm worried about the future, who wouldn't be?' But he said it was his policy through life to drown each moment of sorrow with more laughter. He doesn't smoke, but that evening he sounded breathless and chesty after years of suffering from bouts of bronchitis and emphysema.

The theatre staff had observed the comedian closely. One of them, Mervyn Sperrin, said, 'Some nights they pack the place and you often hear them discussing Ken's problems. However, they all seem to be on his side. I've not heard one word accusing him of being a cheat or a fiddler. They love him up here.' And the comedian's booking manager, Keith McAndrew, said he was amazed that he carried on cracking jokes. 'Even I expected that Ken would suffer during these difficult times and perhaps get a bit weary of it all. I've got to admit he hasn't. There are times when I know he is worried about it but he never once lets his audience feel it. Ken knows they are behind him and it helps him to carry on. When all this is over he won't have changed one little bit. He will be the same man who only really comes to life when he's on stage, warming up the audience until he's got them eating out of his hand. His is a very rare talent and he knows it. That's why he keeps on working so hard – he'd hate to think that anyone had missed out on the fun'.

Back in the Grand Theatre, Blackpool, people relaxed with drinks in the bar or ate their icecreams; others remained in their seats talking or reading their programmes. Leafing through the pages they were instantly reminded of the highlights of Doddy's glittering career in showbiz. He was pictured with royalty as well as politicians and colleagues such as Norman Wisdom, Ted Ray, Jack Benny, Bud Flanagan, Terry-Thomas and Frankie Vaughan. There was a smiling photograph of the comedian himself with the caption, 'Ken Dodd, OBE'. And in between the photographs, Doddy had this to say: 'To me the finest music in the world is the sound of rich human belly laughs cascading cacophonies of chuckles – great giggling guffaws. I'd like to form a laughter orchestra – we could practise in the House of Commons.'

In *'In Praise of Laughter'* he observed, 'There's nothing quite like laughter – it's a tonic – it's a cure for the blues – a relief in times of tension . . . a universal language that everyone understands.'

Such words seemed to provoke some discussion on Doddy's own problems. But these people in the dress circles were his fans; he could depend on their loyalty. To most of them Lester Piggott was a star jockey with a string of wins to his credit. Doddy was different. He provided them with laughs on cold nights. It was inconceivable that anything awful should happen to him. Even now they could not wait for the curtain to rise on the second half of the show.

CHAPTER 2

'For we all need friends, don't we?'

The 'Evening of Happiness' resumed on time with music-
man Paul Connor entertaining the audience to a medley of
tunes that included a nostalgic tribute to Benny Goodman.
Blackpool audiences, weaned on sea and sunshine, like to
sing along to popular melodies and tonight in the Grand
Theatre they were in good voice.

Nonetheless, everyone knew that Doddy's act would
dominate most of this half of the show and he would not
begrudge the audience an extra thirty minutes of fun.
Like the great Jimmy James, he had no qualms about
overrunning his time, occasionally improvising on the
spur of the moment. They could expect a rundown of
Doddy's colourful vocabulary, words like 'tattiphilarious',
'diddilation' and 'goolified' and phrases such as 'Nikky
Nokky Noo' and 'Bunk-A-Doodle-I-Do'; and if they were
lucky enough he might even entertain them on 'The Great
Drum of Knotty Ash', and perhaps spin off the romantic
escapades of amorous Liverpudlians, Russians and Ital-
ians. Doddy's comedy canvas stretched into every corner
of the globe and he had an accent to suit most of its
inhabitants.

Eventually, when he skipped on stage in bright suit
and shoes, he was greeted by the kind of spontaneous
applause that is reserved for the appearance of the Liverpool football team at Anfield. With a sweep of his tickling

stick, he silenced his boisterous audience and instantly began to roll off with the speed of a machine gun, a dozen gags, most of them with some sexual innuendo. As for the jokes directed at the people in the front rows of the stalls, it was soon difficult to decide whether the women were laughing the most; certainly they were as tickled as the menfolk.

Someone has said that Doddy doesn't tell a joke – he detonates it. His act was now proving to be a carefully planned succession of *double-entendres* and he was heard to quip above the applause, 'For all those people who like good clean fun we have the exit.' He looked as if he meant it.

On stage Dodd's laughter is raucous, his energy incredible. To entertain his audience, he spares neither himself – nor them. He sees them as a collection of old friends. 'You gain their trust and then it becomes like a party.' In thirty-five years he claims never to have given the same performance twice, because no two audiences are the same. 'I never do a show *at* an audience. I do a show *with* an audience.'

In reality, what he offers an audience is a mixture of inspired one-liners, whimsical verbal invention, refined insults and unrepentant rudery. He seems obsessed, as one North country critic observed, by 'the anatomical absurdity of the human body'. Dodd's plans for the reorganisation of the human frame are surreal. He favours a mouth in the top of one's head so that one can pop a sandwich under one's hat and eat it on the way to work. An eye at the end of the index finger opens up possibilities that need no further elaboration.

It is no coincidence that when he recalls a particularly successful performance, he will say, 'By heck we took no prisoners tonight.' Looking at him now, sending ripples of laughter through the crowded theatre, prompted the question: 'How has he hooked his audiences? What makes them howl helplessly at him?' Sometimes it's his brand of absurd mockery, his mad invention, and his comments about people's habits, television and topicalities like the birth pill and the occupant of 10 Downing Street, have a happy honesty about them which forges an unbreakable bond with the audience.

Doddy is the only North country comic to turn a common-or-garden phrase for a slice of bread – a jam butty – into a huge joke, and is now confronted with varieties of this gag wherever he goes. The Lord Mayor of Liverpool once entertained him to lunch and instructed the butler to serve the star a silver tray-full of jam butties. Doddy was greatly tickled. And tonight he laced his madcap humour with some jam-butty jokes of Knotty Ash vintage. It was clear there was a loving relationship between the comic and his audience. He is devoid of the cynicism of Tommy Trinder, and the smooth delivery of Dave Allen; instead, he gets his results by a happy combination of frenzy and zaniness. He doesn't complain, except when his gags are pinched, especially when pinched by Liverpool comedians.

He had by now warmed up his audience to the point where they answered him back good-humouredly, and occasionally one of his musicians acted as his feedman. He began a quick rundown of British seaside resorts, describing them as glamorous places with palm trees and sunshine. 'Widnes,' he continued gleefully,' you'll find on the banks of the Mersey, where the fish bribe the anglers to pull them out.'

Once before in his television show, *Wait While . . .*, Doddy had run into trouble when he reported on 'Beautiful, Breathtaking Widnes' which he described as a holiday resort on the banks of the sun-soaked 'Costa del Mersey'. He told thousands of viewers that Widnes was famous for its five-star chip shops and multi-storey betting offices – showing a picture of the town's police headquarters as he made this quip.

There was swift reaction from the townspeople. An

esteemed Alderman thought the programme was very good and admitted he laughed his head off. Two house-wives, on the other hand, found it 'offensive'. One com-mented, 'I thought that Doddy was just slurring Widnes by showing the slums and derelict parts of the town. He could have shown some of the nicer parts.' However one local gentleman thought that Doddy's comical look at Widnes presented a true picture. 'If any councillors,' he said, 'were watching the programme they ought to feel ashamed.'

The irony was that hundreds of people who tuned into BBC-1 on Channel 2 were disappointed, because they got the Jimmy Savile Show instead. Doddy didn't feel ashamed and admitted he loved Widnes. 'By jove, it's breath-taking,' he quipped.

Because he is essentially a visual comic and pulls a variety of funny faces to colour his gags, as well as deploy-ing lots of accents, it is virtually impossible to capture in dry print the full flavour of Ken Dodd's act. The heady atmosphere in which he operates is also difficult to convey to people outside the theatre who have not witnessed his garish appearance. A critic once claimed that Doddy was a 'manic comedian'. It is true; his whole approach is fren-etic and, mentally, he is invariably ahead of his audience.

What endears him to women in particular – and they form sixty percent of his audience – is that he is neither aggressive nor cruel. When he says, for instance, that he brought his grandad to Eastbourne 'to meet girls of his own age' he is celebrating old age, not denigrating it. Obviously he has studied the ways of old people. Age holds a curious fascination for him in the same way that the language of ordinary people fascinates playwright Harold Pinter.

With his indefatigable zest for life, Doddy likes to say he is young at heart and never wants to be described as 'a veteran entertainer'. Yet he enjoys retailing jokes about old people, though never wickedly. Tonight, as he aimed his tickling stick towards the balcony, he asked with a smile, 'How does a lady know she is growing old?' and almost instantly he began to answer his own question, 'Ladies, you know you are growing old when your children begin taking you home early from parties. "Come on Gran, you have to go home now. You have a big date to-morrow: you're having your feet done." '

The critic Michael Billington tried to analyse the Ken Dodd cult in the Sixties and Seventies and decided he was 'a comic genius'. Doddy, he reckoned, owed much of his stage success to 'outrageous gear' and his zany appearance. He saw him as a liberator of instincts, 'a man who speaks from the back of his mind to the back of ours and who rids us of many of our inhibitions, guilts and fears'.

There were others who saw Doddy as the complete entertainer, a comic for all seasons. They were fascinated by his eccentric appearance on stage. 'He looks like a startled rabbit,' commented one Southern critic. Once, in Bournemouth, he darted on stage in a mustard-yellow suit with bowler hat to match and sporting an outsize sunflower with obvious connotations. Everyone remarked on his communication with the audience, something he has cultivated since the early fifties when he was a part-time entertainer.

To author Eric Midwinter, it was the Ken Dodd technique that made his act endure after the acts of many other comics had faded from the variety stage. Immaculate timing coupled with audience rapport were, in his estimation, two of the comic's greatest assets. And he saw merit in his singing. 'Ken uses his unpretentious love-songs as balm for the sore carcasses of his watchers, relaxing them with the warm, quiet sentiment of those melodies, the lull before another hailstorm of wisecracks. Not that he is averse to sending up these same popular ditties, changing *Love is Like a Violin* to *Love is Like a Set of Bagpipes!*'

Billington also speaks of 'Dodd's complex and paradoxical nature,' and came to know the man as well as the performer. He was saddened by the disclosure of the comedian's tax problems. 'Whenever I have seen him there has been a two-way current of affection between him and the onlookers; they came out charged and refreshed from seeing him and he obviously gets a kind of high from their laughter and delight.'

Just now it seemed that Doddy needed all the support he could get to keep his morale, as well as confidence, high. Yet he was coping well, even if at times his bronchitis and emphysema made life a little uncomfortable; he admitted he had his 'highs' and 'lows'.

It was after 11 o'clock in the Grand Theatre and Doddy was still firing a fusillade of jokes at his audience. His humour touched on 'television filth' and 'video nasties' and he said he was outraged by the scenes . . . 'Fancy anyone paying good money to watch someone with long hair and buck teeth!' He parodied the popular musical, *The Maid of the Mountains*, as well as Mario Lanza: 'Be my love, and no one else will do my laundry.' And *Trees*: 'I talk to the trees, that is why they took me away.'

It was time to dispense with the tickling stick and replace it with a big Sally-Ally-style drum, and he proceeded to bang at it furiously as he sang snatches of old songs. At odd moments he seemed on the brink of running out of inspiration, but relied on his technique to pull him through, as well as a few songs that might have been best left in cobwebs. The tempo rose when he began to sing *Tears*, the ballad synonymous with his act. The fans joined in the chorus.

To some members of the audience it seemed that Doddy sang the lyrics with more than ordinary feeling. He looked visibly moved. Did it suggest that at times on stage now he was being assailed, ever so fleetingly, by the awesome spectre of the court trial awaiting him? The comic would say it was not true, so would Sybie Jones, but there were those close to him in the theatre who suspected that he was haunted by his own personal trauma. Tonight his laughter sometimes seemed forced, if not downright nervous, yet it was almost impossible for the majority of the audience to detect anything unusual in Doddy's appearance or performance.

In his light grey suit he looked less eccentric than usual. He introduced little Dicky Mint, the tiny ventriloquist's dummy who was once described as Doddy's leading Diddy Man. Known to millions of television viewers, Dicky was once stolen from Ken's car and a special reward was offered for his return. Now the duo carried on a lighthearted conversation, with Doddy showing the skills he had learned years before when he acquired his first dummy. Suddenly he broke into song, 'Where there are grey skies . . . I don't mind those grey skies . . . You make them blue, sonny boy . . . Friends may forsake you. . . .'

Inevitably, a few people in the theatre were reminded of the comic's private problems by his singing of 'grey skies', but Doddy gave no hint whatever of his private anguish. He was constantly being reassured by the laughter around him. And in a quiet voice, he added, 'For we all need friends, don't we . . . *I do.*'

It was time for what Doddy called 'the Grand Eurovision Song Contest'. He began to sing, 'There's nothing left for me of days that used to be. . . .' Once more the exuberant audience joined in the singalong. Doddy's voice is baritonal in quality, sonorous in tone, and warm in texture. He sings with great feeling for the words and is part of that tradition of comedians who like to finish their act with a song.

True, there was a time when the audience did not take his singing seriously, but that had changed. Like Harry Secombe, Doddy was now accepted as jester and singer. Secombe, with his four-octave tenor voice, charmed audiences and his talent in this field, as well as his clowning, gave him mass appeal. Doddy's singing, though enjoyed by audiences, never quite equalled Secombe's, but it remains a real boost to his comedy act.

Now, as Stanley Clarke and the orchestra serenaded the audience, Doddy performed a tap dance in rhythm with the music. Dedication time arrived. He announced, 'I dedicate this song to all those silver blondes present. It is *The Sunshine of Your Smile*. We sang it the other night at the mission and, believe me friends, I was more than a little touched!'

The audience joined in the chorus and their voices filled the grand old theatre. Suddenly, Doddy exclaimed, waving his tickling stick at nowhere in particular, 'There are a few ugly people in the audience tonight. I won't say who they are. They know where they're sitting.' He chuckled as he tried to repair the damage, 'I'm kidding. You're a beautiful audience. Some lovely brunettes among you, some gorgeous blondes. We have also some lovely silver blondes. If there is any gentleman in this theatre looking for a steady girl – or one a bit unsteady – find yourself a silver blonde; they are the most wonderful women in all the world. Get one over fifty, they're the best. Why? They don't yell, they don't tell, and they are as grateful as hell.'

As though eager to increase the tempo, he switched to funny one-liners. 'He is a comedian who works in terms of images,' remarked one critic, and tonight he wise-cracked about the 'absurdities' of the National Health Service, foreign medicos, frisky ladies and transplants. To the older members of the audience, Doddy's act doubtless recalled memories of the Music Hall, of comics like Billy Bennett, famous for his bizarre fantasy coupled with down to earth humour, George Formby's 'cheeky gentleness', Frankie Howerd's broad and brazen approach, and the genius of George Robey.

However, they would all agree that Kenneth Arthur Dodd was unique, a stand-up comic who made them cry as well as laugh. Although obviously tired, the older members of the audience remained in their seats anxious not to miss a single gag. It was by now pushing midnight and Doddy, as usual, had overrun. In quiet tones, he recalled some of the famed comedians who had played Blackpool, Dave Morris, little Jimmy Clitheroe, Frank Randle and others. And he reminded them, 'I have been coming here since the early Fifties and that is a long time and I thank you once again for proving that Blackpool is the greatest show town in the entire world . . . here is a little song that says thank you. Let's all sing it together. We have such a lot to be thankful for. . . .'

To the audience, the song was more in the nature of a hymn and began with the words, 'Oh, Lord, my God . . .' Doddy sang it with deep emotion and afterwards was greeted with prolonged applause. For his friends in the audience, it was undoubtedly a reminder of the comedian's faith in the Lord, something he had never disguised. As long as the shadow of the impending trial hung over him the song, like most other things, seemed at this time to have a deeper meaning.

The mood changed as Doddy burst into his favourite song, *Happiness*. He sang it with gusto: 'Happiness, happiness, the greatest gift we possess. . . .'

Doddy was still singing on stage as the audience filed slowly out of the theatre.

CHAPTER 3

'I think he must be a sad man'

Outside the theatre some of Doddy's faithful fans hurried in the direction of the stage door, a short distance around the corner. It was by now 12.15 a.m. and the night was still fine, the Blackpool air bracing. A few minutes later the comedian opened the door and greeted the fans warmly.

In the half-light, he laughed as he exchanged words and he did not hesitate to autograph their programmes. For a worried man, he looked relaxed. Despite two shows that evening, he did not seem tired. Two women pressed forward: 'We'll pray for you, Doddy.' He shook their hands, 'By jove, that's nice of you,' he said gaily.

He wished the fans good-night and closed the stage door gently behind him. They walked away, happy and reassured. They liked to think they were his friends as well as his fans. Not a few would go back to the Sunday show. It was the kind of loyalty that Doddy instilled in people; the loyalty that he himself expected from the people he entertained. They were all his audience. In turn, the more sensitive of them recognised the anxiety he was feeling, the cloud that hung over him. It was something they had never visualised would happen to their favourite comic.

It was known in the business, however, that Doddy was able to laugh about his personal problem. There was the story of the comedian going into the Inland Revenue and planting a Stradivarius on the desk and saying, 'How's that for a million-pound fiddle!' And the one about Lester Piggott, who at that time was serving a prison sentence for failing to pay tax demands. Doddy would joke, 'If Lester is still in prison when I get there, I'll throw a house warmer for him!' Bernard Manning, as owner, compére and top attraction at his own Embassy Club in Manchester, liked, as he said, to remember his friend Doddy in his gags. 'At the club I make jokes about Ken and his prosecution by the tax-man, and they love it. I tell them, "He's stage-struck and won't come off. This trial of his, if he gets two years, he'll do four!" '

Doddy's dilemma was a talking-point wherever his old colleagues in the business met. The Irish tenor, Josef Locke, who once shared top of the bill with the comedian in Blackpool and who is now living in retirement in Ireland, felt sorry for him in the same way that he did for Lester Piggott. 'Ken has entertained so many people and made so many of them laugh that he deserves better than this,' argued Locke.

During his golden years in Blackpool, Josef Locke had always been billed as 'The World's Greatest Music-Hall Tenor' and he enjoyed enormous success. But in the late Fifties he was beset by tax problems and faced a bill of £17,000 from the Inland Revenue. He quit England and the entertainment scene there for some years; however he later returned to pay his tax arrears.

'At the time,' Locke recalled good-humouredly, 'Ken Dodd used to joke about Joe's tax problem and he kept the joke going for a long time. There was no malice in it. I didn't mind a bit. I have always regarded him as a marvellous comic.'

Now, the tenor was able to identify with Doddy's tax problem, and knew the anguish he was going through. 'Pay up,' was his advice to anyone entangled with the Inland Revenue. 'Join them, you can't beat them. I learned that.' Like Locke, comedian Harry Bailey was a favourite with Blackpool audiences and thought that Ken Dodd owed much of his success to his funny appearance on stage and his fine voice. Now retired in a seaside resort outside Dublin, Bailey was surprised when he first heard of Doddy's tax troubles and felt sympathy for him. 'I know what he's feeling,' he said. 'When I came back to Ireland and built an extension to my bungalow the Irish Inland Revenue came down on me like a ton of bricks. I had no option but to pay up.'

The ebullient Frank Carson likes to say, 'I was born to make people laugh. It's my mission in life. I'm a very happy man.' He first met Ken Dodd when the Liverpool comic was a guest star at a Butlin's holiday camp in Wales and they have remained good friends. Carson himself left Northern Ireland twenty-three years ago but still speaks about 'going home' to Belfast. He admits his roots are strong and childhood memories remain vivid. As a little boy, he wanted to go on stage; later he had a special ambition 'to play Blackpool'. He was to achieve it in the early Sixties, where he soon joined stars such as Josef Locke, Dicky Valentine, Frankie Howerd and Ken Dodd in the popular summer shows.

When the news of Doddy's tax problems was first revealed in court, Carson was one of the first people in the business to sympathise with him. As they worked together in radio in subsequent weeks Carson was prepared to listen if Doddy cared to raise the subject of his personal problem, but mostly they loved to share jokes. 'Ken always makes me laugh,' says Carson, 'and I think I can do the same for him.' He decided that Doddy was bearing up well, though on occasions the strain showed.

To Carson, who is a funny man both on and off stage, it was important that Doddy should keep working so that he would forget the anguish. He had always regarded him as a gifted comic. 'I like his style; he is a quick-fire comic who can go on for hours and hours telling jokes. It is his face, though, that is his greatest asset. Ken has only to walk on stage to raise a laugh. Where else would you get his teeth? They're a comic showpiece. And his hair? It's a marvel of invention. He is easily the best front cloth comedian in the country – and he is brilliant on radio. We want nothing to happen to him.'

That morning in the plush foyer of a Blackpool hotel Frank Carson sipped a beer and paused for a moment. He was no longer smiling when he said, 'This is a terrible trauma hanging over Ken. I feel for him. As a performer though, I know it will not affect him. I was once fighting a case in the courts – not a tax case – and I was six hours on end in the witness box. It was a gruelling experience. But each evening I went along to the theatre and did two shows. As soon as I walked on stage and took the mike in my hand the old adrenalin flowed and I forgot the court experience altogether. The truth is that audiences don't want to know about your problems. They have paid their money to be entertained, but in Ken Dodd's case I expect many people in his audiences secretly sympathise with him.'

The attitude of the media has been important to Doddy during these difficult times. It is known that he was hurt as well as angered by some reporting of his tax problems; a few of the tabloids became 'personal' and raked up stories about his past. Long before this, he had blacklisted all but two Fleet Street Sunday papers because, he asserted, they had invented stories about his showbiz career and his personal life. When one reporter accused him of telling an old joke he replied bluntly, 'There's no such thing as an old joke. Only one you've heard recently.'

But the press in Liverpool had been, for the most part, fair and balanced in its attitude to the comedian. Two of the city's leading show business critics, Philip Key and Joe Riley, have followed Doddy's career closely. The perceptive Key refers to him as 'Doddy' or 'old Doddy' and is an undoubted admirer of his talent; Riley, a lively columnist as well as a respected critic, invariably calls the comedian 'Ken Dodd' out of respect and friendship.

To Philip Key, a Londoner who settled easily into the more leisurely pace of Liverpool life, the Dodd phenomenon had endured because of the sheer professionalism of the comedian. 'I think he is married to show business, and is a workaholic.' Since Doddy's court case he himself was placed under certain pressure to get *that* exclusive story. It was pressure from outside. As a newspaper man, he was always in the market for 'exclusives', but for a long time he enjoyed a good relationship with Doddy and was reluctant now to exploit that friendship.

To Key, who had spent hours talking to the comedian since the Seventies, Doddy had the sympathy of the Liverpool people, though there were people who reckoned he was foolish to 'find himself in such a situation'. He himself was inclined to blame the professional advisers around him, the accountants. What he really needed was a very astute business manager.

Key, a staffer on the *Post*, the Liverpool daily newspaper, has long regarded Doddy as 'a loner', yet he dismissed the allegation made in a Fleet Street tabloid that the comedian was 'mean'. He was aware that he had done a lot for charity. Always in his own dealings with him he had found him sincere and unpretentious, never mean.

By early November Joe Riley, who is attached to the *Echo*, Liverpool's evening newspaper, had given a lot of thought to the Ken Dodd case. He knew it was being discussed in private, that people in the city were wondering how Ken was 'bearing up to the problem'. He himself had no fears in this respect.

To Riley, as he sat by his desk in the open space of the *Echo* newsroom, there was a good deal of irony in the case. As he explained, 'The irony is of a comic in the dock. The whole imagery of that before you even get to Ken Dodd is ironic inasmuch as that here is a man who has brought a lot of happiness to the world now enduring a lot of sadness. That in itself is emotive and should anything happen to him as a result of this case there would be a dreadful sadness of a really nice man being affected.'

As in Blackpool and Manchester, the Dodd *cause célèbre* had become the butt of numerous jokes. Joe Riley was aware of the trend and thought it was not surprising to find it happening in Liverpool. 'In Liverpool we call it the humour of survival; it is black humour based on the fact that Liverpool is all about irony and cynicism, but there's nothing malicious about it.'

He had studied Doddy's stage technique and decided he was by far the best manipulator of theatre audiences he had ever encountered. 'He is the last of the theatricals who served their apprenticeship in the theatre and not in the hi-tech of television where you can do a take and retake until you get it right. The chemistry between Ken Dodd and his audience is absolutely unrivalled in any genre. I always find his performance funny because I enjoy the enjoyment of the audience.'

To Riley, Doddy's stage act was not unique as some people claimed. It was based, he felt, on Max Miller. 'If you look at a Max Miller script and the way he worked an audience in the old theatrical garnish sense – funny hats and baggy trousers – you can see the comparison.' Another irony existed in regard to Ken Dodd; it was the popular conception that he was tight-fisted. He thought that this had sprung from the fact that the comic himself had avoided a glamorous life-style and instead chosen to live in the house in which he was born. He never moved away from his roots. Furthermore, his own shows were run on a tight budget and little money was spent on supporting acts and this gave the impression of meanness.

None the less, Joe Riley considered the Liverpool comic generous with the thing that rich men were not generous with – their time. As he explained, 'Ken Dodd gives his time to people; he visits friends in hospital and doesn't forget the sick. This can occupy a deal of his spare time. After his shows he may sit in his dressing-room and talk to friends without any eye on the clock. In my own case, I have sat with him until midnight and I was not treated as the critic of the local paper, but rather as a friend. In conversation he avoids small talk and prefers to bring you up to date with current news or about mutual friends. So it annoys me to hear him labelled mean. In fact, he is one of the most generous people I know.'

Since the August court hearing, Riley had shared drinks with the comedian and concluded that he must be a very sad man because he must feel let down and perhaps a sense of disillusion too. The majority of people, though, in Liverpool were on Ken Dodd's side.

As far as Philip Key was concerned the year 1988 had opened brightly for Ken Dodd. He had driven to the resort of Southport to review the latest Doddy Laughter Show. The format was familiar, he had heard a few of the jokes before, yet he laughed – and that was important to him. As Key recalled, 'Doddy likes his audience to talk back, often involving them in the show. One of his gimmicks is to get a confederate to enter the auditorium as a late-comer looking for a seat. He makes the side-kick sit on the lap of a suitably jolly-looking lady in the front row. This can prove dangerous for the confederate. On one occasion he was fondled in enthusiastic fashion by the chosen lady, and on another, an angry husband laid the poor fellow out.'

As usual the show overran, but no one seemed to complain. Philip Key decided, 'Anarchic as Doddy's act might seem, it is honed with a professional craftsmanship to the last word. He is a great believer in using the right rhythm of speech, selecting the proper word and getting everything as exact as possible for the greatest possible effect. The result remains the fastest and funniest act in the business.'

When Key popped round to the comedian's dressing-room at the end of the second house performance, he found him in loquacious mood. He joked about his friend Frank Carson and the radio game, *Pull the Other One*, in which both regularly participated. Said Doddy, 'Frank went secretly, without my knowing, to the show's producer and complained that Ken Dodd wouldn't let him get a word in on the show. Frank Carson! There's not many people who could be accused of out-talking him.'

The conversation turned to show business. Doddy was convinced that the whole pattern had changed. As he put it, 'Now it's a case of one or two-nighters. Southport, which doesn't follow trends, it sets them, started it off. Llandudno will be another regular stopping-off place on my summer schedule.'

He now reckoned he covered 75,000 miles in a year on the whistle-stop tours, playing motorway yo-yo. Southport appealed to him. He produced his own shows there, thus combining performer and presenter. He laughed as he described it as 'the Monte Carlo of Merseyside', and added, 'You may need a calendar to discover the day of the year on which the tide comes in, but it has golden beaches – it is the centre of the egg industry – and the largest donkeys in the country!'

As Doddy reminisced about his childhood and why he always 'dared to be different', Key found him even more forthcoming than usual; yet as he prepared to leave the dressing-room and drive back to Liverpool he could not have guessed that inside a few months the comic would be assailed by anxiety about the future.

As the general manager of the Theatre Royal, Norwich, Dick Condon met, or engaged, most of the current British showbiz stars. He became friendly with a few, among them Ken Dodd, and regarded him simply as a 'comic genius'. Condon, grey-haired and articulate, at that time also managed the revived D'Oyly Carte Company and this morning was relaxing over coffee in the ornate setting of the Savoy Hotel in London. Upstairs singers were being auditioned for forthcoming Gilbert and Sullivan productions.

When Condon first heard the news of Ken Dodd's tax dilemma he felt instant compassion, as if a close relative was unexpectedly charged with a serious criminal offence. Ever since he had first met him in the early Seventies, he had liked him as an individual. As a performer, he now felt there was tremendous pressure on him and occasionally he wondered if it would not prove too much. Nothing had been proved against him, but the burden of suspicion must be great.

'I find it all so sad,' he reflected. 'I mean, Ken Dodd has contributed enormously to the entertainment industry. How can you pay a man who virtually works round the clock? The PAYE tax system was designed for a different kind of worker altogether. I'm sure Ken Dodd has contributed large amounts of money in taxes over the years but, more important, he has given his time and energy generously to bring pleasure to people – and continues to do so in spite of his troubles. The number of work-hours he has given in this respect will never be known.'

The previous summer Condon had engaged Ken Dodd for a series of seaside shows and he completely stole the show. 'I plan to have him back again,' reflected Condon. 'It is a fact of life that Ken Dodd is keen to earn money; he has always been a highly paid entertainer who can command high fees because he has the ability to draw full houses. He is also a workaholic who simply loves every moment on the stage. He keeps on working, he doesn't like to be unemployed for a day, He is prepared to travel anywhere – and overrun his show – if the fee is right.'

Cyril Critchlow runs a small variety theatre over his café in Blackpool's Coronation Street. He is also a founder member of the Blackpool Magicians Club; among its twenty-five members is Ken Dodd, who is a past-honorary president. Years before he had been invited to join the club, but first had to perform some magic tricks. As Critchlow recalls, 'Ken passed this test with honours. We were delighted to have him.'

Unsurprisingly, the club members were taken aback by the tax charges against the comedian, but decided to a man to stand by him. Cyril Critchlow, who came to know Doddy well through meeting him at functions, always found him friendly and courteous and never pretentious. 'We treated him as just another member of the club and Ken wanted it that way. I cannot understand what has happened that he should find himself in such a plight.'

In London show-business circles Doddy's 'tragedy' was viewed in a different light. There was far less sympathy for him. His dilemma was regarded with the kind of cynical detachment one has come to expect in a large capital city. In places like the Palladium and British Broadcasting House the same words were echoed, 'Why did he let it happen?' There was no answer to such a question, so Londoners were inclined to dismiss it from their minds.

Up the street in the Grand Theatre Doddy was still sitting round talking to friends, including Sybie Jones. Conversation was his way of relaxing. The subject of tax was avoided as much as possible; instead they talked about his future shows, his forthcoming Christmas pantomime in Halifax. With the make-up off. Doddy's face can look a little lined, indicating his age, and now perhaps the new stress in his life. Friends felt he had aged somewhat since the court hearing but that could well be a delusion.

Although he took a long time to unwind after shows, he was still energetic, a phenomenon that amazed many in show business. During this difficult period it comforted him greatly to realise that his friends stood by him; it was something he expected. And it delighted him that in a few weeks he would be the recipient of a top Rotary award for his charity work. Despite being nominated for the award before the court hearing, the organisers made it known to him that the tax case would in no way have influenced them. It would be the highest award made by Rotary world-wide.

The comedian's attitude however tended to puzzle some Fleet Street journalists. One wrote, 'It is almost impossible to say what lies behind the jovial Diddymask because Dodd regards all questions about his private life as an insult. It's as if someone said, "Can I look at your bank account?" Small wonder that since the court hearing there was obvious frustration in their ranks as they realised that the comic was not going to open his heart to them.

Cheque-book journalism held no appeal for him. When one of the tabloids accused him of being 'mean', they cannot have known that Doddy had once discussed the subject of money and his attitude to it. At the time he said, 'I am not mean. But I am nervous of money. Nervous of having it. Nervous of not having it. I'm not a tycoon – not a rich man who shows it. In fact I'm not rich at all. I'm only as rich as my last show.'

Although that was in the Seventies, his words were not universally accepted. By then he had been labelled a wealthy man and it was a fair assessment considering his earnings in the theatre and on television. What did emerge was his extreme caution in his approach to life. As he stated, 'I've just begun to taste success. Now I'm learning to savour it – never to swallow it. Once you swallow it you begin to believe all they tell you. It's horrible to see the effect your money has on other people's attitude towards you. You can see it in their eyes. Once I had achieved a degree of success and met again people I had known for years I could see in their faces the change in their feelings towards me. But with a very steady Northern brain, trained to caution, I have managed to sidestep the temptation to think that money can buy you anything.'

By then his success had brought him four cars, a country estate, Ken Dodd Enterprises, Diddy Limited and Happiness Music. 'I am,' he declared proudly, a 'one-man industry. But I've got a long way to go yet in terms of success, in terms of being a *real* comedian.'

Was Doddy being unnecessarily modest? Was he carrying his humility too far? Friends asserted he had always been a cautious man, a throwback to his childhood in a Liverpool hungry for employment and money. Although he wanted the status symbols of success, he was careful not to get above his own people. Perhaps he felt that as long as he stayed among them he would always have an audience. To his colleagues who moved away, it was a contradiction in terms. Most of them would say that Doddy's talent extended far beyond Liverpool. Yet he preferred to remain Doddy, the local funny man.

In an interview in the *Liverpool Post* in the late seventies he asked himself, 'What is money?' and went on to muse . . . 'except a lot of noughts in a bank book? It's only there for the tax-man – and how do you think it feels to write a cheque for £39,000 for the Inland Revenue and know that's only an initial investment? But it can buy the best brains in the country to advise you along the way. I earn a lot of money – I'd have to ask my two accountants to say exactly how much – and I make no apology for being a supporter of the star system.'

Doddy did make it clear that he was never ashamed of having money. As he stressed, 'It gives me the freedom to hand over a hundred pounds to charity and not feel it.' He sometimes liked to talk about investments, but here again displayed his cautious approach. 'I'm cautious with what I've got – about investing it. I've seen too many show-business people come unstuck putting their money into things that they knew nothing about. I have my country house, my little piece of England, simply as an investment because all the greenbacks in the world won't save you from inflation.'

Perhaps it was this caution bordering on fear about the future that motivated him to work so hard and led others to label him a workaholic. Unlike most comedians, Doddy's dream embraced being one day 'a great impresario' and already he thought about producing his own laughter shows.

CHAPTER 4

'My home is Liverpool and it always will be'

It was early morning when Ken Dodd drove his Volvo through the dark, empty streets of Liverpool and south-wards in the direction of Knotty Ash, five miles away. Normally Doddy preferred to return home after his one-night stands, irrespective of the distance. Soon he reached the village and veered right towards Thomas Road until he come to a halt outside a double-fronted Georgian farm-house with its mellow red bricks; the house in which he was born on 8 November 1927.

Doddy Towers, as he likes to describe it, has a faded look, and an air of solemnity more in keeping with a vicar's home than a millionaire entertainer's. It cannot compare in grandeur with Wogan Towers, although Doddy, never one for ostentation, would frown on any such vulgar comparison. He is proud of his eighteenth century house which was originally a small farm, but the land dwindled as the City of Liverpool expanded.

As the Squire of Knotty Ash, he held a unique position. He was invited to open fêtes and supermarkets and carry out other public engagements befitting a squire. The chil-dren treated him as a kind of king. To outsiders, the name Knotty Ash was somewhat puzzling, suggesting to some a tree or perhaps a plant, instead of a friendly village. Lounge bars, shops, garages, post office and a community centre – all bore the name. The main area, which has an almost rural look because of the acres of greenery, is dominated by the imposing Calvary Church, a solid if austere-looking building.

Knotty Ash is well signposted and taxi-men have no difficulty locating Doddy Towers, though some of them claimed that the comedian never tipped them. 'It has been a longstanding joke between us,' said one, 'but it's true.' Since the court hearing they have conveyed pressmen and photographers to Thomas Road, Knotty Ash, to look over the house and area, and they like to remind visitors, 'Doddy loves his privacy.' It was true. Only a tiny number of journalists were ever invited inside Doddy Towers. To the hard-working comic, home is sacrosanct.

Undeniably the court case focused new interest locally on Doddy. Friendly gossip abounded. As the weeks and months passed, people wondered what was going on in his mind, if he would be able to stand up to the ordeal. A few even thought the strain might become intolerable and secretly worried for him. The people of Knotty Ash found it a strange experience, for they had mostly seen Doddy in high spirits. The more perceptive among them suspected that it was a most trying time for the comedian and wished the 'whole damn business was over and done with.' Others, who regarded him as a very private person, did not quite know what to think, though being a comedian they reckoned he was tough and resilient and would pull through.

By now autumn had come to Knotty Ash. Tree-lined Thomas Road was strewn with withered brown leaves and a sad air hung over the district, almost in keeping with the mood of Doddy Towers. Doddy himself was determined, though, to carry on living a normal life, and accepted invitations as usual to perform public engagements. As Squire of Knotty Ash his esteem had in no way been diminished because of his tax problems. The people were philosophical and hoped nothing would happen to him. Their loyalty was never in question. Doddy knew that and it reassured him. But in the back of their minds was the disturbing Lester Piggott case and the harshness of English justice. It could reduce men to the same level. Piggott had discovered that grim reality to his cost.

If he cared to reflect – and probably this was the time for reflection – Doddy could look back on a very happy childhood. He had been christened Kenneth Arthur Dodd, and he later claimed, 'I was a very happy baby. But my mother found she was holding me upside down and powdering the wrong end.' His parents, Arthur and Sarah Dodd, were a devoted couple, and told the world that their son was born with a smile on his face. He did not contradict them. In celebrating his past, Doddy loved to joke about it. 'When I was born' he reminded an audience once, 'the midwife held me up by the legs, slapped my face and punched my dad'. Arthur Dodd claimed the story was not entirely true.

Doddy did not quite know if he was born 'comical'. As he recalled, 'I am told that at the age of two I walked into the living-room and told my mother, "I've made you a nice new draining board" – having smeared a half-inch layer of cocoa all over it, and smoothed it down so it was a nice brown wood. I remember at the age of three, I wanted a kite like all the other kids had, so I crossed Queens Drive and went to the shop – it was a bit silly really because Queens Drive was dangerous in those days. I could have got run over by a stage-coach. The lady in the shop was very kind; she sold me two broken kites for a penny. I thought it was a marvellous bargain. As a little boy of three, you see, I thought it was better to have two broken ones for a ha'penny each, than a proper one for threepence. This confirms what everyone says: I'm a marvellous businessman.'

Doddy was one of three children and he remembered his grandmother with pride. 'She was a remarkable woman. She brought up sixteen kids and also became Liverpool's first lady magistrate. And each of those kids was taught to play at least two musical instruments.' Music was in the Dodd family. Arthur Dodd was a coal merchant and a part-time musician. Originally he played the bass fiddle, then the clarinet and later the saxophone. Sarah, his wife, played the piano.

One of Doddy's earliest memories was the birth of his sister June when he was about three. Two years before, his brother Bill was born. From an early age, Doddy saw how hard his father worked and the struggle it was for him to build up his coal merchant's business. It was something that young Ken does not forget. 'Every Christmas Eve we would go to bed and my father was still out trying to sell coal until after midnight. In those days people would get their coal in during the week and then pay at the weekend – or whenever you could catch them in. So my mother would start collecting the coal money on a Thursday when some people had been paid, and she would be out from the afternoon until 11 o'clock in the evening. It was the same on Fridays. On Saturdays she used to set off from Knotty Ash about nine in the morning and come home just before midnight. She would get a tram back from Prescot having walked all the way in the day collecting money. Yes, it was dangerous carrying money in a handbag, and once she was set upon and robbed by four men. Mum was 5 feet 1 inch tall.'

Ken and the other children helped as much as they could, but still their parents continued to work 'too hard'. Because Arthur Dodd could not get away from work the family rarely, if ever, had holidays. The coal trade was so competitive that any length of absence would jeopardise his business. There were other people in those days who were also unable to take holidays, but they partly made up for this by enjoying day outings. Young Ken Dodd, with his brother and sister, was taken to New Brighton. 'Usually it was a great day out,' he recalled. 'Southport was like going abroad; and going to Scarborough was the equivalent today of going to Australia.'

Despite hard work and long hours, Arthur Dodd tried to make time to take the children on a Sunday outing. Driving a Riley, he would take them on a trip to North Wales and in the evening they would return and have pineapple chunks or pears and cream for tea. Young Ken was close to his parents; he loved the way his father treated children.

'He was very good with kids. He used to put on daft hats, tell us jokes, pull funny faces, and sing comic songs for us. He entertained all the family, and he was my favourite comedian. At other times, he'd play games with us. When I told him I had read in my comic, *The Wizard*, about this boy who had a bike that could fly, he took all one Sunday building these wings that jutted out about four feet and fitted them to my bike. I pedalled furiously on it up and down the yard, and roared down a field trying to take off on this bike.'

Knotty Ash was no different to other areas in Liverpool. Young Ken and his pals sought adventure; they wanted to be cowboys, and dressed for the part, or swashbucklers. Even today it amuses him to recall those 'fantastic' days and he soon decided 'all kids are actors'. He remembered fastening his navy blue gaberdine mac by the top button like a cloak and with his left hand holding imaginary reins and right hand flogging an imaginary horse's backside, haring up and down the road singing at the top of his voice, 'We are the mystery riders. We ride the prairie in search of gold.'

Saturday was a different day. Young Ken went off with his pals to the Tuppenny Rush at the Regent ('no posh miners' matinées in those days') and before they sat down to watch Flash Gordon and the cartoons they found time to shout greetings at one another, yell at their rivals and throw orange peel at one another. The real joy for Ken was the freedom he enjoyed and the images created in his young mind as he watched the wonders on the screen. Later, his dad used to take the family to Liverpool's variety theatres such as the Olympia, the Royal Court, the Empire and the Pavilion. Ken loved every moment of the entertainment; the colour, the excitement, the laughter. Afterwards he would say to his Dad, 'I want to go again, I really do.'

What he did not realise then was that Arthur Dodd was endeavouring to foster in his young son a love of the theatre and of music. 'You must take up music, Ken,' he would urge.

Soon the boy had a succession of blowers, tooters and squeezers. There were the cornet, the accordion, and the piano, and he tried to learn all three. He joined the church choir and surprised himself by quickly acquiring a liking for music. 'It was my first attempt at being in any kind of show business when I became a choirboy just over the road at St John's Church in Knotty Ash. Together with other nine-year-old gangsters I used to go along there and look angelic – twice on Sundays. We were paid sixpence a service, and I loved all that church music. You could sing out, let it rip. It's great music to sing. Furthermore, I learned something about music and the theory of music in the choir, and we could wink at all the girls in the congregation. We were not cherubic in the least. For we used to flick paper pellets across the chancel and whisper terrible things. I guess choirboys haven't changed in a couple of thousand years.

At home in Thomas Road, young Ken was industrious and helped his parents as much as he could. He grew fond of animals and birds. With a large space behind the house, there was ample room for the horses, cats, dogs and canaries. The dogs were given some fancy names such as Prince, Patch, Skippy, Nicky, and later Touche and Mark. His father kept stables and Ken helped to muck out the horses and groom them.

One of the most unforgettable days of his young life was when he went to the Wrexham horse sales with his dad. 'I remember we bought Duke. Duke was a vanner, which is a light cart-horse. I loved watching all those horse dealers. I'd hear them shout "Trot 'em on the hard," and the horse would be taken on the hard part of the ground. Then: "Bring 'em down on the soft." It was a marvellous thing to watch when they sold a horse. They spat on their hands, and there were fine handclasps. Then the man who sold the horse would give a bit of money back to the buyer, usually a silver coin. They called that "luck money". Visiting horse sales gave me a great insight into animals and human nature.'

Being a sensitive boy, it saddened him, even made him cry, when an animal he loved died. In time they buried quite a number of animals in a little churchyard at the back of the house. But the memory would stay with him for a long time. At that time he was showing an individuality not noticeable in his friends. In retrospect, he says he must have been a strange youth because he liked doing things differently and that would later be one of the basic requirements of a comic. 'I used to try to walk backwards to school just to see if I could do it. I've still got the lump on the back of my head – lampposts, you see. And doing things differently – that's how I got my sticky teeth. I tried to ride my bike with my eyes shut, which is something you should never do because ultimately you hit the kerb. I did, and I sailed over the handlebars and landed smack on my choppers, and that jutted them out.'

He was lucky in his background. His mother was stern but fair-minded and his dad took a genuine interest in his life. Young Ken was athletic and adventuresome and enjoyed open air pursuits enormously. Later, he had a racing bike and would cycle with his pals from Knotty Ash to Betws-y-Coed, a respectable distance. It was gruelling, he would say, but worth the trouble. He got some insights into the Welsh. 'Welsh secrecy is the finest in the world – of course we were more interested in the foreign women. We learned to say Cariad Bach!'

Growing up he remembers he was seldom out of mischief, but he and his pals never needed to do anything illegal except perhaps light fires and dig holes. They were never bored. 'There was so much to do,' he says, 'when our world was young, and that is probably the answer to vandalism and things like that – give the kids plenty to do. I don't remember doing anything that meant I had to go along to the police station. I broke a few windows in my time but I hadn't the slightest desire to steal anything because I had a very good family life, and I didn't need to.'

Education was a priority with the boy's parents. Young Ken had started school at five years of age, when he was dragged along to Knotty Ash Infants' School. It was during the first day there that he developed a distaste for a certain malted milk drink which was forced down his throat. 'The smell of it knocks me flat on my back even now.'

The headmistress was a Miss Hill and she had 'a magnificently genteel habit of wandering around the classroom. She would sniff the air, and then announce, "Someone does not smell sweet in this room." Whoever it happened to be had to leave in disgrace.'

Although shy, young Dodd was not a well-behaved pupil. He recalls, 'I was always being called off for chattering and talking. All through my schooldays I've always been able to talk myself into trouble. But I was intelligent and picked up knowledge easily enough.'

It was the gift, however, of a Punch and Judy set from his parents for his eighth birthday that first launched the boy into the world of public entertainment. As he recalls, 'I practised like mad, built a stage out of orange boxes and organised concerts in a hen-coop in the yard.' He was always an imaginative boy, eager to try out new ideas, and in this respect he was never once discouraged by his parents. They both suspected that somewhere inside their son was the urge to be a showman.

One day he read an advertisement in a comic that ran,

'Amaze Your Friends, Fool Your Teachers. Send Sixpence in stamps.' He applied straight away and in return for a tanner, he got a booklet on *How to become a Ventriloquist*, along with a leatherette Swiss Bird Warbler. By now he was able to throw his voice into a trunk, on to a bed, or anywhere called for. Earlier, he had been given a ventriloquist's doll by his parents and he experimented with all kinds of funny voices,

He called the doll Charlie Brown and came to like it as though it was a tiny brother. He had lessons in ventriloquism from an old variety artist in Liverpool who gave him tips on how to keep his mouth shut. 'All ventriloquists are a bit odd, including myself,' he says today. 'After all, talking to yourself can't be a very steady living.'

He made his début at the age of eight at the St Edward's Orphanage, Knotty Ash. His dad wrote the script, and as well as the chatter with Charlie Brown, the act included tap-dancing and performances on piano and saxophone. His first appearance was considered such a success that he was invited to other functions in the area. Arthur Dodd told his wife, Sarah, 'Our Ken's pretty talented, don't you think?' Mrs Dodd never had any doubt of it. Even at this early stage she saw the little boy making a name for himself on the stage. She set about encouraging him as best she could.

The studious side of the boy surfaced as he continued to read more and he liked to send for things he saw advertised in papers. Throwing his voice appealed to him and he worked on his ventriloquist's act. He loved whimsical wheezes. His parents let him do what he wanted to do; at that time he was independent and knew what he wanted. A month after his début in St Edward's Orphanage the Father Superior sent for him. 'I thought I was going to get a good hiding for being a rotten ventriloquist,' he recalled. 'Instead he gave me half-a-crown.'

Shortly afterwards he did a concert for the Knotty Ash Parent-Teachers' Association and received a shilling for his act. He saw the joke in the reduction of his fee. 'I had to learn my first lesson in show business – how to take a cut gracefully.' It pleased him that his dad was writing the scripts for him. He had a sailor script, and a jockey script, because his dad was crazy about racing. With his frilly teeth it was an advantage to young Ken to be a ventriloquist because he always had his mouth partly open whether he liked it or not.

As an aspiring young showman, he was in demand. He did charity shows, Boy Scout gang shows, anywhere they would have him. 'Wherever there was an audience I would be there with my suitcase and all my props. The case was bigger than me and I used to lug it all over the place on the bus.'

Sometimes he went to places like St Helen's, Widnes and 'exotic' Ellesmere Port. 'I did a show at the Scala in Widnes at the age of ten and I played the Philharmonic Hall when I was twelve.' He listened attentively to what his father said; he respected his advice for he had a feeling for show business. 'My father's advice was that you must be original, that you must have you own style, and I have always tried to do that. Obviously I have been influenced by early heroes, particularly Arthur Askey and Rob Wilton. The basic philosophy from my mother was that you can do anything you want to do and be anybody you want to be – if you really try hard enough.'

Young Ken continued to find stimulation as well as enjoyment in books. *The Wind in the Willows, Coral Island* and adventure stories filled his bookshelf. At Knotty Ash Junior School he got a scholarship to the Holt High School. The change was, as he recalls, dramatic. 'Suddenly I was thrown into this clinical, disinfectant-smelling establishment where everybody, all the teachers, looked just like the man you see when you go to pay your rates – stern, forbidding, and not wanting to know. I'm sure there's a lesson for educationalists there – when you are trying to build a little personality, giving future citizens confidence in their powers, trying to mould them into the kind of people you want them to be, you should ensure your own self-importance doesn't get in the way.'

It was in the *Liverpool Post* that he saw an advertisement, 'Dancers Wanted for Pantomine' and he reckoned with his amateur experience he had as good a chance as anyone else. When he went along to the Pavilion he found to his horror that it was girls they wanted, not boys. 'I saw these little girls dressed up, and I thought, "Oh no! It's not me – I'm not stripping off." I was about twelve at the time and they offered me the job of props boy. The job lasted about four weeks in the school holidays. One night I was actually caught on stage during the transformation scene. You see, there was this rat-trap and the pumpkin on stage, and the Fairy Godmother said, "Right, you shall have your wish, Cinderella. You shall go to the ball." The stage was blacked out during the time the coach was supposed to arrive and I removed the rat-trap and pumpkin. I think I must have been a bit slow getting off, and when the light came up I was still there. So that was how I made one of my first appearances, and got one of my first laughs – standing on a stage with a rat-trap in one hand and a pumpkin in the other. And the coach and ponies galloping towards me.'

At that time he was enjoying life. Besides school work, and the occasional stage engagements, he helped his father at the coal business. By now he was able to drive and used to take the lorries round the yard until one Sunday he backed one of them down a fifteen-foot hole and did not drive again until he was seventeen and got his first licence.

It was wartime and the Dodd home, like most homes in Liverpool, followed the key events. Young Dodd knew about the sinking of the *Bismarck*, reckoned at the time the most powerful battleship in the world. The *Liverpool Post* carried columns of news about the Allied progress in the war and, being a good reader, the boy realised that by 6 June 1944 the war was running in favour of the Allies.

That morning the *Post* carried large headlines about the mass invasion of Northern France, with an extensive map of the invasion coast. Under the heading, '4,000 SHIPS, THOUSANDS OTHER CRAFT, INVADE NORTHERN FRANCE,' the report began. 'The Second Front was opened today. The Battle for the Liberation of Europe has begun . . .'

Despite wartime food rationing, the Dodd family had not experienced the pangs of hunger. It was the excitement of the war battles that appealed to young Dodd, but like everyone else he was looking forward to the end of the long campaign. He had been too young to play a vital part. Now, at the age of fifteen, he was still interested in the stage and one day saw an advertisement asking for performers to entertain Her Majesty's Forces, so he went along to Priory Road School in Anfield. It was the Air Training Corps Cadets. He went on and did his show with his ventriloquist partner Charlie Brown. He was terrified. There was a concert party on called The Spitfires, very professional and very good, and the two Dooley's Boys – two lads just starting like himself, a singing act full of vibrancy.

Young Ken felt he must have been accepted as a 'turn' because first this man came round who said his name was Billy Caton and he was an agent. 'I had only read of agents in books, and I thought "Blimey! This is it! Stardom at last." Then a young woman came backstage, Hilda Fallon. I was a teenager and she was an attractive girl. She asked me if I would do some shows with her concert party, The Mersey Mites. I thought, "By jove!" I couldn't sleep for weeks thinking about these amazing offers I'd had. They asked me if I would like to play in a nightclub. Now the only nightclubs I had seen were in Hollywood musicals where everyone went round supping champagne. The men were in evening dress and the girls beautiful in evening gowns. In these films one room was as big as the Adelphi Hotel, and there was a 90-piece orchestra playing . . .'

Although apprehensive, he agreed, so they said, 'Right! Meet us at the Pier Head and we'll get the ferry – which did not sound like Hollywood for a start. They went on the Birkenhead ferry and got the Crosville bus to Ellesmere Port, which was where this big nightclub was. It still seemed a bit strange and a bit odd to him, but finally they arrived there – Flatt Lane Labour Club!

The atmosphere did not excite him. He remembers, 'When I saw the inside of this club, I knew there was something different from the ones I'd seen in Hollywood musicals, because there were a lot of people sitting around in flat hats, sipping pints. The ladies all seemed to have Guinnesses in front of them – and meat pies.'

That was his initiation to the nightclub scene. He received 1s. 9d. which was considered good in those days. More shows followed in Bootle and Walton. He did a lot of work for Hilda Fallon who was a great communicator. 'There are certain people like circus trainers who have a psychic ability to communicate in some way with animals and train them. In exactly the same way Hilda Fallon is one of them. She could train people to be entertainers. She could take a boy or girl and mould them into a smashing little artiste.'

CHAPTER 5

A letter from David Forrester

At the age of seventeen Ken Dodd left Holt High School for good harbouring no serious personal regrets. Young Dodd had no ambition to pursue higher education or study for a career in the professions; he was at that time more anxious to help in his father's coal business and, in addition, earn some extra money entertaining in halls around Liverpool. Years later he quipped, 'I had a body like Tarzan and muscles like Samson then. I was fit and healthy and doing the job I liked.'

Delivering coal had its grim as well as its light side. 'It was hard work,' he remembers. 'I was out in all weathers. Every night was bath night – we would have 365 baths a year. More, actually, because in the summer you would get really black. But a bit of coal dust never hurt anybody.' He derived enjoyment from going round all the houses, laughing and chatting together with his brother Billy and it was there the word 'Missus' came from, the one he used often in later years. He was paid a good wage, but he worked hard for it.

After almost four years he decided he wanted to branch out on his own. He felt it was all right for someone else, but he now sought control in his own affairs. He had powerful ambitions to become a businessman. A tycoon. Soon he made a humble start with a mobile shop. He bought a small furniture van, and a carpenter friend, Fatty

Oldham, fitted it out with shelves for him. The eager young salesman began to spend many hours promoting and selling Kaydee products: pots, polishes, lotions and many other things. With his dark, bushy hair, funny teeth and beaming smile he became a familiar figure around the sprawling housing estates and he found that 'the ladies' liked to be addressed as 'Missus'. He was now twenty years of age, self-employed, and a young capitalist to boot. Even then he believed that individual endeavour was entitled to be rewarded. Proudly he went about building up his little business, secretly hopeful that one day he might become the tycoon he wanted to be.

As a house-to-house salesman, he was observant and quickly learned what working-class humour really meant; the language the people spoke, the jokes they enjoyed. To his surprise these people responded with a laugh when he wise-cracked, 'We're not frightened of work in Liverpool. It fascinates us.' He discovered amusing irony in the friendliness of these Northern people: 'Had your tea?' they would ask as the visitor entered the door. 'Pity. We've had ours.' On his rounds he found he was becoming a showbiz performer. 'On wet days, when the clouds were low in the sky with rain, I tried to cheer the old ladies with a joke. They loved it.'

All the time he was a part-time entertainer, much in demand. Every shilling he earned went into his own business. Becoming a professional comic did not cross his mind then: he was too busy selling his wares. Without capital he knew he could not expand his business. His plan now was to sell equipment and supplies to bars and clubs in Liverpool, but before he could develop the idea any further he found that his nightly show business engagements at parties and functions were taking up more and more of his time. More important, party-goers, diners and audiences liked his zany act in which he sang, did his ventriloquist's act with Charlie Brown and told a joke or two. He was colourfully billed as 'Professor Yaffle Chuckabutty, Operatic Tenor, and Sausage Knotter'.

Mrs Sarah Dodd wondered when her son would make the decision to turn 'pro'; his reluctance to do so disappointed her, for she had no fears about his ability to make people laugh. She had urged Ken to try more comedy in his act, but for a long time he had said he was too young. 'Plenty of time, Mum, for that,' he'd tell her. 'I'm too young to be a comic yet.' However after a while he began to take advice and it paid off. His brand of comedy was proving successful. Meanwhile, Arthur Dodd played sax and bass around Liverpool.

Entertaining people brought some quiet chuckles to young Dodd. There was the funeral director's annual dinner at the Bradford Hotel and as he and the other four entertainers waited in the ante-room he was reminded of the fact that 'if you didn't go on you didn't get paid'. As often happens on such occasions, the speeches dragged on and on. They knew the licensee was a bit miserable and in his book 11 o'clock meant just that. Everybody out.

Fifteen minutes before 11 o'clock, the door opened and this man said, 'All right, now the show.' They all looked at each other and thought, who's going on? because whoever went on was going to get paid and the others were going to be unlucky. Suddenly they realised that if each did two and a half minutes they would all get paid. 'You've never seen anything like it,' recalls Ken. 'We were laughing more than the audience. Each one went on, told one and a half jokes and was practically yanked off stage by the next artiste waiting to go on and collect £1.'

Another dinner he remembered was supposed to be a posh affair at the Sandon Hotel, a beer and stout bottlers outing. Ken arrived about 10 o'clock and had to crunch his way through about two inches of broken glass. The bottlers had evidently been having a good night. He was engaged to do his first all-male stag dinner and approached a tenor there named Earnest Reynolds, who was a detective superintendent in real life, whether he should 'mix it a little'. Reynolds looked hard at him. 'Look, son, these are intelligent men and you can tell any sort of joke, white or blue, as long as it's clever and doesn't insult their intelligence. That's all you have to remember with stag shows.'

In those days he did a lot on the after-dinner circuit, with people like Len Annett, Phil Kernott, Ada Taylor and Jack Ray. They played after-dinner shows in most of the hotels in Liverpool and Birkenhead and would often do two or three dinners in a night. When they were doing a double shuffle it was a question of getting on and then getting off as quickly as possible to the next engagement.

At that time young Dodd began to make a study of humour and bought books about it. He had set out to be the comedian who never told a gag – he wanted to be a visual comedian. However, as time went by he found that words were his hobby and he compiled files of gags. 'I developed into a talking comedian, really, because I had radio shows in mind.'

By now he was finding that sales chat was hard work. Deep down he would say he was the sensitive chap and a bit reserved. Putting one foot in the door and selling vacuum cleaners takes nerve that he had not got in abundance. When he reflected that perhaps after all he should try a career as full-time entertainer, he was not totally convinced. His mother put it down to his love of home. As she said, 'I think that's why Ken is taking so long to make up his mind.'

Up to now, he and his friends had devoted most of their time to Liverpool audiences. Now they were eager to spread their wings. At that time he used to double up with a tenor called Ken Pike, and they decided this would be a good 'in' to Manchester. Today Ken Dodd says, 'I hadn't realised that, being a Jewish community, so many people had relations in show business on the executive and business side. From one particular show I got five offers from London agents like Bernard Delfont, Lew Grade, and others. I was tickled by the interest in me. I went home asking myself should I give the "pro" game a try. My colleagues were all for it and said I had nothing to lose. But I was a salesman and I was yet to achieve my ambition to be a tycoon.'

Everything changed on a spring morning in 1954 when he received a letter from a London theatrical agent who signed himself David Forrester. Now in his twenty-seventh year, Ken Dodd instantly realised that he would soon have to make the biggest decision of his life. Forrester pointed out that he had heard about him and was interested in his future in show business. He suggested a meeting at the Adelphi Hotel, Liverpool.

That a London agent had thought it worthwhile to contact him gave the salesman a lift. Maybe, he chuckled to himself at his home in Knotty Ash, stardom beckons. When they eventually met, he thought that the agent looked like his dad – and that was a good start. There was the air of a gentleman about him, and he spoke in a rather husky voice.

'I'm having tea and cakes,' he said. 'Is that all right with you?'

The young comedian nodded. He felt he could trust this man. He was about the same height as his father and had a head shaped like an egg. He guessed the agent was in his early fifties and he seemed slightly ponderous, not as sharp as he expected. But in conversation he showed he knew the business from A to Z, and by the time they had finished their light meal he had agreed to go on his books.

'Good,' said Forrester. 'I never make promises, but I think you will not be disappointed with me. I would not take you on, or suggest you become a professional entertainer, unless I thought you had potential.'

In the excitement of the meeting, Dodd found he himself had paid for the tea and cakes. He thought: 'This fellow must be a good agent if he looks after my money as well as he looks after his own.' So he chose him, not because he was a good agent – but because he looked like his dad. It was a logical enough reason for Ken.

Dave Forrester, as he was known in the business in London, enjoyed a good reputation and he had his own philosophy about grooming unknowns to possible stardom. He did not believe in rushing them. 'Be patient,' he would tell young singers or comedians. 'I think we can make it with you.' He was not known to make extravagant promises; if anything he was over-cautious. But Forrester had a sharp mind and was reputed to be honest.

They did not sign a contract that afternoon in the Adelphi, but inside a few weeks Ken Dodd found that his agent was working on solid lines to launch his professional career. At home in Knotty Ash, Mrs Sarah Dodd expressed delight at her son's decision, and her husband felt that all those scripts he had written for his son were at last leading somewhere. All Ken knew was that he was no longer a salesman. It was a jolting thought. At least he had Charlie Brown and his mobile van. About his immediate future he was unsure.

There was someone else in Ken's life who felt like his mother; that was a young nurse named Anita Boutin, who at twenty-four years of age was prepared to give up her profession to be with him. At first she would be his secretary, and eventually perhaps, his wife. She had a sweet disposition and lively sense of humour. For a long time she was Ken's most enthusiastic fan – an attractive young woman with a winsome smile who was among the first to encourage him to turn 'pro'.

For six years she had been a nurse. Daughter of a French Canadian, she was determined to see Ken make it to the top. Later she said, 'I moved from the sad side of life to Ken's mad, zany world – and I loved it. The only thing that has really changed my life is the hectic pace. When

I was nursing I used to dash off duty and go by train or bus wherever Ken was appearing – now I dash backwards and forwards with him.'

There was another reason why Anita had become his secretary. She had Ken's fans to thank for it. She was all set to go to Canada to see her father's relations when Ken plaintively mentioned that he had three hundred letters from fans and no time to answer them. Anita set to work to keep him up to date with his fanmail and thereafter began coping with over fifty letters a week which he conscientiously signed. Correspondence took up most of her time.

After the pain and grief Anita had seen in hospitals, she was thrilled to be part of show business with Ken. He was the only serious boyfriend she had had up to then. As her brother Bill Boutin would say, 'Anita was a probationer nurse when they first met in the early Fifties. I think it was at the Vaudeville Club in Tweed Street, Liverpool. Anita became a State Registered Nurse, but she had no hesitation about giving it all up when she met Ken. I think it was she who talked him into becoming a professional entertainer – when he was a salesman. He was able to make her laugh and she knew he could make others laugh.'

Ken had once told Anita that he had ambitions to become an opera singer, but he made such funny faces while singing that no operatic producer would think of taking him seriously. Gradually Anita convinced him that he was a comedian and that he should try to develop his act. She had wonderful confidence in his talent and was able to say what jokes people laughed at.

It was natural that the people of Knotty Ash should ask about Ken and Anita. Romance was a constant topic of conversation in the village, where families knew each other, and a white wedding was eagerly anticipated. The women wondered when Ken Dodd would pop the question now that he had turned professional. They were aware Anita got on well with the Dodds, Arthur and Sarah. Would it then be only a matter of time until Ken moved out of the house into his own house? Or would he put it off while he established his show business career?

The fact was that Ken paid Anita a weekly salary to look after his affairs. She set about improving her wardrobe. She had her own house in Liverpool and Ken continued to live in Thomas Road, Knotty Ash. Although Anita knew that Ken's career came first and he thought of little else, she could say that she was deeply in love with him, but if he wanted to defer marriage she was agreeable. There was no immediate hurry, she told herself, and it was time enough when Ken was making more money. She admired his ambition; he was strong-willed and she had no doubt he would be wealthy one day.

Ken had his favourites in show business. Among them was the great Al Jolson whose dynamism he adored. 'The greatest showman of them all,' he said. Arthur Askey made him laugh, so did Jimmy Edwards. Soon any trepidation that he had had about turning professional disappeared. He had come by now to have complete trust in Dave Forrester who worked quietly to find him good engagements. The agent fixed his professional début in variety on a bill at the Empire Theatre, Nottingham, in September 1954. It was a strong bill, with singer Tony Brent topping the programme and including also trumpeter Kenny Baker and the singing group, The Kordites.

Afterwards he reckoned he made a fairly good impression, though no one went exactly wild about his zany act. It had not helped that he found some difficulty in getting theatrical digs. Eventually he landed up in 'a commercial travellers' hotel where one was expected to have breakfast at six a.m. and be out of one's room soon after'. As a result a rather melancholy young comedian spent much of the week sleeping in his dressing-room on a piece of board suspended between two chairs.

Undeterred, he was not given much time by Dave Forrester to think about the Nottingham 'experience'; some other good dates followed in Leeds and Manchester where he got the first of his many love-letters. Anita chuckled and made him sign them. The *Manchester Guardian*, which took a serious look at show business, described his performances thus at the Hippodrome: 'The trammels of gentility still cling to the splendid down-at-heel madness as portrayed by Mr Ken Dodd at the Hippodrome last evening.'

The talented comedian was learning the realities of the business – and there were some aspects that didn't appeal to him. There were the off-putting back-stage notices on the lines of 'On June 4th 1896, an artiste was fined £5 and costs for using unsuitable material – please see that this does not happen again.'

On occasions it was disconcerting to discover the theatre manager standing out front while the comic went through his act, wearing 'the slightly blasé look of someone who had heard it all before'.

He was prepared to learn. If a gag had failed to make an audience laugh he asked himself why. He would try to improve on it. He listened to the other pros and took their advice, if he thought it was worthwhile. He got useful tips from them about pacing his act and tightening up this or that gag.

In those days he sang ballads such as *The Floral Dance* and funny versions of *The Road To Mandalay*. He dressed in bright clothes and his hair was plastered down. He looked slightly bizarre and eccentric. Initially he used to go on clutching a battered euphonium which looked as if a steam-roller had run over it. As he explained to Michael Billington, 'The reason I used to carry it was that it represented music. It was the most musical symbol I could find. I hadn't realised then but it was also very phallic.' The joke was, of course, that he never played it.

By now the salesman-turned-pro comic was on the road to fame. He was being talked about as an 'original talent' and set to join the Merseyside crop of comedians, which in itself was an attainment.

CHAPTER 6

'You must see this new comedian'

In August 1954 Ken Dodd was in variety in Colwyn Bay when he was told that BBC producer Barney Colehan wished to see him. He expressed instant surprise. He had heard of Colehan and knew he produced the popular television programme, *The Good Old Days*, but could he be really inviting him on the show?

The young comedian had no illusions about himself – he was a virtual unknown in the business and he liked to reassure himself by recounting Dave Forrester's words, 'Don't rush. Take time.' None the less, he agreed to see the producer in his dressing-room after the show.

Barney Colehan was a likeable, if direct, Yorkshireman who had declined all offers to live anywhere else. He had started as a pharmacist, joined the army as a gunner, gravitated to British Forces Broadcasting in Hamburg, and was demobbed as a major. In 1947 he joined the BBC as a production assistant and toured the country setting up the radio show, *Have A Go* for Wilfred Pickles. Six years later he produced a modest little programme about the music-hall, compèred from one of the boxes at the renowned City of Varieties Music-Hall in Leeds. Soon *The Good Old Days* television series was born.

As a go-ahead producer, Colehan was always on the lookout for new talent. He had given Frankie Vaughan his first TV date, after discovering him in a student show at the old Leeds Empire; also the comedian Jimmy James, and Wilfred Pickles. That August he was staying at an hotel in Llandudno and met Jess Yates and his mother. The former, who would later become a television personality, remarked to Colehan, 'You've got to see that new comic over in Colwyn Bay. His name's Dodd and he's got potential.'

'Do you think he's that good?' asked Colehan casually.

'Yes, I do, Barney. I think he's good enough for a spot on your show.'

Next evening they drove to Colwyn Bay and joined the packed audience. Barney Colehan liked what he saw. As he said later, 'Ken Dodd had immediate rapport with the audience. He looked funny and his humour was original and his warm, infectious personality captivated everyone.'

At times during the performance the producer chuckled to himself, first at the outrageous costumes paraded by the comic on stage, then at the rapid succession of one-liners. Dodd, he decided, was zany, and different, in fact a throw-back to the oldtime music-hall artistes. Backstage he found a shy man taking off his make-up before a large mirror. 'Ken looked at me and seemed surprised to see me, but when I told him how much I had enjoyed his act he smiled through his funny teeth and was relieved.'

'I want you, Ken, for my show, *The Good Old days*,' Colehan told him in a strong Yorkshire accent.

There was a momentary silence.

'I don't think I'm ready,' replied Dodd. 'As you know, I'm only a newcomer in the business. Come and see me in Leeds in a few weeks' time and tell me what you think.'

Colehan was in no hurry. He suspected that the Liverpool comic, probably on the advice of his agent, wanted to be sure he was really ready for the big time.

When the comedian eventually arrived in Leeds, he sought out good theatrical 'digs'; this was not as easy as it sounded. As he recalled, 'I was at the Leeds Empire, and there I was lucky to find one of the last remaining theatrical landladies. Her name was Mrs Hartley, and she kept a big Victorian house she had even styled Vauda Villa, and she did cater – and how! – for theatricals. The first day there the diddy lady, who helped her, staggered from the kitchen with this huge meat pie covered with gravy. But when I cut it there was no meat inside. Silly old biddy, I told myself, she's forgotten the meat inside.

'Anyway I scoffed the lot because I was hungry. I was sitting there all bloated when she brought in a huge dinner that would kill a navvy. I looked at her and said, "I've had my dinner . . . the meat pie." She bellowed, "Meat pie? What are you talking about, you creckpit? That was the Yorkshire pudding. *This* is your dinner!'

It was Dodd's only eccentric moment. The rest of the week went well and the audiences loved his act. True to his word, Barney Colehan called round to his dressing-room and promised him a date on *The Good Old Days*.

'What did you think?' the comedian asked.

'Your performance gets better all the time, Ken,' the producer said cheerfully. 'I think you'll be another of my discoveries.'

Being himself a born optimist, Ken Dodd was delighted to meet a fellow enthusiast in this blunt but genuine Yorkshire man. He made his television début in *The Good Old Days* on 11 March 1955 and was paid a fee of £32. 9s. 4d. He was pleased with his performance, even if his spot on the bill was relatively short, and afterwards he quipped, 'By Jove, I didn't overrun this time.' One of the other artistes was Hylda Baker who had been doing the rounds of the music-halls without notable success. For her television appearance, which did something for her career, she was paid £49. 3s. 8d.

Looking back on the show, Barney Colehan says, 'Ken Dodd was a very funny man even then. He was an instinctive comic with visual magnetism. Other comedians dressed smartly and often didn't look like comics, but Ken never left you in any doubt at all. In my book he had exceptional talent. His patter was quick and topical and his face was his fortune. The audience laughed at him before he spoke a word.'

Clearly the demands of the profession were shaping his personal life and career. For the first time he realised the work to be done if he was to become a star of stage, radio and television. Discipline was essential – and dedication. He was fortunate that he had none of the self-destructive forces that affected some people in the profession. He didn't smoke, he drank moderately, and Anita Boutin was loving and supportive. As other comics moved from Liverpool to try their luck elsewhere, he was happy to stay in Knotty Ash. And he accepted Dave Forrester's advice, 'Be patient, and I think we can make it with you.'

The practical Forrester had so far not promised anything that had not come off. The bookings he accepted were aimed at putting his client up front with the stars and eventually top billing. It was inevitable that his mind would turn to opportunities in radio. The Fifties was proving a golden era for funny men in this medium, with Tony Hancock about the most popular of the lot. *The Goon Show* had changed everything – and zaniness was in. The Goons, Sellers, Milligan and Secombe, had managed to create images as well as destroy them. They had broken new ground in radio comedy.

However, when Ken Dodd eventually got his break in radio it was through a performance at the Sunderland Empire in 1955. Jimmy James topped the bill and his son Jim Casey was one of two stooges; he was at the time also writing radio scripts for the BBC. Ken Dodd was the second spot on the bill and made an immediate impact.

'He was tremendous,' remembers Jim Casey. 'I was seeing his act for the first time and I laughed as I stood at the side of the stage. As a stand-up comic with visual impact, he had star quality. My father, who was not easily pleased, agreed with me. In retrospect, I think it was his machine-gun attack on the audience that bowled me over. As gag followed gag, he left the audience breathless with laughter. Not surprisingly, they missed a few of the gags, but so did I.'

Dodd's singing he found pleasing to the ear and it undoubtedly enhanced his act. When Casey joined the BBC shortly afterwards he remembered that performance in Sunderland and mentioned the comedian's name to Ronnie Taylor, Head of Light Entertainment in BBC Manchester. He thought he should be given a chance to prove himself. A meeting was arranged for the following Monday morning at 10 o'clock in Taylor's office when scripts and ideas for a radio series would be discussed.

'It was 11 o'clock when Ken arrived,' Casey says. 'He said his car broke down. We believed him and got on with the discussion. It was agreed that he would feature in a series of six programmes which I would produce and script for him. Although he was breaking new ground in radio, I can say that Ken was a success from the start. The only fault was perhaps his quick delivery which caused him to fluff lines if he happened to be working from a new script, otherwise he adjusted easily to the technique and his voice recorded well.'

It was thought by some people in Manchester that because he was essentially a visual comic Ken Dodd would not be a success in radio, but Jim Casey disagreed. 'Yes, it was true that a few people at the BBC reckoned Ken was a better stage comic, yet they came round to the view later that he had succeeded admirably in radio.'

Workers' Playtime, which attracted millions of listeners, provided the comedian with ample scope. Producer Jim Casey was surprised one day to find him entertaining the workers on the factory floor immediately after he had finished his own eight-minute recording spot. 'For more than twenty minutes Ken made them roar with laughter and the workers loved every minute. I can't say the same for the bosses. Undeterred, he continued to entertain the workers wherever the programme was recorded. All he wanted was an audience, the location wasn't important.'

On another occasion when the series came from Barton Power Station, Charlie Chester was top of the bill. 'Charlie was very kind to me,' Dodd remembers. 'You'd be surprised with some of the stars you see, and you think, "Buy Jove, he looks hard" – they are usually the ones who are charming people. On the other hand some of the people you think look like Father Christmas turn out to be real big-heads. I reckon you should never judge a sausage by its overcoat.'

As an individual, Jim Casey liked the comedian. Off-stage, he found him quiet, even serious, and unlike other comics he knew Ken Dodd did not try to be funny all the time. 'He never fooled around retailing gags. He preferred to talk about ordinary happenings. Even then, Ken had a lot of time for the public: he was nice to them, and he became popular because of his affable manner. In those days Ronnie Taylor reckoned he was the funniest man under the age of fifty in the country.'

Casey found that Dodd was obsessed with comedy. 'I'd do it if they didn't pay me a penny,' he remarked to him one day. Soon they were working together on a new radio series which was the comic's first in the Light Programme. It was through working with Dodd that the producer met Eddie Braben, who had shortly before joined the comedian as his script-writer. Casey recognised his tremendous talent and reckoned he would go places in radio comedy. Braben had come from a working-class background. In his youth he was tall and quick-witted with a gift for wise-cracking. He had been a barrow boy in St John's Market in Liverpool and used to give his customers so much lip and gags that one customer who could appreciate the lingo suggested to him one day, 'Why don't you write for comics, Eddie? I hear there's a lot of money in that.' Eddie became interested, but he had to start from scratch and learn the alphabet. And at home at night he worked hard to write down funny gags. Eventually he sold a page of jokes to a local funny man for fifteen shillings and this was his spur. At that time he was making fifteen shillings a week out of his market-stall jokes when he met Ken Dodd and convinced him well enough to become his gag-writer.

They got on well from the start, each appreciating the other's sense of humour and penchant for comedy. More important, they began to work well as a team, and Ken Dodd used most of the gags provided by Eddie. He was honest, too. 'I am only a gag-man,' he would tell the comedian. 'I've never done situation comedy or sketches.' Dodd was not worried at that time about sketches for all he required was funny gags and Eddie's supply never dried up.

In September 1958, Jim Casey and Frank Roscoe sat down to write a new radio series for Ken Dodd. *It's Great to Be Young* would include in the cast Peter Goodwright, Judith Chalmers and the Barry Sisters. Music was provided by the BBC Northern Dance Orchestra and the recording took place on Sunday afternoons at the Manchester Playhouse. Casey, who also produced the series, felt that the comedian was learning decidedly more about radio techniques and this was showing in his performance, though he still fluffed lines when he talked too fast.

Judith Chalmers' bubbling personality came through in the opening lines: 'Yes, it certainly is great to be young, especially when you're with that laughable Liverpudlian, the nut from Knotty Ash, Ken Dodd. But to tell you more about Ken here is our brilliant young impressionist Peter Goodwright.'

Goodwright: (impersonating Arthur Askey) 'Hello, playmates. How do you do? I'm here tonight to introduce a fellow comic from Liverpool, Ken Dodd . . .'

Goodwright, a most accomplished radio actor, was particularly good at voices and very convincing in a variety of roles. In sketches with Dodd he could be brilliant. Miss Chalmers also proved an excellent foil for the comedian, as can be seen here:

Judith: It may surprise many listeners to know that Ken Dodd has his serious side. He is a great student of history.

Ken: 'She's right, Missus. I've read all the books – "The Arabian Nights", "The Decline and Fall of the Shepherd's Bush Empire" – but none of 'em mention the people who matter. You've all read about Henry the Eight and his six wives, but nobody ever mentions his executioner. You don't even know his name, but I do. His name was Fred – known as Fred the Chopper. The famous ancestor of Mack the Knife. Fred was an easygoing sort of bloke, but he wasn't happy in his work.'

(Door opens and shuts)

Judith: 'Is that you, Fred?'

Ken: 'Yes. Is my tea ready? I'm worn out.'

(Clang of metal on floor)

Ken: 'Give that axe a rub-down. I'm past it.'

Judith: 'What kind of day have you had, dear?'

Ken: 'Oh, shocking. I've never stopped. King Henry's been doing his nut. I've had five ducks during my tea-break.'

Judith: 'Well, you would go in for this Executioner's job. You were doing very well with your firewood round.'

Ken: 'Well, I couldn't be mixing with the peasants. I mean being the King's Executioner, I meet a better class of people altogether.'

Judith: 'Well, it's no use complaining. You've got the job so make the best of it.'

Ken: 'It's not the job. It's the hours. And I get no overtime. I should have insisted on piece-work. Ten bob a nob. I wish King Henry had never offered me the job.'

Judith: 'Offered it to you? That's a laugh. When you

heard it was vacant, you were never off his drawbridge. Three o'clock in the morning – by his portcullis.'

Ken: 'If you don't stop nagging, I'll start bringing my work home.'

Later in the sketch, when Peter Goodwright enters, there is an amusing scene between Dodd and himself.

Peter: 'His Majesty King Henry the Eight requires your presence at the Royal Palace immediately. Bring your axe.'

Ken: 'Don't tell me he's had a row with the wife already?'

Peter: 'Come along at once.'

Ken: 'But it's ten o'clock at night. I was just going to put the pig out and go to bed.'

Peter: 'Do you refuse to obey His Majesty's command?'

Ken: 'Tell him I'm jacking it in. And that axe stays here till I get my cards and my holiday money.'

Peter: 'Insolent varlet. His Majesty is outside in the state coach. Do you refuse to come?'

Ken: 'Yes.'

Peter: 'Then it will be on your head . . .

The sketch ended on a neat note:

Peter: 'Well, we've sorted it out Fred. Clarence'll be taking over the axe from now. And we'll see your name is remembered in history.'

Ken: 'How?'

Peter: 'You're Clarence's first customer.'

Judith: 'Oh, Fred!'

The script ran to twenty-two pages with certain lines and brief passages edited out. It was one of the occasions that the recording did not overrun to any great extent. 'I wish it was always like that,' quipped Jim Casey. 'Sometimes I had to use the knife quite liberally to get it down to size'. Ken Dodd never interfered with the editing and accepted that in that area Casey, as producer, was the boss.

CHAPTER 7

'I'd Like You For Blackpool'

The prospect of playing his first summer season in Blackpool excited Ken Dodd. He was told that Jack Capstack, manager of the Central Pier, was eager to have him on his variety bill. To the ambitious young comedian from Knotty Ash, it was another step up the showbiz ladder. 'Blackpool's a shopwindow for comedians,' Dave Forrester used to say.

It was more. There was nothing like it anywhere else in the world. In the Fifties it was a veritable Mecca. With a population of a million people during the high season, Blackpool could support more live theatre shows than any other resort in Britain, and in addition could point to cinemas, nightclubs, the Golden Mile with its glaring lights, side-shows and some excellent eating places all over town. In some you could order oysters with champagne which you could buy by the glass.

It was a long season, from the beginning of April until mid-October, enlivened by a show business community that was large and gregarious, and an artist's standing was judged by the sort of theatre he played. At the top of the league was the Opera House. 'In those days a pro couldn't miss in Blackpool,' commented Eric Morecambe. 'What with the regular employment, high wages and no travelling expenses, many bought new cars. Some took up golf and flying.'

65

Although Morecambe and Wise topped the bill at the Central Pier, Ken Dodd was prominently featured in the show, *Let's Have Fun*. His act proved a smash hit with the lively holiday audiences. When he burlesqued a sentimental ballad, they sang along with him. Jack Capstack was delighted by the enthusiastic response and told the Liverpool comic, 'One day you'll top the bill in this town.' The theatre critics and showbiz columnists wrote nice things about his performance. The columnists were eager to know more about life in Knotty Ash and Ken assured them that it was a real place inhabited by real people. When they quizzed him about romance, he introduced them to Anita Boutin and more than one reporter featured her prominently. The critics concentrated on his comedy and his stage appearance.

'Ken's humour has a touch of Marx about it (Groucho, not Karl),' began the review in the *Blackpool Gazette*, 'and a giddy unpredictability that has his audience in stitches. His appearance too is quite something. He has a shock of black hair, mischievous eyes and teeth like kerbstones.' Doddy was tickled for once, and remarked, 'I wouldn't mind but they do look like kerbstones! However, it's a change from being told they look like dominoes.'

Magician Cyril Critchlow, whose favourite comic was Frank Randle, described Blackpool in those days as a place of glitter and sand and the most important theatre town outside London. In the Fifties it fulfilled an important function by providing entertainment for the masses. He rarely missed a show and was attracted to the Central Pier because Morecambe and Wise topped the bill, but to his surprise it was Ken Dodd who proved the show-stealer. 'The audience loved him,' he remembers. 'He clowned, wise-cracked and sang – and overran. His line in patter was topical and very funny and he appealed to both parents and children, although quite a number of his one-liners were above the heads of the children.'

To Critchlow, the Liverpool comedian was a rising star.

'I had no doubt he would make it. I had seen comics "die" on Blackpool stages, but here was an unknown making people roar with laughter. He was fresh and enthusiastic and he did not spare himself. He knew above all what he was about.'

Today Critchlow, who measures the greatness of comics by their timing, has a fascinating theatre museum in Coronation Street in Blackpool, a short distance from the Opera House and the Grand Theatre, and he is also co-author of a book about the history of theatres in the resort. Among the two thousand or so exhibits in the museum are photographs of Ken Dodd and programmes from his early shows at the Central Pier and later at the Opera House. There are also reminders of famous comedians who made their names there. Critchlow ranks Ken Dodd among the best comics he has seen. As he says, 'Ken captured the town by his outlandish appearance and dynamic approach to comedy. Unlike other comics, he gave his audience no time to relax between gags and seaside audiences loved him for it. It was fun and gaiety they were after and they suddenly discovered a man who could make them laugh. At the Central Pier they did not want him to go off, so he overran, but I don't think Jack Capstack cautioned him about that.'

In that summer, 1955, there were as usual seventy acts at eight theatres and it was customary for the show business crowd to gather each day at the Savoy or Winter Gardens. There, they gossiped about personalities, shows, cricket and who was next for golf and flying. Ken Dodd nearly always missed the coffee and the gossip as he had motored home to Knotty Ash on the previous night. But his name came up whenever new Blackpool performers were talked about. He was a rising star in a town that loved stars – and most of all comedians. Since there was only one matinée in the week the entertainers liked to sunbathe or swim or merely relax with a drink.

The pace was leisurely, the atmosphere exciting and the crowds swarmed over the Golden Mile.

By the end of August Ken Dodd was able to invest in a second-hand Jaguar and for a change arrived in style at the Central Pier. Soon the car became the butt of his jokes. 'Every day I discover something new in it. So far I've found a radio, a cigar lighter, and a heater which does everything except toast. I believe the car used to belong to a titled lady who sold it because one day she found it pointing in the wrong direction.'

When the show ended its run the management announced that it had broken all box-office records. Dave Forrester, who normally did not betray emotion, was overjoyed for Ken Dodd's sake. He remained cautious, though, about pushing the comedian too fast. London offers did not interest him at that stage. Back in the quiet seclusion of his Georgian house in Knotty Ash the young comedian regarded his career with new-found confidence. As his mother had never tired of telling him, 'Anything is possible,' and now her advice seemed to be coming true.

That November he was appearing in variety in Manchester when he was visited by London-born impresario, Peter Webster, who was then living in Blackpool. Webster spread before him on the dressing-room table a blank contract and remarked earnestly, 'I'd like you for the next Blackpool summer season, Ken.' The comedian, who was still in his make-up, stared at the contract and wondered what to do. He would have to discuss it with Dave Forrester.

Webster started to fill in the contract, then looked up at Dodd and said as an afterthought, 'I almost forgot . . . it's a three-figure salary. Will that be all right with you? The comedian gave a short laugh. He did not want to appear overwhelmed before the impresario. He merely said, 'That's fine, Peter'.

Before Ken set out for Blackpool he had an important date in his home town. In early May 1956, he was given top billing at the Liverpool Empire Theatre. It was the ambition of every Scouse comic to top the bill at the Empire Theatre, which was one of the leading variety houses in the North of England. Growing up, he had seen Arthur Askey, George Formby and other comics there and he enjoyed them immensely. The Liverpool *Post* noted, 'Ken Dodd not only deserves his success but has earned it the hard way – via the clubs, dinners and social occasions as a semi-pro entertainer. And what fine company he is in! Jimmy James, that popular comedian who will surely introduce us again to his "bloke from Bootle", The Kordites and Joan Turner'.

The Empire, an attractive and spacious theatre, was not easy to fill to its capacity of 2,500 seats, but on the first night few were empty. Among those who laughed at the string of Knotty Ash gags were Arthur and Sarah Dodd, Ken's parents, who were as proud as punch about their son's showbiz success. Anita Boutin was there to mark as usual the response to his gags. The comedian was nervous before the curtain rose but he quickly got into his stride and even managed to overrun.

By now he noticed that his singing appealed more and more to audiences, and the Empire audience was no exception. It encouraged him at that time to find suitable ballads to sing at his performances. Several recording companies shared the view of his fans that he should make records. 'They wrote to me about recording,' he recalls, 'asking me to make an LP. I wonder which voice I should use? The octave voice that enables me to sing soprano, tenor and baritone songs, or should I concentrate on pop songs and try for a Golden Disc? Last year in a BBC *Blackpool Night* I sang *Brown Eyes*. I got many written requests for an encore, including dozens from Anita who has brown eyes!'

The recording companies were reputed to be impressed

by the 'feeling' he put into his singing, although at that time his primary commitment was to comedy. 'Maybe I should have singing lessons?' he remarked to Dave Forrester. Perhaps he was reflecting on the time when he wanted to be an opera singer and only dismissed the idea when Anita Boutin reminded him of his protruding teeth. However, he still saw himself in the mould of John Hanson and in variety he found singing relaxed him between the patter and the gags.

That summer in Blackpool he could be counted among those people who fell under the spell of Josef Locke's voice as the tenor thrilled audiences with ballads like *Goodbye* and *A Soldier's Dream*. Locke, in turn, regarded the comedian as the funniest he had ever seen in a theatre. 'He took the Central Pier by storm,' he recalls. 'I did something I rarely did at the time – I watched his performance from the side of the stage and found it hilarious. Everything about him was funny – his face, teeth, hair, and his delivery was so fast I missed some of the gags. He overran but the truth was that we wanted him to stay on stage.'

Locke, who was a larger-than-life character, was sufficiently impressed by Dodd's baritone voice to say that he could perhaps make a living as a singer. 'I think it was a big asset to him as a comedian and it helped make his act more enjoyable. It was his dedication, though, that struck me forcibly – Ken lived for the stage. The sound of laughter did something to him and I feel that is why he overran.'

When Ken Dodd introduced Josef Locke to Anita Boutin he was taken by her sense of fun and obvious love for Ken. 'Nobody except Ken Dodd was alive for that woman,' says Locke. 'In the business I had heard about Anita giving up nursing to be with Ken but I hadn't expected to find such loyal devotion. She watched him from the wings, she listed all his gags, and she never missed a show. I knew they weren't married, but seeing

Ken's obsession with the stage it did not surprise me that he was still a bachelor. I don't think I ever expected him to marry Anita.'

To Locke, who liked a drink after a performance, it seemed peculiar that Ken and Anita would not stay overnight in Blackpool, but instead drove home to Liverpool. Most of the other artistes drank and chatted about the business into the night. It was the practice in the Blackpool showbiz scene of the time. Josef Locke decided that the comedian was somewhat of a loner in a business where it was usual for performers to seek reassurances in conversation with colleagues and friends.

Ken Dodd was, for instance, a notable absentee from the 'Battle of the Roses' cricket match played by the stars of that season's summer shows. When a trial match was arranged for Stanley Park, he felt that the conditions of the £10,000 insurance on his freak teeth would not permit taking any chances of getting in the way of a bumper. However, the comedian was respected by his fellow professionals who found him unpretentious as a person.

When the season ended he returned as usual to Knotty Ash and prepared for the Christmas pantomime in which he was to play Jolly Jenkins in *Red Riding Hood* at Sheffield. Pantomime held genuine appeal for him, mainly because it appealed to children and he loved entertaining children. It was in his view also good for theatres because it filled them and so helped them to stay open. At that time he played a lot of variety with star names on the bill and it was something that he welcomed.

At Coventry Hippodrome, he teamed up with Jewel and Warriss, Jill Day, Tommy Cooper and Arthur Worsley. There was one snag: when he was asked to follow Tommy Cooper he refused because he thought it a bit daft since it meant 'one grotesque after another'. Instead, he was given the spot following a Jewel and Warriss slapstick act (one in which Jimmy, dressed as a plumber, ended up rising from the tub of a nubile bather with a cry of, 'I'm here, you bloody fool') and he admitted later, 'Coming on top of an audience-rouser like that, my own act went like a rocket.'

He was a good listener and heeded advice. 'Jimmy Jewel was generous with his time. He used to give me my riding instructions before I went on. And Ben Warriss was equally good to me. I couldn't pass his door without him calling to me and introducing me to all kinds of important showbiz people.'

The comedian was developing his own philosophy about comedy and the role of the comic. He reckoned it was much easier to steal a show than to star in a show. 'A new comic can steal a show with ease because he has the quality of the unexpected.' He didn't mind being called a show-stealer, in fact he was tickled by it; there was, in his own view, still enough time to be a star.

To attain stardom needed perhaps something extra: a prop, a popular catch-phrase, a lucky break, or the creation of an original stage character. He gave it a lot of thought and when he eventually decided on a tickling stick he knew it was by mere chance. As he explained, 'It came partly from reading about jesters and their familiars on a stick. The jester always used to carry around a pig's bladder on a stick and, if he liked you, he always used to hit you on the head with it. Charming. He also had a red-hot poker, which is another phallic symbol, and his own little image on a stick which he used to talk to as if it were a straight man. He had this terrific licence – he could mention the unmentionable.'

The tickling stick was to become synonymous with his act in the same way that the catch-phrase, 'I theng you' was associated with Arthur Askey. Ken Dodd reckoned that the tickling stick was more potent than any catch-phrase and this was borne out by audience response. Laughter usually exploded when he aimed the stick at some pretty girls in the front row or some silver blondes and exclaimed, 'Have you ever been tickled under the circumstances?'

He used a variety of tickling sticks, big ones, small ones, thin ones, and on occasions great big ones as high as himself. He also made use of the fact that he addressed a mythical lady in the audience as 'Missus' and it helped him to establish a warm rapport, besides being very effective as a comedy device. It went back to his days as a salesman when he sold things to the ladies in the housing estates in Liverpool and he used to say, 'Missus'.

Despite his growing success, Ken kept close to his parents. There was never any real likelihood that he would move out of their house in Knotty Ash. His private life was his own and if he wished to sleep in in the mornings, which he was inclined to do, no one complained. As always his mother fussed over him, ensuring that his shirts were washed and properly ironed, and that he ate the right food. They were intensely interested in his career and they had no doubt that he was destined for the top. It did not escape their notice either that he was earning more money than ever before.

To Bill Boutin, Anita's brother, the comedian was level-headed and seemed to take success in his stride. He always wanted to achieve bigger things and did not disguise his ambition. Boutin found him to be 'a careful individual who did not indulge himself in either food or drink, nor did he go in for smart clothes.' It struck him that Ken Dodd worked extremely hard and holidays did not seem to interest him. He continued to be good to Anita, though Bill Boutin sometimes wondered if he intended to marry her.

For her part, Anita had grown philosophical and was satisfied to be Ken's partner. They often discussed the possibility of marriage in those early years and there were times when she thought he wanted her to be his wife, but he would forget about it because he was too busy.

She was committed to helping him become a big star. She went to any lengths, for instance, to ensure that he got local laughs in towns he visited. The first thing she did when he arrived to play a town was to go to the library where she would spend hours poring over local reference books so that Ken could bring local gags into his act. Jokes like, 'Have you read the new item, Missus? Liverpool man steals three tons of jelly – remanded in custard.' She carried around with her a stop-watch and timed the length of laughs. She made notes in an exercise book about every gag – a 'V.G.' for a big belly laugh, and 'X' for one that didn't go at all.

By now she had filled more than a hundred notebooks and kept them for reference, so that whenever Ken played a town she could look back and see what jokes had gone down well there before. Jokes like, 'I'm not married, Missus – I've always been round-shouldered.'

Sometimes Anita and Ken had tiffs and she would threaten not to attend that week's performances. The trouble was that he had, as he used to say, 'a very short fuse and flew off the handle quite easily'. He also liked having his own way too much. However, they made up quickly and he would be relieved to know that 'his Nita' was back in the theatre with him. It was a relationship that was admired in the business and Anita seemed to leave a lasting impression on people she met. A few people, however, regarded it sadly and thought at that time that Ken should pop the question. It seemed such a natural thing to do since he always told friends he loved children.

But stardom beckoned – and Anita could wait.

CHAPTER 8

'I Caught a Whisper That He Was Good'

'He explodes on to stages wearing the garish hues of the fairground – bright pinks, vivid greens, glaring checks – and often carrying the tickling stick.'

It was an accurate description of Ken Dodd in the late Fifties and reflected the excitement he generated. It was the impression carried away from performances by a young Mancunian, Eric Midwinter, who had a burning interest in comedy and comedians and in no time at all could describe the comic mannerisms and stage styles of Billy Bennett, Rob Wilton, Jimmy James and Max Miller. It afforded him also tremendous satisfaction to be able to draw comparisons between their fame and achievements.

As a youth his father used to take him on Sunday mornings to Manchester railway station to watch the comings and goings of shows and acts booked by the week. 'One can imagine,' Midwinter recalls, 'Jimmy James on the steam trains with their newly painted BR or in one of those oblong-shaped saloons of the post war travelling slowly and deliberately from Preston to Portsmouth or Warrington to Wolverhampton.'

He was convinced that part of being a great comedian lay, consciously or unconsciously, in being attuned to the refrains of society, in hearing its melodies, in orchestrating them, and in playing them back. When he first watched Ken Dodd perform at the Manchester Palace he saw in his act reminders, if sometimes slight, of Jimmy James and Rob Wilton. The comedian made a powerful impact on him, so much so that years later he wrote, 'Where Jimmy James or Rob Wilton might steal up unawares and sap a corner of the fortress, Ken Dodd takes the fortress by storm. The barrage is laid through his "what a wonderful day it is for . . ." artillery. "What a wonderful day it is for trooping the rentman, or "grandad-biting" '.

Midwinter made a close study of the comedian's art and decided he possessed highly individualised comic flair, range and versatility, which were matched by his diligent technical application. Even without the tickling stick, he reckoned that Ken Dodd, because of his eccentric stage appearance, automatically passed for a clown. Later he visited his home in Knotty Ash and felt that a sense of place was important to the comic and essential to his act. He marvelled at his work-rate and this resulted in some 'hectic conversations' with him and tended to make Dodd an elusive subject for interview.

Midwinter tells the story of calling at the comedian's home one evening to find that he had not yet returned from a mission, with his door being knocked by someone trying to persuade him to do a charity show in Worsley, prior to a long drive to Stratford-upon-Avon for a late-night cabaret, with several urgent phone calls in between times. Anyone else except the zealous Midwinter would have given up in despair, but he was committed to discovering how the comedian coped and to try to 'grasp the historical roots of his comic gift'.

He was amused when Dodd told him, 'You look tired, you shouldn't overdo it!'. Coming from an entertainer who worked nearly sixty hours in the week it seemed an ironic, even absurd remark. He was puzzled by the comic's frenetic tempo and wondered about this inner compulsion. He had rarely encountered it in other comics, for in Dodd's case his life-style was far removed from his dynamic stage act. There were elements of frenzy in both.

He was perhaps at that time more interested in the influences on the comic's work, something that Ken Dodd himself was not slow to acknowledge.

'He is an admirer of comic actors,' Midwinter said, 'and is quick to mention Alistair Sim and Cary Grant. Will Hay, master of the long double-take and the disdainful sniff; Frankie Howerd for being – in Ken's word – "outrageous" – and more, latterly, for the exquisite deftness of his expertise, Jimmy James – these are some of the influences on the comedian.'

In their conversations the eager Midwinter found that Rob Wilton's name cropped up quite regularly. Stories about the great comic are legendary. Jimmy James used to say that 'he was the greatest timer in the business'. And there were celebrated anecdotes too about his ad lib humour. Midwinter would say that Ken Dodd always spoke warmly about Wilton and actually honoured him with a funny and lovable impersonation.

He felt, though, that Dodd's tempo was brisker and more audacious than that of the 'Confidential Comedian'; he was, in his own expression, a 'fireworks comic'. But there was much of the same domestic commentary. 'The lugubrious Wilton's exasperated reply to his wife's suggestion that he wouldn't know who Hitler was if the Germans landed – "I've got a tongue in my head, haven't I? – is not too far removed from Ken Dodd's notion that to discover the time during the night, one might bang a bass drum, on the grounds that someone is sure to yell, "Who the hell's banging a big drum at half-past two in the morning?" It is the same dotty combination of the alien concept and the homespun rejoinder.'

It was inevitable that the comedian's modern approach to comedy would attract a wide cross-section of people. It was accepted that he drew on Liverpool for a lot of his material, though he also relied on general comedy. By now his shrewd analysis of audience reaction had inspired the label, 'the slide-rule comic'. Papers began to take more notice of his unique record of how, night by night, audiences reacted to his gags. What puzzled more people was how he found time to fill his notebooks. Among those fascinated by his log-books was Eric Midwinter, who thought they reflected the respect he showed for his audience while at the same time helping the comedian in his own choice of gags on particular nights.

He concluded that Dodd was a 'comic genius'; a clown and jester, but without the Pagliacci touch, eschewing that hint of pathos which was the ruination of popular comedy. He personified the chief characteristics of professional comedy. Ken Dodd was a rarity.'

By now the enterprising comedian was affectionately known as 'Doddy' in Liverpool, Blackpool and Manchester. It was an indication of his popularity and the warmth of his personality. Further appearances on *The Good Old Days*, as well as radio's *Blackpool Night*, widened his personal appeal and charisma and made his name better known outside the North of England. Because he did not spare himself, he quickly realised when audience response was less than enthusiastic. On such rare occasions he was more inclined to put the blame on the audience rather than on his own performance. As he argued, 'There are some people who cannot take part in this very English form of evening. It is not a question of jokes. It is a fantasy and high-flying exuberance. Some people don't respond. They're born like that. They're cold. Bawdy is as meaningless to them as the loneliness of men's legs, kilted tables and sleeping on the right-hand side of the bed in the comic market.'

Doddy's reputation did not extend as far as London. Dave Forrester, his agent, was not concerned by such lack of recognition. His approach, as ever, remained quiet, if over-cautious. He liked to say, 'I have seen many good artistes who had star potential, but have gone by the wayside because they have been impatient, often moving to another agency which has not been good for them at all. Good management is very, very important in the entertainment business.'

The Liverpool comedian had no intention of leaving the theatrical agency of Forrester George Limited. He hadn't as yet signed a contract but that did not worry him. Their working relationship was solid and there was no shortage of offers. Sometimes, in discussions between the agent and comic, the London offers were mentioned and invariably Forrester showed lack of enthusiasm, preferring, as he said, to wait for the right opportunity to come along to launch his client.

Few in Fleet Street took any notice of the rise of Kenneth Arthur Dodd and, for all they cared, Knotty Ash could well have been a remote island off the coast of Scotland. Eventually John Barber of the *Daily Express* was urged by friends and a few colleagues in the North to catch up with Doddy in performance. 'He's a star in the making,' they assured him. Barber would say, 'I caught a whisper that he was good. I wanted to take a wary London eye to this new Mr Funny.'

He made the pilgrimage to Bristol in order to give his verdict. He set out with an open mind and with only a slight sense of anticipation, he remembers, though he suspected it might after all be worth the journey. He was in for a surprise. 'I ran into the most formidable chunk of cool calculation since Laurence Harvey upstarted,' he later wrote. 'Dancing onto the stage he resembles a tailor's dummy escaped from bedlam. Hair like a frightened haystack. White cuffs exploding from his dress-coat. What made me sit up was his happiness. His hopping vitality. His pace. And his instant grasp of music-hall essentials.'

That evening in the theatre, the critic was captivated by the comedian's opening words, 'I'm as fit as a lodging-house cat. Every morning I wake and punch the bag for half an hour. She doesn't like it.' He pointed to his protruding teeth. 'I'm the only man in our house who can eat a tomato through a tennis-racket.' And: 'At school I was teacher's pet. I used to sit in a cage at the back of the classroom.'

Barber checked his watch. Doddy had been one minute on stage, yet around him in the dress circle and stalls the audience was convulsed by his lightning attack. In that brief space of time he had covered sex, matrimony, childhood, self-degradation, the Oedipus and inferiority complexes – every basic joke except the one about cheese. 'And if you think that is being over-analytic about humour, you don't know Mr Dodd.'

To Barber, it had been an exhilarating evening in the theatre, at once fresh and vibrant. Like many others seeing Doddy's act for the first time, he was amazed by the rapidity of his attack and the impact on himself. He decided Ken was worthy of closer scrutiny so he made his way into the street and around to the stage door. He quickly discovered another side to the comedian as he sat in his dressing-room poring over a notebook. At that moment he looked serious, like a bank clerk counting notes. Every page of the notebook was covered with scribbled hieroglyphics. And every big laugh Doddy got scored a VG. Or the reaction to a joke might be marked S-L-O-W. A real roar of laughter got a square box sign. A feeble one drew a firm X. Suddenly Doddy exclaimed, 'I'm worried. I've got one laugh I can't account for.' Puzzled, he again examined the ledger.

He anxiously scouted Henri Bergson's theory of humour as incongruity. He quoted Freud. But the psychology behind that extra giggle escaped him, as it had done Anita Boutin. As the comedian concerned himself with the ledger, Anita told the critic that she usually listed all responses to Ken's jokes in a notebook. Enthusiastically she explained, 'Every joke, every show. Both houses. Plus times, summaries, and outspoken comments. Ken has now a reaction to everything he has done on stage since he became a professional.'

Barber was fascinated by the scene around him. These people, he thought, treated comedy in the same way a scientist worked on a new theory – with method and calculation. Doddy, in his estimation, was the 'Scientific New Comic' of his generation. His success was obviously based on his thorough homework. While he was an instinctive comic, he was undoubtedly above his colleagues in intelligence and left nothing to chance. He was fighting his way to stardom by slide-rule methods. It was extraordinary. The comedian was able to tell, for instance, what was needed to get laughs.

In Scotland, Doddy told Barber, they wanted quick laughs – one-liners. In the North of England audiences were more cynical. It was aggressive, poker-faced comedy for them. In the Midlands, they loved singing ('Harry Secombe began there') and in the South they wanted lovable clowns. Fun was gentler there. It was where Sid Field struck gold.

Barber was surprised by the comic's energy; his mind was alert and his concentration sharp, despite his performances earlier. He was in loquacious mood, as he pointed again to the ledger. 'In Yorkshire friendly comedians are most popular, while in Lancashire they must be warm-hearted, but with a more abrasive, cutting edge. Welsh audiences go for wild, zany comedians possibly due to the Celtic element, thus the success of Tommy Cooper. London seems to like comics with a Chaplinesque feature of pathos.

Barber considered his journey a worthwhile pilgrimage. For his paper he summed up, 'Sooner or later you will see this restless loon with the wild hair and kempt voice. I predict that you will laugh. Be not fooled. His steely, streamlined performance, his ruthlessly calculated act is geared for maximum laughter output. He is fighting you with ledger statistics, joke categories. Freud . . . you may as well give in.'

Back in Knotty Ash it was rumoured that Doddy had become engaged to Anita. Romance again was in the air and women in shops and hairdressing salons talked in terms of a white wedding. Wherever Doddy and Anita went they were confronted by the news and the inevitable questions: when is the wedding? In order to cool the situation, he told the *Liverpool Post*, 'Well, I can tell you the wedding won't be in October.'

'Will it be in December then?' asked the reporter.

Doddy was cautious.

'I can't say. One thing I can assure you is that it will be in Liverpool . . . when it happens.'

The young reporter was disappointed. If she expected a scoop, she wasn't going to get it that morning from Doddy. She switched her attention to Anita Boutin and congratulated her on her engagement and expressed the hope that it would work out. She inquired about marriage plans, but Anita was hesitant. All she would say was, 'I really don't know. It's up to Ken. Why don't you ask him?'

'I did,' sighed the reporter, 'and he said he'll be discussing his plans with you.'

The *Post* missed a scoop and the reporter hung up frustrated. It was not the first time that the rumour had circulated that the comedian intended to wed. At least there was confirmation of the couple's engagement. But that was not enough for the friendly women of the village of Knotty Ash. They felt cheated that Ken and Anita had still not provided them with that white wedding.

As for Doddy, he made no secret of his admiration for women. He liked chatting them up in restaurants and round the theatre and he saw nothing wrong in mild flirtation. In turn, women found his charm irresistible and he was good company. Jealousy was not part of Anita's make-up and she understood that comics had women admirers as well as fans. Ken, she knew, was no exception. In his dressing-room she had seen women greet him with kisses and laud his success. In their eyes he was a star. It was part of the glamour side of showbiz and she had learned to accept it, even if sometimes it could be irritating. She felt reassured that Ken wanted her round him; she never doubted his love.

Doddy was not reluctant to discuss the subject of women and his views over the years did not change greatly. As he said, 'I would definitely count myself as an expert on the subject of what turns a man on. After all, I'm a professor of tickleology. But let's take the sensual bits first: with a man, certain parts of a lady have definite appeal. Some are leg men, calf men, ankle or cheek men. I'm an upper arm man and shoulder man; that's definitely one of the nicest bits. Upper arm and shoulder men are in evidence at parties, boilermen's soirées and Hunt Balls. In the springtime you can even see them in St John's Garden.'

Merseyside women, in his view, were the prettiest in the country. 'We have the best of the Celtic and the best of English together.' He thought that girls were more beautiful at that time than they had ever been in history, mainly because they could afford to dress better, but how they did it on their husbands' money he would never know.

At that point, Doddy could not resist a bit of whimsy: 'I like paying compliments to ladies wearing a particularly nice necklace or piece of jewellery. I tell them that whoever bought them that must have loved them a lot, and they invariably say, "I bought it for myself".'

He had his own romantic notion of his ideal woman. He saw her as a mysterious nymph-like goddess. He abhorred in those early years mannish women who wanted to drink, smoke and curse like the lads. It was his opinion that a woman in business could achieve a lot more with femininity than by trying to match a man by being forthright. Only one thing was worse than a bossy man and that was a bossy woman. Charm was the key, and he never tired of extolling its praises. 'Charm is what it is all about. I remember a lady in a pub in West Derby who could empty the place at closing time quicker than anyone else. "Come along, sunshine," she'd say. "There's a good boy. Empty your glass." That's much better than the usual, "Time" or "Ain't you got no 'ome to go to?".'

In the theatre Doddy used another kind of charm to ingratiate himself with women in his audience. Like Max Miller, he often seemed to talk directly to them, but unlike Miller his patter was never suggestive – it was funny. And his sexual innuendo appealed to both men and women. He could not be labelled a cruel comedian, even when he joked about placing old folk safely in nursing homes or wickedly poked fun at grandad, or at 'imported' doctors deployed to prop up the Health Service.

To theatre audiences, Doddy's singing of romantic ballads held undoubted appeal and occasionally he would inject a measure of pathos, although he was always careful to stop short of sentimentality. Invariably, he aimed his tickling-stick gags at women in the front of the stalls while at the same time he mischievously tried to reach them with the wandering stick. He never ceased to win laughs as he quipped, 'how tickled I am by all the goodwill. Have you ever been tickled by goodwill, Missus? Good old Willie.' Or when in full flow, he cajoled,'Would you like a moonlight dip, Missus? You'll have to warm your hands first. Would you marry a man in a kilt and green socks – or would you wear a wedding dress?'

It was this kind of intimate rapport that he missed on television and to a lesser extent on radio, for as one critic succinctly put it, 'It is in his theatre performance that one can analyse the compound of flair and technique, of art and craft, which makes him a champion comic.'

CHAPTER 9

'Ken Has Hypnotised The BBC'

Everyone agreed, including Doddy, that Tony Hancock was the first of the great television comics.

He owed his success not only to his face and voice but to his clever utilisation of situation comedy and to his versatility: changing from crooner to Shakespearean actor to impersonator came easily to this introspective comic. Yet Doddy, while admiring Hancock's skills and mastery of television comedy techniques, was 'disturbed by his excesses of melancholia'; such excesses ran contrary to his own conception of comedy, which was to heighten the gaiety and promote laughter at all costs.

At that time Bob Hope blamed television for virtually killing off vaudeville in America, and music-hall in Britain, none the less Doddy saw the value of the medium. It created overnight discoveries, forged international reputations, and was ignored by entertainers at their peril. Television was on the advance. As it expanded it would provide opportunities for variety artists made redundant by the end of music-hall. It would in time create its own stars, Stanley Baxter, Benny Hill, Ronnie Barker and, hopefully, Ken Dodd.

Ever ambitious, Doddy embarked on his new career with the enthusiasm and purpose that marked his approach to stage and radio. He was optimistic. Morecambe and Wise had after all transferred their stage performance successfully to TV, so what had he to fear? As far as he was concerned, nothing. However there were factors to be considered. The advent of the comic actor – a new phenomenon – meant fewer opportunities for comedians. Comic actors such as Wilfred Brambell and Harry Corbett would be soon attracting millions of viewers in *Steptoe and Son*. One television critic voiced his concern: 'By the Sixties there was scarcely television for top-rate comedians. There would be variety spectaculars with slots for comics and some feeble efforts to encompass comedians within the confines of domestic serials.'

For Doddy there were the permissive Sixties to consider, and whether he was prepared to take advantage. In reality, it was a time more suited to biting satire than any zany comedy. The Liverpool comic neither possessed the outrageousness of Frankie Howerd nor the allure of Danny La Rue. Doddy's lunatic poses that rocked theatre audiences might seem unfunny in camera close-ups, and the simple virtues of his stand-up patter comedy could similarly misfire.

Television producers who had watched him in the theatre privately expressed some doubts. There was a question mark over his discipline. His record for over-running in the theatre was appalling. Could he adapt to television techniques where a single expression was sometimes more important than a round of jigs and hand motions? In Doddy's favour, though, was the fact that he was a visual comic whose style appeared easily adaptable for the small screen.

Barney Colehan, who had given him his first opportunity in *The Good Old Days*, was confident that the comedian could make the transition successfully. As he said, 'I kept bringing Ken back to my show. With his combination of funny patter and popular ballads, he was popular with viewers. I could not see why he shouldn't be funny in his own TV show.'

When Doddy did get his own show in 1960 it was at

peak viewing time on a Saturday night. Not only that, he had persuaded the BBC to allow him to record it in Bolton in circumstances that would have made more experienced TV comics shudder. Actually he had forced the Corporation to slap on his show with only a day's preparation.

Ostensibly it seemed absurd, a decided risk for a newcomer, however talented, to television. But Doddy was undeterred; he just could not spare the time for days of preparation, as was the case with other performers. Usually comedy shows had meticulous rehearsal lasting up to a week. Why then had the BBC thrown their rules overboard? There was but one answer – their implicit faith in the comedian. As one observer noted, 'The BBC think time will show Ken Dodd to have the genius touch, for they are paying him good money to work the Saturday peak variety hour for some months. Certainly he has hypnotised the BBC into what for them amounts to sheer recklessness.'

Doddy arrived for rehearsals at the Continental Theatre in Bolton, Lancashire on Sunday mornings at 10 o'clock and worked almost non-stop with his musicians, stooges and fellow artistes until 7 o'clock to ensure an integrated show. To enliven proceedings, the audience was admitted after seven and the recording begun. It was all-action Doddy, as he threw himself about, fired gags at the audience, pulled faces, shouted in a corncrake voice, and suddenly changed the whole tempo by plunging into a romantic ballad that had some of the older people in the theatre in tears.

To all intents and purposes, it was little more than a televised stage show, with Doddy wildly poking fun at his audience. Yet it quickly made its impact. The sheer vibrancy of the comedian's performance bowled over not a few TV critics. Kenneth Bailey in the *People* observed, 'I imagine that most viewers watch mesmerised, unable to decide whether he is just a jumped-up funny man from the end of some pier – or a sheer genius. Mind you, I think the shows have a thrown-on look, yet I feel this is part of their mesmeric power. You keep wondering if Mr Dodd is going to get through, or fall off the stage in a stroke.'

Anita Boutin's presence in the theatre did not go unnoticed. As ever, she filled her little black notebook with comments on Ken's performance and audience responses to his gags. Surrounded by cameras and lights, she found the scene both challenging and exciting and felt that Ken would soon be a television star in his own right. She was perhaps too close to him to be the best judge of that; moreover it was the viewer, not the audience, who now called the shots. At a time when Morecambe and Wise were refining their stage act for television, it was understandable that critics should comment on Doddy's approach. As one wrote, 'The whole pleasure of Mr Dodd's act is that he is an old-fashioned, stand-up comedian. He isn't way-out, off-beat, sick, black or goon. He springs straight from the old music-hall tradition.'

Visually his show was fun and ensured agreeable family viewing. Whether such an approach would in time lift him into the top rank of television entertainers was too early to predict. But he was prepared to devise, shape and plan for the new medium. It was imperative, though, that he should find more time to prepare shows and thus avoid the impression that they had been thrown together. Someone observed, 'Personally I find the whole Ken Dodd set-up engaging. It's just got me on tenterhooks, like a cliff-hanger. What will happen to Ken in the end?'

It was a question the comedian had scarcely time to ponder, although it left his producer with an understandable sense of trepidation as he entered the Continental Theatre in Bolton on Sunday mornings for rehearsals, not quite knowing what to expect, or whether at the end of the long rehearsal session they would have a programme for recording. It was a predictable pattern and would continue as long as the show lasted.

Meanwhile press interest in his career was increasing. He was attracting a wider audience through his radio and television programmes. By late 1960 he was earning £600 a week, though he was quick to remind reporters that he was paying out £8,000 a year for comedy material. For an entertainer who was not yet a big star, he was remarkably confident. 'I know I am on the right track,' he boasted. 'I know I can get more laughs in twenty minutes than anyone in the country. By laughs I mean real whopping belly laughs. The kind of laugh that makes you drop your tensions and relax.'

By now his success allowed him few breaks for privacy or relaxation. He was tireless, restless, ceaselessly working, forever on the move. In his sleek maroon Jaguar he drove thousands of miles to fulfil dates, including dinner and cabaret spots up and down the country. At that time he never tired of saying that the biggest mystery in the world was what made people laugh. By his own admission he said he had turned to Freud, Kant. Schopenauer and Bergson for the answer. 'The result,' as one observer put it, 'is not egg-head humour.'

There were critics who still could not make up their minds about his television show. Came the comment, 'At times tonight in his BBC show, Ken Dodd, with his kerbstone teeth, barbed-wire hair and grotesque dress, looks more like the village idiot.' That prompted the comedian to remark, 'Ah, this is the part of my act where I'm trying to make friends. I'm out to make them like me as just an ordinary fellow. Nothing very clever. When we're all friends then I can get down to the real stuff and enjoy myself. People want humour about things they can appreciate with all their senses. About things they can see, touch, smell and see in their minds.'

Even then, five years after turning professional, he was, it seemed, still burdened by the tag of provincial entertainer. He admitted he was better known in the North than in the South, yet it irritated him increasingly to be labelled a 'North Country comic'. He repeatedly said, 'I'm a British comedian and my ambitions are to come to London with a review and also to make the first comedy film musical.

Significantly, Doddy's efforts to be a star coincided with the rise of the Beatles and, like the comedian, the group at that time were finding it difficult to attract recording companies. With the emergent Beatles it was a case of desperation and in turn Brian Epstein's approaches were rejected by Pye, Phillips, Columbia and HMV. Doddy, on the other hand, had been trying for years to get people to take him seriously as a singer. It was not easy. The great majority of people saw him primarily as a comedian, despite the popularity of his singing with theatre audiences.

Eventually he achieved a lucky breakthrough. Jimmy Phillips, the boss of Keith Prowse Music, told him they were going to back him to make a record. 'He played me a few songs,' Doddy recalls, 'and then I said aloud, "That's it! That's the one!" It was the song that was magic, and Jimmy looked at me and said, "Oh . . . *that* one".'

After a pause, Doddy asked, 'Anything wrong, Jimmy?'

Phillips replied calmly, 'Nothing, except that's a French song and the lady who owns it has never allowed an English lyric to be put to it before, but I've managed to persuade her. There's a man called Jimmy Kennedy sitting on top of a mountain in Switzerland right now trying to think of a lyric.' Kennedy by that time had a string of chart-toppers to his name, *Red Sails in the Sunset*, *Harbour Lights*, and *South of the Border* being only three of them.

The song was titled *Love Is Like a Violin* and the English lyrics made it into a haunting love song, one ideally suited to Doddy's light baritone voice. He recorded it in the spring and by August of that year, 1960, it was number one in the hit parade. To his surprise, he was now a chart-topper and it meant he would in future be taken seriously as a singer.

Tenor Josef Locke was in no way surprised by Doddy's success. 'Ken always had an appealing voice and recording companies should have recognised this long before 1960. Funny thing was that in my Blackpool days he used to listen to me sing and he liked my singing. I'm sure he learned something from me. I also sang songs with a love theme.' Likewise, comedian Harry Bailey, a favourite in Blackpool, reckoned that Doddy's singing made him a more complete entertainer. 'At the beginning I don't think he took singing seriously, but as audiences loved to hear him sing he realised it was an asset to him.'

Doddy would say that it was pressure of public opinion that made him a singer in the first place. As he said, 'On stage I smoothed my hair and really went all out for a straight rendition of a ballad. It was this complete contrast between gags and the songs which appealed to the public.'

The turn of events amused him, for in the early days he wanted to sing and not tell gags. 'At first it was my singing which led me to comedy and now it is my comedy which has led me to emerge in public as a singer. I really enjoy singing a straight song and love romantic ballads with good orchestration. I like songs to have something to say and a sensible way of saying it. A lot of songs today are merely words and music without a message. I believe a singer should try to communicate with his audience through his song. And to be a good singer, one has to be an actor so that one can put over the song in the way it can be most appreciated.'

Success in the charts was, he conceded, important to the advancement of his career. It boosted his name and when *Love Is Like a Violin* stayed at the top he found he was asked to sing it by audiences and he included it in his act. When he went to Manchester to play at the Opera House, he surprised not a few people by enrolling at the city's School of Music, He hoped to fit lessons in between stage performances. Privately, he knew that he needed more insights into music if he was to sing effectively with a full orchestra.

He was tired, as he would say, of being 'high-hatted by music directors and orchestra leaders who tell me to "tacit" when all they mean is cut out a couple of bars.' When friends heard about his attendance at the School of Music, they wondered if the comedian was actually serious. 'It's not just a gag,' Doddy protested to W. Kindley Taylor, the Academy's principal. 'I would give anything for the chance to sing at Covent Garden.'

As his friends argued there was 'No money in opera for him' they were relieved when he forgot about the notion, as they called it. Doddy quipped, 'My father had a musical ear – it was shaped like a French horn.'

Unsurprisingly, as his popularity rose, his act began to attract London interest. Leading impresario Bernard Delfont travelled North and, after seeing Doddy's performance, told him, 'Bring it to town and don't change a word.' Later different dates at the Palladium were mentioned. The comic admitted, 'I was offered various deals by Val Parnell. He came to see me and he seemed to be impressed. But Dave Forrester said, "No, this isn't the time, or that isn't the show, nor is that the kind of deal we should accept." I took his advice and was prepared to wait.'

The time factor always seemed relevant in Doddy's case. He knew he must be ready when the opportunity came along. He never hesitated to blame lack of time for his failure so far to marry, and he was inclined to say the same thing about West End offers. 'Just haven't the time,' he would say. It sounded too simplistic by far as an excuse and wasn't always accepted. He did admit though, that he wanted to see his name in 'big lights' in the West End.

At that time he made another admission. He was

exceedingly frank: 'I can't say I like the West End scene. Scares me a bit. Everybody's so reserved and tight-lipped. They always remind me of those characters in a bad gangster film who all hate each other. It's different back in Liverpool.'

It smacked of a provincial man's view of the big city at a time when Liverpool, with the dramatic rise of the Beatles, looked likely to be the music capital of Britain. Was there a danger that Doddy would perhaps leave it too late to make an assault on the West End? Assured of his own success in Blackpool, Manchester and Liverpool, there was about his attitude a curious reluctance to venture beyond the North of England. He could be accused of being smug. By late 1962 he was earning nearly £1,000 a week and stated he wanted to be the greatest entertainer in the world – and saw no reason why he should not make it. As he explained, 'There's no point in aiming any lower. I hope there's a lot more ahead of me. I'm comparatively young. Thirty-four is nothing in this business. And I'm opportunist enough to know where I'm going. This doesn't mean I'm excessively vain or conceited. But if I don't know, and if I'm not going to go all out to get what I want, no one's going to do it for me.'

While it was an understandable ambition, the nagging feeling remained, even among some of his Liverpool friends, that he was not prepared to take a gamble with his career. His studious approach tended to make him more cautious than his colleagues. In Liverpool they were talking about a young comic, Jimmy Tarbuck, and his ambitions to emulate other Liverpudlians like Arthur Askey, Ted Ray and Tommy Handley.

A year later, in December 1963, Doddy had still given no serious thought to the West End; instead, he was preparing for a lavish show at the Royal Court Theatre in Liverpool. He was now without question the biggest box-office draw in the North and his show at the Royal Court Theatre was sold out within a few weeks. He stood to gain £11,000, minus the taxman's share, which was two-thirds, and even then it was nothing to laugh at.

By the time the show had finished, Doddy, who was now being described as 'one of the most sensible men in the theatre', was at last prepared to focus his vision beyond the North of England. One day, as he sipped a beer in his dressing-room, he reflected on his position – and popularity – and mused, 'I could go on pulling faces and telling jokes and keeping people happy and warm, but it's not enough to stay in one groove even if it is lucrative and comfortable. If you live for work as I do, and you know you're not fully extended, you must go on. But at the moment I'm still finding myself. I mean what sort of character am I? Am I a bully or a little man? Or the fool who gets everything wrong? Or the Phil Silvers greedy man?'

It was the enigmatic Doddy talking, assuming unwittingly the role of a Beckett character as he asked himself, 'Who am I?' Presumably the question was not inspired by any search for personal identity but rather the kind of character he was at the time. To those who knew him as a serious person outside the theatre or TV studio, it was not a disturbing question. Neither his fans, nor the critics, concerned themselves with such soul-searching.

It was four years since he had played in his home town of Liverpool. As expected, he got a rapturous reception from full houses every night. The *Liverpool Post* commented, 'The level of his consistency is a show business marvel. Even on a third hearing his gags ricochet around the theatre with deadly effect. And his communication is lethal.'

It was the time of the onslaught of Beatlemania and Doddy acknowledged the new phenomenon on the show's opening night, when he pranced on stage as 'Ringo Dodd' in Beatlemania suit and clutching a monstrous guitar. He wise-cracked and led a singalong of Beatle numbers. 'He had,' as another critic put it, 'whipped up near-Beatlemaniacal enthusiasm' among his audience. 'It is achingly funny, and rounds off a show which is pretty well excellent.'

Doubtless he was driving himself hard. Too hard, his friends feared. He was advised by his doctor to take a short rest before he embarked on his summer show in Blackpool. Sarah Dodd, his mother, was also concerned. 'When he returns home next time,' she said. 'I'm going to see that he puts his feet up and has a really good rest. Summer shows can be a terrible strain and I want to be quite sure he's fit before he starts.'

Doddy could be stubborn, as his mother and Anita Boutin found to their cost. He was an independent spirit who had a life-style of his own choosing. He still found it hard to rise early in the morning, despite occasional urgent commitments. It was not unusual, either, for him to keep people waiting in the parlour with tea served by his mother.

The phone in the kitchen seldom stopped ringing for him. The scene so intrigued a young woman reporter that she wrote, 'In between making tea, calling the plumber to fix a burst pipe outside in the yard, and answering the door to a young lad wanting autographs, Mrs Sarah Dodd acts as a filter passing messages on to Ken or fetching him to the calls needing his attention.'

She quickly decided that Kenneth Arthur Dodd, the most popular comedian in the North of England, urgently needed a manager, secretary and perhaps an agent in Liverpool. The trouble was that Dave Forrester lived in London, and George Bartram, his publicity man, lived in Birmingham. Even his regular dresser was away which tended to add to the chaos.

In the midst of it all, Doddy found the time to take out his Jaguar and make the long journey to Dartmoor Prison to entertain six hundred prisoners. A gun was used in the concert sketch and when it was fired he quipped, 'If you do that you'll end up here!' The entertainers, led by

95

Doddy, gave a two-hour show, the girls winning most of the applause. He said afterwards, 'One of the prisoners asked me to sing *The Key*. I didn't see its significance until later. It opens with the words *There's a key which can open all doors for me.'*

For a man like Doddy who loved an audience, the prisoners of Dartmoor were a match for the best.

CHAPTER 10

'You're Ready to Top Palladium Bill'

By January 1964, Doddy had twice declined offers to star in *Sunday Night at the London Palladium* and the chance to play before a multi-million audience. On the face of it, it seemed a mutinous act, one not only disrespectful to viewers but to impresario Val Parnell. The problem sprang not only from the Liverpool comic's doubts of being a star at the greatest variety theatre in the country, but his anxiety to negotiate a big deal and big money.

To some people in show business, who knew he was the highest paid comedian around, his refusal was inexplicable. Doddy replied, 'The longer you put a thing off the more nervous you get about it. I'd like to make one or two little try-outs first – some concerts or one-nighters to see how it goes.'

Coming from an entertainer who could earn as much as many a pair of Palladium performers put together, his hesitation baffled not a few of his colleagues. Despite the success of his radio and television shows, Doddy was not convinced that he could automatically win the same massive following down South. When someone suggested that an appearance at the Sunday Palladium would be a reasonable way of dealing with his doubts, he argued, 'The audience don't pay to come in so they're half-way happy before you get them. It wouldn't prove anything, you see.'

He was being described as a 'thoughtful and sensible comedian'. Anxious to make more records, he searched round for new songs to follow up his latest success, *Still*. Films at that time also interested him. 'My ambition is to have Peter Sellers as director. Filming would be a new, exciting experience, but I'm not going to rush into a scrappy job that would simply be cashing in on what little name I might have made.'

In showbiz circles it was felt that Doddy's agent, Dave Forrester, was too uncompromising in his efforts to clinch a gilt-edged Palladium deal. He never tired of telling his clients, including Doddy, how long it took Morecambe and Wise to make star status, which was another way of telling them to be patient. Furthermore, he was aware of Palladium intrigues and rows that occasionally led to the postponement of artistes' debuts, even the scrapping of contracts. He was adamant on top billing for Ken Dodd; better still, he thought: why not his own show?

As Forrester moved cautiously, the rest of Liverpool was on the march. On 10 January, the Beatles smashed into the US charts with the record, *I Want to Hold Your Hand*, and inside ten days had sold 500,000 copies; the self-effacing Cilla Black was on the way to becoming a singing star, and Jimmy Tarbuck would soon take over as compère in *Sunday Night at the London Palladium*.

It prompted Mike Yarwood to say wistfully, 'Jimmy has leap-frogged from the Yew Tree Inn at Whythenshaw to the London Palladium almost in one bound – and why can't I become a name quickly, too?' It was a sentiment echoed by many aspiring stars of the time. Yet neither Doddy nor his agent seemed in a hurry to join the Liverpool cavalcade.

Never the one to be envious of other artistes' successes, Doddy was impressed by Jimmy Tarbuck and the way he had managed to emulate the long line of top-line Liverpool comics. The ebullient Tarbuck had made his Palladium début in October 1963. He had wanted to be a star

there ever since, at the age of eighteen, he saw his first
Palladium show. On his subsequent début, he said, 'I
was over the moon. I felt as if I'd just been capped for
England.'

Like Doddy, he is a born comic and humour fascinates
him. 'I enjoy making people happy,' he says. 'It gives me
a great deal of honest enjoyment to be out there on the
stage telling jokes. It's fun for me. That's for sure. And if
it's fun for the folks out in the audience – well, could you
ask for more?'

A patient Doddy stood by his agent. He agreed that
Dave Forrester was cautious with his promises, though
generous with his encouragement. And the agent had a
habit of saying to his clients, 'I might be able to have
something very nice for you. But I'm not telling you in
case it doesn't happen.'

Early in 1965, he did disclose his 'secret' to Doddy,
when he told him, 'I've booked you into the Palladium.
You are ready to top the bill and it's in your own show.'
Doddy did not argue. If his agent considered he was
ready, he accepted his word. It was the big glamour date
of that time, the prestige booking every entertainer
sought. As Mike Yarwood said later, 'For me the prestige
of playing the Palladium was marvellous, but I think the
act must have been awful, for a friend of mine taped it
and I heard it. I was raw, and the timing was bad, and
just the rehearsing made me recall that I couldn't walk on
and off the stage properly.'

The same experience was unlikely to happen to Doddy.
Years of success in variety and pantomime had made him
stage-wise. He knew his craft. Yet he had no illusions
about going South in search of stardom. 'I'd starred all
over Britain, collected all sorts of records and awards, and
here I was a Northerner, a Liverpudlian, going to London
where they had absolutely chopped down Northern comedians for years. The critics had murdered geniuses like
Frank Randle, whom they had permitted to play in the

late suburban halls, but when he went to the West End –
well, they assassinated him.'

Lacking the brashness of Jimmy Tarbuck, Doddy was
perhaps being too sensitive to what he saw as the tough
Southern audiences. By now he was twelve years a 'pro'
and there seemed no need for him to be scared. He was
realistic enough to accept that unless he achieved success
in the West End his reputation in the North counted for
little. Not that he ever lacked self-confidence. As he said,
'I am not worried about the way Southern audiences will
react to my brand of humour. I am sufficient of an entertainer to be able to use material that they will enjoy. I will
still have to be Doddy but there may be a little less about
Merseyside. Jam butties, for example, I think they call
them sandwiches down there.' He admitted that up to
then he had been offered better deals up North, and
bigger money; it was one of the reasons why he had
delayed his Palladium début. 'I was waiting for the right
show, at the right theatre, and the right money. I admit
the longer I wait the worse the thought of a London début
becomes. I know the knockers are gathering, but I'm not
afraid of them.'

The press bombarded him for interviews and photographs. He quickly realised the new pressures stardom
would bring. Never lost for a word, he was prepared for
their pointed questions, though he drew the line where
his private life was concerned. Some questions he answered over the phone, others in face to face interviews. The
Daily Express elicited the following revealing responses:

Why don't you live like the big showbiz personality you are?

It's part of my philosophy, you see. I have seen so
many others as they've climbed towards the top surround
themselves with bodyguards of every kind and a payroll
of hangers-on. I have a first-class agent, Dave Forrester,
who believed in me in the beginning and has looked after

me ever since. You must have one person right in the know, to talk things over with.

Why not the status symbols?

I don't want all the flash things, all the status symbols. I don't want a gleaming new Bentley, or to eat in smart restaurants. I want to stay just where I am. I never forget that it's the audience, those ordinary folk, who have put me where I am, and I mean to stay one of them myself.

Who is the real Ken Dodd?

He is a buffoon, a jester, and people like him because he symbolises the innocent little man who refuses to be crushed. He started life selling pots, pans, disinfectants and detergents, now he makes jokes about them.

Anita's a charming woman. Why haven't you got hitched?

Marriage . . . what . . . I'm not married. I'm too round-shouldered. Seriously, though, I have just not got round to it – but perhaps in the near future.

Do you think you will be saved at the Palladium?

I just don't know. I feel the moment has come when I must have a shot at it. My mother has a saying that all the family uses at different times: you can only do what you can do. I am one of the last comics to stand in front of a back-cloth and tell jokes. That's all I can do.

One Fleet Street journalist, who talked to the comedian in the privacy of his home in Knotty Ash, suddenly got the urge to see the other rooms in the house. He found that one room was given over entirely to Dodd's 'props', a hilarious collection of rude noises, funny faces, and foam rubber bric-à-brac of a most intimate kind. Bouncing brassières, squirting milking stools, false hands, a doctor's bag with ten feet of stethoscope – fiddles, policemen's helmets and cushions you sit on at your peril.

Doddy explained, 'I don't care what I do for a laugh as long as I'm with 'em. I'll bite, scratch, and kick as long as I can communicate. And when I've got them with me, then Knotty Ash is paradise and I am ten feet tall.'

Diminutive comic Arthur Askey was in no doubt that Doddy would become a star at the Palladium. Although a Liverpudlian, he emphasised he wasn't being biased. Doddy's radio and television shows had amused him, yet he felt his real place was in the theatre. 'Ken Dodd is a genuinely funny man, just as funny as Tommy Cooper,' Askey said. 'There are people like Dickie Henderson, Max Bygraves, and Des O'Connor who are excellent entertainers. But they are not what I would call funny men.'

Askey, the little man with the wide-rimmed spectacles, was by now thirty-two years a professional comedian. When he gave up his job in Liverpool's education offices in 1923 to go on the stage and take his act South, he was advised to drop jokes about diddy men, jam butty mines and treacle factories. They were considered unsuitable. As he recalled, 'They were the local jokes of the day. I was a diddy man. My Uncle Arthur, who was 5 feet 3 inches like me, he was a diddy man. Everybody used to crack gags about the treacle mines at Oglett and the jammy butty mines at Otterspool. Once radio and television started that sort of humour spread.'

Askey was aware at the time that Doddy told diddy jokes but they didn't dominate his act, so he wasn't at risk. Doddy's humour was more general and tended to appeal to a wider audience than the Liverpool Empire. Like himself, he was a genuinely funny man and people usually started giggling before he uttered a word.

To Askey, the London Palladium was a lovely theatre. 'I have done numerous shows there and it can take a large audience, but it's still an intimate theatre.' In his view if a comedian could not succeed at the Palladium, he would not succeed anywhere else. He was thinking particularly of the audience who was never slow to applaud new talent. It gave him great satisfaction to watch the success of a new generation of Liverpool comics, such as Doddy and Jimmy Tarbuck.

Doddy was his favourite funny man at that time. He

considered him one of the best comics in Britain, if not the best. As he explained, 'I sometimes ask people if they have seen Doddy and they say they have seen him on telly and weren't all that keen. I just say, "Have you seen him in a theatre? He is a genius".' The other comedians who made him laugh were Bruce Forsyth, Frankie Howerd, Dickie Henderson and Jimmy Tarbuck.

It was the warmth of Doddy's personality that first endeared him to Arthur Askey. 'There needs to be a lot of warmth in a performer,' he liked to say. 'Ken Dodd has it. So has my old pal, Ted Ray, and of course Tommy Cooper. It can get through to the viewer and the audience. I see comics now on television – and you can see gags going in the ear and coming out of the mouth. It doesn't go into the brain or around the heart.'

That Liverpool continued to turn out comedians did not surprise him. Askey himself was part of 'that great apostolic succession of Liverpool comedians that runs from Rob Wilton and Ted Ray through to Ken Dodd, Jimmy Tarbuck and Tom O'Connor'. There was only one answer in Askey's view – 'I think it's inbred'.

Another thing that pleased Askey was that relations between comics themselves had greatly improved. When he started out it was not the done thing for comics to like each other, but that had changed. He expected Liverpool comedians and funny men not from the city to turn up at the Palladium to applaud Doddy. It was the natural thing to do, and he hoped to lead the way on the first night.

Godfrey Winn was not only one of Fleet Street's best writers, but he was also a colourful personality and the author of popular books. When he set out by rail for Liverpool on a bleak, wet March morning, he was feeling weary and was befogged by a bad cold. His mission was to take in Doddy's performance at Liverpool's Royal Court

103

Theatre and convey to his readers the type of comic they could expect to see at the London Palladium.

Although he had never seen him in action in the theatre, he had been briefed by colleagues, though the last word in his ear was, 'You've got to see the man for yourself, Godfrey.' By the time he booked into the Adelphi Hotel, he was feeling slightly better. When he eventually reached the theatre a chaotic scene greeted him. Crowds from the first house were struggling to make their way out of the theatre while the second house audience was furiously struggling to get in.

Despite his cold, Winn was gripped by the 'sense of jollity' around him and wondered if the Palladium would witness similar scenes when the comedian came to town. After a struggle through the masses, he took his seat in the stalls and waited for the curtain to rise. When Doddy, dressed in scarlet as a court jester, pranced on stage he clutched a long tickling stick in his hand instead of a traditional sceptre. The house rocked with laughter. Winn had never heard such rich, rumbustious laughter coming from people of all ages.

To catch his lightning patter and his *double entendres* which were more saucy than smutty, he had to lean forward in his seat, but even then he could not catch all the gags. People were doubled up in their seats around him, some wiping the tears from their eyes. Mercifully, thought Winn, the laughter ceased for a short while as the comedian sang a romantic ballad which was greeted with cries for an encore. To Winn, Doddy's performance was not only remarkable but contagious, for his cold had virtually disappeared and the fatigue had left him. On a few occasions he found himself chuckling quietly at the more topical gags. Although the show overran, he decided to stay in his seat until the end; in fact, he reckoned, it might be a good idea to go backstage to confront the comedian in his dressing-room.

It was a struggle. A score of well-wishers and fans

crowded round the dressing-room door and it was with difficulty that Winn finally managed to get to the comic. 'Join me for supper later,' Doddy suggested amidst the confusion. Winn thought it a good idea. Eventually he was joined by Doddy and Anita Boutin for a light meal and to his surprise the comedian looked remarkably fresh, as though he had not run through two hectic shows.

After the laughter of the evening, their conversation was quiet and enjoyable. Winn found the comic modest, very articulate about the science of humour, and full of good jokes against himself. Doddy said, 'I shall never forget the first time I played in Glasgow. On the Monday night the manager met me and gave me my marching orders. "All football jokes are out," he explained gruffly. "They lead to riots here and you will get the bird on Friday night. Everyone does." You can imagine how I felt waiting for my entrance on Friday. A drunk in the second row took one look at me, rose to his feet, and shouted out, "What a dreadful sight!" and collapsed. A great roar of laughter went up and I was saved.'

To Winn, Anita Boutin was a charming and good-humoured woman who was obviously a key link in the comedian's career. She was a good listener and rarely, if ever, interrupted the conversation, although the journalist suspected she must have heard a few of the funny stories more than once. Doddy talked about famous comedians and how pleased he was to receive a letter from Lady Robey telling him that he was in the tradition of her husband George, not like him of course, but carrying on the same comic tradition. Sid Field was another of his heroes as a boy, as were Arthur Askey and Nat Jackley. 'I once laughed so much at Nat in the back row of the gallery here at the Liverpool Empire, that I fell forward a couple of rows.'

Winn at that moment could not resist asking, 'Is that how it happened – I mean your front teeth?'

Doddy was amused. No one ever left his teeth alone.

Once more he explained how he fell off a bicycle as a lad. It gave him an opportunity to reminisce about his childhood in Knotty Ash and, in particular, his parents. Winn found the story fascinating, partly because Doddy wasn't trying to impress him. He was telling him his life story in a quiet voice.

They discussed the study of humour and Winn said he found it unusual for comedians to probe too deeply. Doddy reminded him that for years he had studied the subject. 'When I was playing in Oxford I went to see a couple of professors in psychology to talk about humour, and I've read Freud and Jung from cover to cover. But in the end it all comes back to getting the audience with you. When I do my serious singing spot, I can tell how things are by the number of matches being struck to light cigarettes. If there are only a few out there in the darkness, I feel good.'

It was getting late and Winn wanted to get back to his hotel. Doddy must have been impressed, for he invited the journalist to come round to his home in Knotty Ash next morning to carry on the conversation. Godfrey Winn, who was finding the evening an experience, agreed.

When he called at Doddy's home in Thomas Road, Knotty Ash, the following morning, he was in for a few more surprises. After a warm welcome by the comic, Winn was introduced to Mrs Dodd, a small, kindly woman who obviously adored her son. She handed him a cup of tea and hoped he would enjoy it. 'I made it myself for you, sir.' Winn decided that Doddy lived in a house untouched by the Mersey tide. It was late Georgian, small and neat, with a green country porch, and cream-colour windows. He thought: 'A proper setting for members of the Diddy tribe.' The front parlour was like the sitting-room in good theatrical digs. It was, it seemed, the way Doddy himself liked it, and that's how he intended it to stay.

Even at that hour in the morning, Doddy was proving

himself a compulsive talker. He had taken to the elegant Godfrey Winn, who like him loved cats. In conversation, Dave Forrester's name came up and Doddy said, 'My agent has suggested that I should take a break between the Liverpool and London shows. A fortnight in Majorca? I've turned down the idea flat. I might catch cold or some horrible disease.'

Winn smiled.

'Sounds like a good idea to me. Why not?'

Then Doddy said something that rather startled the much-travelled Godfrey Winn.

'I've never been outside the British Isles, and I've no yearning to see Naples and live.'

Incredible, thought Winn to himself. How could he entertain all those people and not escape to the sun occasionally? He listened as the comedian talked about his forthcoming appearance at the London Palladium, which he described as the Leaning Tower of Pisa, the Colosseum in Rome, and the Statue of Liberty all in one.

Winn asked, 'Will you change your act for the Palladium?'

Doddy calmly replied, 'I'll take out a few of the local gags, of course. But as it is I always try out half a dozen new jokes every night. It's my way of keeping up to scratch. Not getting stale or smug.'

'And I do hope you'll sing?'

'Of course I'll sing. The audience expect it.'

At that moment Doddy burst into song:

> *Happiness, Happiness*
> *The greatest gift that I possess*
> *I thank the Lord that I've been blessed*
> *With more than my share of happiness.*

Godfrey Winn did not join in the chorus. It was enough that the house exuded happiness. He knew he had enough material for three articles, but his editor had asked for one only. After that, it was a profile of Winston Churchill, junior.

As he boarded the train at Lime Street station he collected his thoughts about a rare visit. Later, he wrote: 'I must record I've never seen an audience depart more full of happiness than that night at the Royal Court Theatre in Liverpool. Will it happen like that every night this spring at the Palladium? The knockers will knock, the carriage trade may stand aloof, but I prophesy the coaches will be rolling up. You can only do what you can do. But watch how this new name to London who depends on no stooge, no props, nothing except his own spontaneous flair for communication, does it.'

Shortly before his début at the Palladium Doddy was introduced to the Fleet Street showbiz press corps for the first time. He admitted he felt a little nervous. From the stage he surveyed the empty Palladium auditorium and the 2,500 seats. With its quaint décor, it looked an attractive theatre and, more important, a friendly one. He liked friendly theatres. As he stood on the stage he said, 'This is the first time I've stood here. I feel a bit nervous standing on the same stage as the most famous personalities in show business.'

He pulled the odd funny face and said he did not know how long he would be appearing at the Palladium, although he had been told that the advance booking was good and bookings had been made up to August. Inevitably he talked about Knotty Ash, the Beatles and comedy. 'If a good fairy were to grant me three wishes,' he mused, 'I think I'd choose good health, complete success in my career, and a pay rise for the Amalgamated Society of Cucumber Operatives and Rhubarb Minders.'

He looked confident in his neat suit and bright tie and once again his ordinariness surprised a few reporters who had come anticipating a star performance. They were puzzled that he had not played the West End before; his answer had a familiar ring about it. 'Believe it or not I've always been booked elsewhere. But now that I'm here I'm very excited.'

The place, he decided, breathed theatrical history with the ghosts of variety stars everywhere. He was introduced to old George Cooper at the stage door office. He would be the man who would give him the key to Number 1 dressing-room.

It didn't matter how big or small a star's name was, George always made them welcome. Mike Yarwood, like Doddy, had found him 'nice and friendly' and in his own way a fantastic character.

George was the living sign of the tremendous efficiency around the theatre. Yarwood recalled, 'You can go downstairs in a panic and say, "George! I've come without cuff-links," He'll open a drawer: cuff-links! That's the sort of comfortable man he is.'

If Doddy wanted to know more about the stars who graced the Palladium stage, he had only to talk to the backstage staff: men like Ron Harris, Bill Platt and Dave Grimley. They were not easily pleased.

Harris, a tall, wiry man, joined the Palladium backstage crew in 1948 and remembered the phenomenal success of Danny Kaye. 'The queues stretched up and down the street outside and the audience did not want him to leave the stage. Kaye sat down and asked for a cup of tea and the keys of the theatre. He was zany and a gifted impersonator.' He was able to recall Jack Benny's 'perfect timing' and Bob Hope's funny one-liners and clever ad libbing.

The years between 1948 and 1958 were, in his view, the Golden Years at the London Palladium with outstanding American and English acts. Audiences came to enjoy themselves and almost always got value for their money. When Ken Dodd's name went up on the posters, Harris knew he was the first British comic to top the bill at the Palladium for years. He had seen comedians from the

North of England and Scotland do badly at the Palladium and wondered how this funny man they called Doddy would fare.

They agreed that Palladium audiences came solely to enjoy themselves. Electrician Bill Platt, who had shaken the hand of a score of stars, thought that Doddy had nothing to fear. 'You'd have to be pretty awful for the audience here to turn against you. The management was a good judge of an act and it was rare for them to book a bad one.'

Like his backstage colleagues, Platt had never seen Doddy on stage. They reckoned he must be good.

CHAPTER 11

'I am Completely Overwhelmed'

For his Palladium début it was suggested facetiously to Doddy that he have the mole above his upper lip removed. It was fashionable at the time to treat moles and warts and medical experts approved. The suggestion had been made to him before but he had laughed it off, partly due to pressure on his time and because he claimed the mole enhanced his comic image.

As with his teeth, he had grown fond of the mole and regarded it as a landmark on his face. Moreover he had a more pressing matter to engage his mind than an 'innocent little mole'. There was his tiff with Anita and this time she might even carry out her threat to stay away from his first night at the London Palladium.

The stubborn Doddy had upset her over some 'trifling matter', but in Anita's eyes it was nothing of the sort. She was furious with him. As before, he rushed off to her brother Bill Boutin to discuss the domestic crisis. Tiffs between the lovers tended to amuse Bill for he knew how close Ken and Anita had become.

'Ken couldn't believe that Anita wouldn't be there to see his début,' he recalls. 'I could see he was worried and I assured him that everything would be all right. I didn't want to see the biggest night of his career spoilt in any way.'

Doddy was thinking too, of the house he had rented in

111

Kensington for the duration of his engagement at the Palladium. It was unthinkable now that Anita would not be there to look after it.

As Bill Boutin expected, the pair made up before another day and soon Doddy was telling Anita about his latest plans for London. He could have told her that the posters were already up outside the famous variety theatre with the words, 'DODDY'S HERE', which was the unambiguous title of the show. Groups of fans were by now planning to make the trip by coach to London for the first night. To Doddy, an avid Liverpool football supporter, the occasion resembled the build-up to a cup final. He dared not fail.

Yet his forthcoming début would not be taking place if Leslie McDonnell, the Palladium boss, had not had second thoughts and invested £80,000 in the show. McDonnell harboured serious doubts about the box-office appeal of North Country and Scottish comedians. As he said, 'I'd seen them come down here and die a death. I'd never been happy about the regional idiom.' It wasn't a question of bias but rather that London audiences found neither them nor their humour funny. In the end he was swayed by assurances from Bernard Delfont and other impresarios who had seen Doddy perform in Blackpool and Manchester.

On the late afternoon of Saturday, 17 April 1965, Doddy collected the key of No. 1 dressing-room from George Cooper, accepted the old man's firm handshake and proceeded along the corridor towards the door. Inside the room he picked up bundles of good-luck cards and cables. The warmth of the messages made him feel good. And preparations for his début had gone smoothly. Robert Nesbitt, the director, could be relied upon to stage a classy show, and Dave Forrester had surrounded him with good support acts, the Kaye Sisters, ventriloquist Clifford Guest, the Carmenas and the Ross Taylor Dancers.

Doddy took care with his make-up and was relieved

that Anita was around to assist him with props. As usual, she would list in her notebook the response of the audience to his gags; at the Palladium he was breaking new ground. The first house, he was informed, was completely sold out. As he prepared to leave the dressing-room – a room occupied in the past by Danny Kaye, Bob Hope and Jack Benny – he was assailed by apprehension, yet he knew that once on stage his fears would vanish.

Shortly after 6.12, he pranced on stage and was immediately greeted with the shout, 'Up the 'Pool!' Armed with a fancy tickling stick, he bombarded his audience with a rapid succession of gags, from seaside landladies to his diddy grandad. At first the audience was slow to warm to him, but gradually he beat them into submission. At the end of the first spot he rushed back to his dressing-room, swapping his comical ill-fitting morning suit for a garish sweater with DODDY emblazoned on the back. And for his next appearance he changed his pullover into a natty oatmeal-coloured suit, stuffing his great sunglasses into his pocket, and combing his hair with a comb the size of a hay rake.

So fast-moving was his performance, that his twenty-minute spots appeared less than that, though his third spot ran long over. In fact, the first house did not end until five minutes after the curtain should have gone up on the second house. The audience was ecstatic and refused to let him go. Eventually he ran off and left behind him chaos, inside and outside the theatre.

As the audience struggled to get out another 2,500 people were struggling to get in. To ease the crush, the police had to close Argyle Street in an attempt to restore order. Stage-door keeper George Cooper emerged from his office to tell Doddy that he hadn't seen anything like it for twenty years. He could recall only two or three stars who overran, among them Danny Kaye and Tommy Trinder.

Wielding a long tickling stick, Doddy bounded back on

stage for the second house and set about his audience with typical gusto. True, he touched only lightly on the jam-butty question and neglected the black-pudding plantations and the snuff-quarries, but he changed not a vowel of his 'fur-wur-and-tur' Merseyside delivery. He was making no concessions to metropolitan sophistication.

Unsurprisingly, the second house overran. Doddy was being held captive on stage by his audience who applauded his every gag. Finally he escaped, but only because people were exhausted from laughing. It was an extraordinary scene, even for the London Palladium. Doddy's triumph was complete.

Backstage hands remembered nothing like it since the Golden Years and the 'invasion' of the Palladium by American stars, including Johnny Ray. Although they missed their late-night public transport and pints of beer, the men were not angry with Doddy for overrunning. They wondered, though, if he would be spoken to by the management. It was particularly troublesome when the first house overran, for if the curtain did not come down as scheduled at 8.20 it left little time for the house staff to clean the ash-trays and take away rubbish. In addition, the doors had to be opened for the second house patrons to ensure that the curtain rose on time.

If a star continually overran it was customary for the management to visit his dressing-room to discuss the problem. Backstage, the technicians were asking if Doddy could be stopped. Bill Platt recalls, 'Ken had so many gags he could go on all night telling them. He is a very good pro and works his heart out, but I don't think he had any sense of time. I didn't know how he could be stopped.'

To Ron Harris, the Liverpool comic owed so much of his success to his explosive style and non-stop delivery. 'Ken was involved in almost everything on stage and his own spots were very funny. For years at the Palladium British comics did well to get twelve-minute spots and the majority never overran.'

114

On the way back to his dressing-room, Doddy chatted to scores of well-wishers who crowded round him. 'What about a tickle, Missus?' he quipped, pointing his tickling stick at a woman's head. She burst out laughing. In more serious mood he told them, 'I am completely over-whelmed. The show was fabulous. The audience wonder-ful'. Visitors to his dressing-room had little difficulty find-ing it. Hanging on the wall outside was a large picture of the Liverpool football team signed: 'Doddy's Diddy men, winners cert,' while the comic remarked, 'Doddy at the Palladium and Liverpool for the Cup – I hope.'

As people drifted away and left the theatre by the stage door, others came in. There were Terry-Thomas, Norman Vaughan, Georgie Wood and little Arthur Askey. Seeing Askey seemed to touch Doddy and for a brief moment they hugged, but their words were lost in the buzz of conversation. The night's achievement was summed up in a brief encounter between Terry-Thomas and the Liver-pool comic. 'Son,' exclaimed Terry-Thomas, 'you slayed 'em.' He was followed by Norman Vaughan, who told Doddy, 'I thought you were marvellous.'

Leslie McDonnell popped his head into the dressing-room and assured Doddy, 'It's a winner, Ken.' He said it with relief and satisfaction. For the backers it was the start of a money-spinning run, with advance bookings already breaking records. No one, even Leslie McDonnell, seemed to bother that the show ran forty minutes over. Nor did anyone care that the backstage technicians had been obliged to hire taxis home.

Remarkably, Doddy looked as though he could trot on stage for another performance. He was being carried along on a wave of euphoria. At that moment, as he sipped a beer, he was telling a group of Liverpudlians, 'Did you hear them out there tonight? They knew all about jam-butties! They even know what a moggie is! They were with me all the way. I'll have them diddyfied in no time!'

He parcelled up seven hundred good-luck telegrams

and sighed, 'I was nervous, but if I'd known so many people were keeping their fingers crossed for me, I'd have been petrified.' Never one to ignore his fans, he rose and proceeded to the stage door and outside was greeted by about three hundred people. As he signed some of their programmes, he wise-cracked, and he was tickled by the number of cockney accents.

It was nearly 12.45 a.m. when he and Anita finally left the theatre to join with friends in a late night champagne party.

'DODDY'S THERE!' The headline in a morning newspaper summed up his astonishing success. Another one came just as close: 'KEN DODD WINS THE COCKNEYS'. All the papers rhapsodised about his performance. In Londoners' eyes, he was an overnight star, which rather amused the Liverpool comic who had spent ten years honing his act in provincial theatres and clubs.

Doddy reflected: stardom at last. It promised to be the most exciting period of his life. And Anita was beside him to share in that success. He knew the press would be asking again if he now intended to marry 'his Anita' and he'd try to answer their questions. Women's magazines would want to highlight the romantic side of his success and ascertain what it meant to Anita. There was a price to be paid, he knew, for taking the Palladium by storm, as one paper put it.

To the thirty-seven-year-old star, it was heady stuff. He was unsure if he would not be changed by it all. The trappings of stardom worried him, in particular what was demanded of him. Up to now he had coped with success, but there would be the onus on him now to *act* the star. Privately, he knew he was only reaping the rewards of a lifetime's study of humour, and stardom had come to him the hard way. Not that he had not welcomed it. He admitted he was tickled to death. 'It's all highly tattyphilarious and I'll have to get used to it.'

116

The Georgian house in Knotty Ash
where **Ken Dodd** was born – and still lives.
(Liverpool Daily Post & Echo)

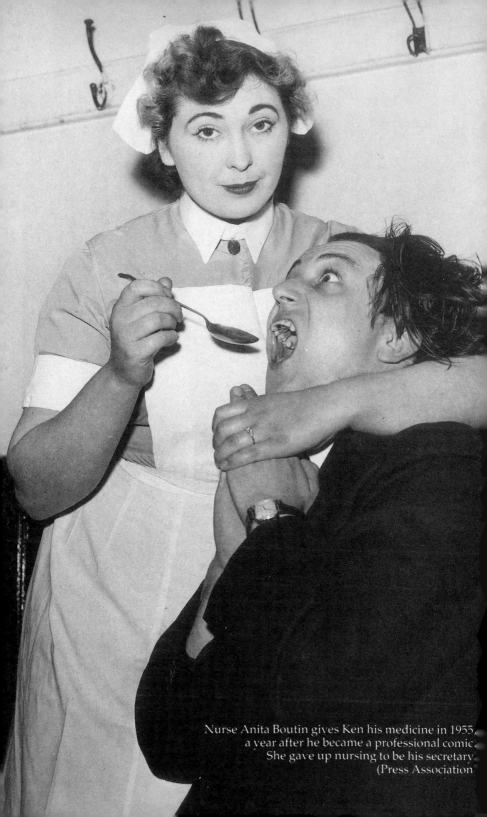

Nurse Anita Boutin gives Ken his medicine in 1955,
a year after he became a professional comic.
She gave up nursing to be his secretary
(Press Association)

The mad, mad world of Kenneth Arthur Dodd.
(Liverpool Daily Post & Echo)

The Squire of Knotty Ash mingles with
his subjects at the entrance to the Jam Buttymines.
(Liverpool Daily Post & Echo)

Top – Ken makes up in the
No. 1 dressing room at
the London Palladium in 1965,
the year he became a star.
(Press Association)

Right – Ken and Anita
during his season at
the Palladium.
(Express Newspapers)

Left – Hallmarks of the comedian:
buck teeth, saucer eyes and
uncontrollable hair.
(Express Newspapers)

Ken becomes airborne after hearing that
his record 'Tears' is top of the Hit Parade in 1965.
(Press Association)

Prime Minister Harold Wilson raises his glass
to Dodd during his season at the Palladium.
(Press Association)

Ken is presented to the Queen at the Royal
Variety Performance at the Palladium in November 1965.
(Press Association)

A delighted Dodd after receiving his golden disc for sales of one million copies of 'Tears'. (Press Association)

Relaxing with the morning papers in his sitting-room in Kensington, it suddenly seemed a long way from the pastoral setting of Doddy Towers. By now he assumed the people would have heard of his success and that evening he expected they would toast the Squire of Knotty Ash. He could see that the showbiz columnists and the critics had pulled out all the stops and he was in danger of being immortalised before his time. With his new-found status, it might not always be the way. Fleet Street, he had been warned, could be a wicked place if it decided to humiliate stars. This morning he dismissed the thought from his mind. It was wonderful to be alive.

'The star who was in no hurry at all slipped into the nation's top entertainment spot – and looks like staying there for ever,' wrote one paper. 'Doddy hit the West End on Saturday with the impact of a long-range missile. Doddy, the lank-haired, wild-eyed Clown Prince of Knotty Ash, was a riot at the World's No, 1 variety theatre. It was his first-ever live appearance in the capital, and the first time since the war a North Country comic has starred in his own show for a Palladium season.'

In subsequent days and weeks the papers out-did each other to record his success. Doddy was pleased that the *Liverpool Post* had sent its own correspondent to the first night and the piece caught the mood: 'If Londoners did not know what a jam butty was before Saturday then they do now. Ken Dodd, the Clown Prince of Merseyside, had them tickled pink on the opening night. Long after the second performance was due to end the self-appointed Squire of Knotty Ash was still on stage catching the laughs and jokes about diddy grandad. He just would not come off and the audience would not let him go.'

The *Liverpool Echo* headlined its report, 'DODDY'S DÉBUT CAUSES LONDON TRAFFIC JAM', and it began, 'Any doubts about the jam-butty humour generated by Doddy were dispelled by the close of the first house for he had an impact which not only wrought chaos to the audience, but also to the usually smooth working arrangements at the Palladium. It is a long time since I heard a theatre echo to such delighted laughter as the Palladium does when that toothy comedian with the hair spiking in all directions fires off his nonstop fusillade of jokes. Here is one of the most exuberant and spontaneous personalities the stage has ever seen. No sick humorist this, no dry purveyor of subtleties, but a happy fount of mirth which bubbles out of him in a seemingly inexhaustible flow with incredible vitality. If Liverpudlians in London don't flock to *Doddy's Here* they will be missing the laugh of a lifetime.'

Doddy always admitted he was tickled when the 'posh' papers sent representatives to talk to him or cover his shows. In the early days he was slightly suspicious of their motives, wondering if they wanted to send him up or dismiss him out of hand. The *Guardian* had been the first to examine his humour and it wrote a weighty piece about his performance. Now he was told it was fashionable for similar papers in London to send along their critics. Penelope Gilliatt in *The Observer* noted, 'The patter is as blue as Max Miller's and the puns come thick and fast. Like Max, Ken Dodd has a trick of innocently just missing a filthy meaning that stares everyone else in the face, like a baby behind the wheel of a sports car careering at a brick wall and swerving at the last moment.'

Alan Brien in the *Sunday Telegraph* spoke of Doddy's 'enormous potentialities as a surrealist clown with the kind of interior monologue you might expect from a character in a bawdy nursery-rhyme'. Later, Michael Billington, one of the most perceptive critics around and a close observer of Doddy's kind of humour, commented in *Plays and Players*: 'Mr Dodd fires at his willing audience an apparently inexhaustible stream of patter that is just shocking enough to make them glow with guilty pleasure.'

There was understandably a tendency for a few of the

critics to read too much, perhaps, into Doddy's humour, as though he were a comic Beckett character rather than a stand-up comedian. When Jonathan Miller was sent along by the *New Statesman* to study Doddy's performance even Michael Billington was impelled to ask, 'What did he expect, Samuel Beckett?' Yet Miller made some telling points: 'Dodd is never still for a moment, fluttering like a conjuror with all sorts of disarming accessory mannerisms. He capers and skips, giggles, goggles and splutters with his upper front teeth. He delivers his most outrageous gags with a shrill, puerile sweetness, and then opens his eyes in amazement at his own daring. And then there's that wild shampooed fright of hair which he whisks up into a Struwelpeter quiff.'

Miller was quick to note that everything Doddy did was rehearsed down to the smallest detail. Every trip, pause, break-up and syncopation came exactly as it did the first time he saw it.

Dave Forrester was overjoyed. Where his clients were concerned, Doddy included, his management policies had paid off. He derived tremendous satisfaction from Doddy's new status, partly because he himself had guided him and found the right show with which to launch him in London. Doddy was ready, that was the secret. He admitted that in early April the Palladium management had accepted bookings for only a limited period, but Doddy's runaway success at the box-office ensured that the season would be extended.

As the weeks passed Doddy had little time to himself. Visits to recording studios took up hours of his day, there was a radio programme to think about, and he was told that BBC 2 was planning a 45-minute spectacular. Photographs revealed that the mole was still prominent above his upper lip, but he had no intention of having it removed.

To his surprise, the brainy set, as he jokingly called

them, continued to be attracted to his Palladium performances. Playwright John Osborne dropped in to the show
accompanied by actors in rehearsal from the Royal Court
Theatre. Osborne saw a similarity between Doddy and
Archie Rice, the leading character in his own play, *The
Entertainer*. As Michael Billington pointed out, 'The playwright's fascination with Ken Dodd sprang from the
Archie Rice-like quality with his jokes. There is a slight
similarity in that both use time-honoured tricks of the
halls like joshing the conductor, chatting up the front
rows and playing on sexual ambiguity. However, Archie
Rice was a failure, throwing out his jokes like a desperate,
bereft trawlerman hoping for a minuscule catch; Dodd is
a pagan, festive celebrant who has the knack of establishing an almost mystic rapport with 2,500 people at once.'

By now the papers were describing Doddy as 'the most
eligible bachelor in town', but he tended to keep a low
profile in public and discounted rumours that he was
about to marry. Everything he did was news. When he
and Anita visited Liverpool on Sundays it did not go
unnoticed. He was getting used to the meaning of stardom but he avoided the trappings. He had no intention,
he said, of leaving Knotty Ash and settling in the south.
His only status symbol was his Jaguar and he wouldn't
change it for a Rolls-Royce. He tended to see the funny
side of things and he knew that as long as he didn't take
himself too seriously he would survive in the showbiz
jungle.

He was enjoying the powerful new glare of publicity.
'May be it's all going to my head,' he would laugh, 'but
I'm beginning to feel that I've got something to say to the
brainy set. After all, I'm just as informed on humour as
an Oxford don and maybe more. Oxford dons don't get
a chance to work the Palladium twice nightly. And a
London audience is ideal for research. They're so sophisticated you can try anything out.'

However, he found that he was in such constant

demand from the television, radio and recording studios that he had yet to get a real look at the territory he had conquered. He was aware, though, he was a star. Old George Cooper treated him as one and at the stage door every night there were people waiting for him to sign programmes. For the first time the cockneys were calling him 'Doddy'. He decided he was at last a star in cockney-land. He was once more tickled to death.

CHAPTER 12

'I'm on the Crest of the Wave'

Incredibly, in that autumn, 1965, Doddy was poised to equal the Beatles record of the previous Christmas with *I Feel Fine*, which topped the pop charts for six weeks. Challenging for No. 1 spot was composer-singer Chris Andrews who jumped to No. 2 with his own composition *Yesterday Man*, while the Rolling Stones with *Get Off My Cloud* and Paul McCartney's *Yesterday*, sung by Matt Monroe, were also pushing for top spot.

Doddy was elated. Paul McCartney was to remark, 'I thought *Yesterday* sounded so good that someone else must have already written it.' It was a slow-moving love song. Similarly, Doddy's *Tears* had a love theme, except that it was a big, emotional ballad that was proving irresistible to audiences at his Palladium performances.

He had recorded two songs and wondered which one he should release first. His company earlier wanted to issue *Tears* on the flipside of *The River*, but Doddy was determined to have *Tears* released separately. He knew it was a near thing, for if it had come out as 'B' side it might never have been played on the air.

Everything about the song captivated him. Particularly the lyrics:

> *Tears for souvenirs are all you left me*
> *Memories of a love you never meant*

I just can't believe you could forget me
After all those happy hours we spent
Tears have been my only consolation
But tears can't mend a broken heart I must confess
Let's forgive and forget, turn our tears of regret
Once more to tears of happiness.

Later, it was planned to release *The River*, another appealing ballad. It was Doddy's recording manager Norman Newell who had written the flipside of these records. A former transport worker from London's Plaistow, he was at that time one of the success stories among British songwriters. His hits as lyricist included the American success *More*, which brought him a regular income, and *Say Wonderful Things*. And he was planning to write a musical to star Peggy Mount.

Soon it was obvious that Doddy's recording company had made the correct decision. By early October *Tears* had equalled the Beatles' record of staying No. 1 in the *New Musical Express* hit parade for six weeks. It would become his most requested song, yet its swift rise in the charts surprised him and it tickled him to equal the Beatles' record and climb over the Rolling Stones, Andy Williams and Matt Monroe. Suddenly, he was a pop star.

To crown his most successful week in show business, he was informed that he was chosen for the Royal Variety Show. Press focus on him now was intense, but so full was his daily schedule that he scarcely had time to think about the pressure. His No. 1 dressing-room sometimes resembled a railway station, with fans, friends and the press battling it out, it seemed, to catch the star's attention. Anita Boutin occasionally looked lost in the midst of the confusion.

Anita and Ken were by now ten years engaged. Women journalists tended to remark on the lengthy engagement and inevitably asked if they intended to marry. 'Goodness, they are still engaged,' wrote one, and added, 'Anita is devoted to him and he would be the first to admit how much he owes not only to her companionship, but to her business-like help in making him Britain's most successful comedian. But now it seems that Doddy's friends and family are pressing him to marry Anita.'

The headline, 'NOW, AT LAST, THEY CAN GET MARRIED,' cannot have escaped Doddy's attention. Nonetheless, he had no intention of being rushed. Imperturbability, and a reluctance to change, were characteristics that even stardom could not shake. The basis of their happy relationship was a firm understanding of where they stood with each other. Would marriage spoil things? That he was the most eligible bachelor in town tickled his fans. Anita's friends on the other hand suspected that she would have welcomed being called Mrs Ken Dodd. At thirty-six, she had little time left if she hoped to marry and have the children she wanted – and that Ken occasionally talked about.

Sadly, in Doddy's ambitious schedule there was little time for sentiment. 'I just haven't the time to get married,' he repeatedly replied to pointed questions. His diary was full, with visits to recording studios, meeting radio and television producers, and brushing up on the latest batch of Eddie Braben gags for his Palladium show. New material, he felt, was necessary to keep the show fresh and topical.

Everyone close to the star knew how he liked to lie in in the mornings, but that luxury had to suffer as he kept important appointments. His old habit, however, of staying up late persisted and he brought back friends to his house in Kensington and talked for hours. It was his favourite way of relaxing and he enjoyed it immensely. His attitude at that time was summed up in his own admission, 'I've sweated for fifteen years to get to the top. I'm on the crest of the wave.'

It invited a reply from one journalist who was thinking of Anita Boutin: 'Sure, you're a great star, Ken – loved by millions. But even a great star needs a happy, settled home life. And so does the girl in the wings. Ten years' courtship is long enough for both of you to make up your minds. Now is the moment of triumph. Surely there is no better time to take the plunge.'

No one could claim he was unhappy. When it came to defining stardom he had his own views. He drew a distinction between national and international stardom and he became more aware of this as Danny Kaye and Bob Hope in turn visited his dressing-room. He recognised them as international celebrities, firm favourites with stage and screen fans everywhere. It was the kind of stardom he wanted for himself and which it seemed very few British comedians attained. He was more determined than ever to work towards that glittering goal.

Paradoxically, Ken was slow to act the role of a star. His ordinariness still puzzled observers. 'He's in the £2,000 a week class, but lives frugally by stars' standards, and has never had a holiday abroad,' commented a columnist in a Sunday paper. 'His dressing-room sometimes resembles a booking-office with the star selling tickets for cash to a queue of working-class friends, thumbing through a ready reckoner because each friend wants tickets for coach-loads of friends.'

Someone else asked, 'Don't you get fed up having so many people invading your dressing-room?' Doddy had a ready reply, 'I don't in the least, young man. I'm certainly not going to turn anybody away when friends like these represent a dozen seats. I want to keep my customers.'

By now he was becoming a one-man industry. It was indicated not only by his involvement in a recording company, but by the invasion of Diddy products on the market: Diddy dolls, slippers, Diddy pyjamas, Diddy cakes. As his box-office value increased so did his earnings from radio and television. His friends wondered about his financial investments, but Doddy laughed off such enquiries. It was acknowledged he was by now a wealthy star.

Stardom, however, wrought no marked change in his life-style. He did not spend extravagantly, he avoided the smart London nightclubs, and gambling casinos did not interest him. He did extend his wardrobe and Anita went shopping in Oxford Street. But Doddy had acquired the name of being tight-fisted; he was not a big spender in lounge bars, and he shared with Arthur Askey and Ted Ray the reputation of being 'careful with money'. Alone among the comedians of that time to admit openly that he was mean was the incorrigible Jack Benny who unashamedly styled himself the 'meanest man in town'. It became a catch-phrase and he promptly cashed in on it.

Undeniably, it was his lack of pretension and ego that endeared Doddy to most classes. Despite his new status, he remained *the* people's comedian and never lost sight of himself. It was no coincidence that fellow-Liverpudlian, Jimmy Tarbuck, was, at the age of twenty-three, enjoying a popular success as Sunday night compère at the Palladium. Tarbuck's idea of stardom, while more flamboyant than Doddy's, was just as realistic. Later, he would say, 'I was a cheeky chappie in my early twenties, not a big star. That would come later.'

Doddy was not easily swayed by public opinion, though he was amused by what the press continued to say about him. They labelled him a 'giggle merchant', a 'genius' and an 'eccentric'. As long as they did not invent stories about Anita and himself he didn't mind what else they wrote. He could have echoed George Bernard Shaw, 'My way of joking is to tell the truth. It's the funniest joke in the world.' At times the showbiz razzle-dazzle got to him and he was grateful to be able to slip away on occasional Sundays to the sanity of Knotty Ash, with its pastoral beauty, private people and friendliness.

Most times he breathed show business, loving every

moment. He admitted he was stage-struck, and he continued to see the funny side of life: 'If my mother knew I was doing this in London she'd be ashamed. She thinks I'm still in prison.' The zany side of his comedy was compared to Spike Milligan's, but the similarity ended there. To the majority Doddy made more sense. 'He's a dotty character who plots hundreds of gags every night with scientific precision, and has got miles of tapes, analytical notebooks, files and books on psychology to prove it,' commented one journalist after a visit to Doddy's dressing-room.

Baffled by such a scientific approach to comedy, he decided the Liverpool comic was unique. Most other comics he had met were content to leave the psychology of comedy to the professors and preferred pretty girls in their dressing-rooms to erudite books on humour. Repeatedly he was asked why he hadn't changed his act substantially for the Palladium, whereupon he replied, 'I won't change for London, for anybody.'

Liverpool member of Parliament Mrs Bessie Braddock, a friend of Doddy's, once invited him to join her for tea at the House of Commons. He could not resist wisecracking, 'I've a shrewd suspicion what's going to be on the menu.' Although he continued to welcome the press to his dressing-room, a few of them regarded him as a 'loner'. One summed him up, 'He loves the worship of fans, yet despite this pressure of people around him, he walks alone in show business.'

It was true. Doddy was different. In Liverpool it was an aspect of his character that was already noted.

By now the popular Doddy had grown used to all kinds of celebrities, from movie stars to politicians, popping their heads into his No. 1 dressing-room. However, when he was told that the Prime Minister, Harold Wilson, and Mrs Wilson were to attend his Palladium show, he regarded it as a 'great compliment'. He was further pleased to learn that the Wilsons would be accompanied by Mrs Bessie Braddock. One thing he did not want to know and that was where the Prime Minister and his party would be seated. 'Please don't tell me,' he begged.

That evening Harold Wilson sat in Row G of the stalls, his wife and son Giles on his left, Mrs Braddock – whose idea it was – on the right. Doddy had no intention of 'softening' his act for his celebrity guests, except to ensure that the rest of the audience knew who was present. When he bounded on stage for his first spot in the second house, he pointed his tickling stick towards the auditorium and exclaimed: 'We have got a posh lot in the audience tonight. We have a special outing from a working-men's club in Westminster. And I've marvellous digs in London. I am staying with a Mrs Wilson at No 10 . . .' He affected to forget the name of the street. 'You know,' he continued breathlessly, 'her husband's a nice little feller – ' 'Arry . . .' The dig, although part of Doddy's act, got a rousing laugh. And he added, 'Yes, 'Appy 'Arry, always walking round the House telling people not to worry.'

Came the inevitable gag about the Prime Minister's pipe. Doddy sniffed loudly into the microphone and quipped, 'Someone is smoking a nice bit of something there.' He could have joked about their respective earnings but refrained. Mr Wilson at the time earned £15,250 a year while the comedian's earnings were reputed to be £50,000. Instead, he said, 'We have a very sophisticated audience tonight. These MPs have the time of their lives with the all-night sessions.'

At the interval Doddy dashed back to his dressing-room and changed into a smart grey suit specially to meet the Prime Minister and his party. He was perspiring freely and seemed somewhat overcome by the occasion. When a young reporter popped his head into the room, he told him, 'I wouldn't dare do anything to send Mr Wilson up.'

Momentarily, he greeted the Prime Minister and his

party in the dressing-room, and presented Mrs Wilson and Mrs Braddock with bouquets of flowers. With that, Mrs Braddock seized a comb and fluffed up the comedian's hair. As Mr Wilson drew on his pipe, Doddy heard him say cheerily, 'It's the first night out we have had since we went to No. 10. We are enjoying ourselves.' Doddy did not try to cross swords with the PM. He had heard that he was particularly good at repartee. Nor did he try to be funny. On such occasions he tended to be serious, and thanked the Wilsons for coming to the show. Evidently, it meant a tremendous lot to him that they wanted to see his performance, though others might say, 'Why not? Isn't Knotty Ash only half a mile outside Mr Wilson's constituency of Huyton?'

It was a vibrant Doddy who ran on stage for his first spot after the interval. He quipped, 'I could do with a knighthood – if only to keep my ears warm at night.' Soon he was in full stride. He sent up 'U Thingi', the UNO arbitrator on the 'uprising in Bootle' and proposed a fish and chip shop for the corner of Downing Street, adding gaily, 'Somebody could send George Brown out for twenty-five guineas'-worth of hot peas.'

A smile was seldom seen to leave Harold Wilson's plump face. Mrs Braddock laughed outright, and Mrs Wilson seemed highly amused. It was doubtful though whether she got all the punchlines, so swift was Doddy's delivery. The jokes kept coming at even more speed – about fat aunties, pimples, kippers and bottoms. Suddenly, the joking ceased, and Doddy's voice was calm as he dedicated *Tears* to the Wilson party.

Although the performance overran, he had time to change back again into his grey suit to welcome back the Prime Minister and his party. It was drinks all round as Mr Wilson shook the comedian's hand warmly, and said 'Marvellous, Ken.' Later, Doddy said that the PM loved the gag about the fish shop. 'He said that I worked very hard and when I asked him if he was really a 'Appy 'Arry tonight, he said, "Certainly I am. I've enjoyed myself no end".'

A morning newspaper noted, 'The Prime Minister had his chuckle-muscle tickled by the Chief of the Diddy Men last night. It seemed, at any rate, to do Mr Wilson a power of good. He left the Palladium looking as if he'd laugh all the way to the next crisis. Few of the audience, though, realised that Mr Wilson was in the stalls until Ken Dodd pointed at him after the interval and referred to a knighthood.'

Doddy regarded Harold Wilson as 'a nice, friendly man'.

The phenomenal success of *Tears* was reflected in sales that now exceeded a million. Doddy was presented with his first gold disc. Later he got a silver disc for sales of *The River*. By November he had smashed all box-office records at the Palladium. Furthermore, it was announced that he would top the bill at the Opera House, Blackpool, in June.

'I'm delighted to be going back to the Opera House,' he enthused. 'It's the logical thing after the Palladium. Just as the Palladium has a special atmosphere, so too the Opera House and it's the biggest theatre in Europe.'

Doddy refused to disclose the money he would be paid, but it was reckoned to be £2,500 a week. It would be his sixth season in Blackpool and the first time he was to go there as a recognised star. Now, however, he was more concerned about his forthcoming appearance at the Royal Variety show. 'I am thrilled and excited at the prospect of appearing before royalty for the first time,' he said. 'I shall try to do my best – and on stage I won't have the time to be frightened.' Sharing the bill with him were Peter Sellers, Spike Milligan, Max Bygraves, Dudley Moore, Shirley Bassey and Tony Bennett.

As the occasion coincided with his birthday, he decided to invite his parents. He felt that he owed them more than he could ever repay. Before they left Lime Street station for London, Mrs Dodd remarked, 'It's a grand birthday treat for all of us and we are looking forward very much to seeing Ken in the show. We'll be staying with him.' Their daughter June saw them off and in their luggage was a large birthday cake for Doddy.

It was noticeable that Doddy was nervous before going on stage and perspired a lot. But he had brought an extra shirt or two along. Most of the other stars had performed before royalty and now a few of them tried to soothe Doddy. Once, however, he bounded on stage he forgot the tensions and quickly ran through his repertoire of jokes, touching on his diddy grandad, the geography of Knotty Ash, and kippers. It was an amusing lesson for Her Majesty the Queen, who appeared to be enjoying herself. Afterwards, when he was introduced backstage, she referred to his season at the Palladium and he assured her that it had surpassed his wildest dreams. He found her 'a very regal and a very beautiful lady'. Prince Philip, it seemed, was more anxious to chat up Spike Milligan, who had shaved off his beard.

'Vintage Doddy' was how the critics described his performance, and the star himself was pleased. That night he celebrated with his parents and friends in Kensington; he cut the birthday cake and gave everyone a slice. But he refused to reveal his age. 'Say I'm twenty-nine,' he joked. Later, they danced and sang and everyone agreed it was 'just like being back in Knotty Ash'. Arthur and Sarah Dodd were immensely proud of their son's achievement, yet it was Doddy's thoughtfulness more than anything else that they remarked on. 'Ken never forgets us,' Mrs Dodd said. 'He's a good son.' Anita Boutin helped to serve more birthday cake and was happy because Ken was happy. No one mentioned marriage, certainly not Doddy. He was delighted to be creating happiness.

He was resilient and durable. He saw more success for himself on the horizon. Reflecting his new showbiz status, he peppered interviews with eminently quotable lines: 'It's been a Doddy year all right. Fantastic. Fantastically fabulous'. You come to the end of a year like this and you ask yourself, "Why? Why have I had such a wonderful year when some other feller got run over or something?" There's no answer. People say, "What's the secret?" There isn't one. It just happened. It's just you know . . . I've been blessed. That's all. I'm not a religious man but . . . things were ordained thus and all I can say is "Thank God".'

Early in December, the day before the show was scheduled to end its record-breaking run, Doddy was visited in his dressing-room by a sharp young journalist who introduced himself as Barry Norman. Fascinated by the things written about the Liverpool comic, he decided to make his own assessment. He remembered what the playwright John Osborne had said, 'We all went away from the Palladium exhilarated and awed by this incredible phenomenon of human invention and overwhelming energy.'

Norman briefly surveyed No. 1 dressing-room. The walls were covered with birthday cards and good luck cables and pictures of the Liverpool football team. In the corner of the room was a suitcase full of jokes. To Norman, the off-stage Doddy was a serious individual. He did not try to be funny, despite the fact that the interview was taking place during the first house performance. From time to time Doddy went on stage and snatches of the act came over the intercom: . . . 'He said, "You'll marry our Dolly or else". I said, "Let's have a look at Else. . . .'.

Doddy came into the dressing-room and tidied his hair with a comb a foot long. With his eyes focused on the large mirror, he mused, 'I'd be a very strange sort of feller if I wasn't delighted by the extent of all this. But you know, success was the object of the exercise.' Asked if he had been surprised by the intellectual cult that had grown around him, he could not restrain from wise-cracking: 'Oh, all the intellectuals come to see me – me dad, the milkman, our dog . . . No, I'm not surprised. If certain people possessed of a very high IQ enjoy what I do, it's because this is a very original performance. People say, "Ken Dodd? He's just a stand-up patter man.' I'm not. I do visuals, a bit of wit, a bit of satire, political lampoons, a lot of way-out stuff – the full kaleidoscope of comedy.'

More than once, Doddy used the phrase 'touch wood', as though somewhere in the back of his mind a tiny sense of insecurity existed. However in his next remark he corrected this impression: 'Success doesn't close doors, you know – it opens them. Films are the next thing I want to try and I'm meeting two producers this week.'

Doddy rose and, clutching his tickling stick, went back to work. Over the intercom came some of his, 'Have you ever been tickled' jokes followed by bursts of laughter. When he eventually came back, wiping sweat from his forehead he turned to Norman and said seriously, 'You see, I know where my act is going. It's whimsical, exuberant, inventive. I make up my catch phrases, characters that people can identify with me. I'm proud of my creation – the diddymen, for instance. I invented them for children. I love children. I still believe in Santa Claus. Well, why not? He hasn't been bad for me this year, has he?'

Barry Norman felt that in the eyes of his audience Doddy could do no wrong. He rose and shook his hand and as he did, Doddy said with conviction, 'It's timing, you see – the right time, the right place. This has been my greatest year so far, but things can still get better.'

CHAPTER 13

'I didn't expect an honour like this'

Doddy's success wasn't complete. Doubts persisted about the merit of his television series and critics claimed it lacked the magic of his stage performance. One of the most influential of them, James Green, was the first to raise the question that was being asked by the star's admirers: 'Why should TV success be so elusive for Ken? I find it remarkable the way the small screen has so far cut him down to size. Otherwise, it has been a phenomenal year for Mr Dodd. Everything he touches, including records, turns to gold. All that is, except one thing. He has still to knock the TV audience for six.'

Green argued that it was paradoxical that Doddy could fill every provincial theatre, break records at the Palladium, make a disc that sold a million, yet he had never known the TV acclaim of a Forsyth or a Hancock.

It was a source of concern for Doddy, but it was early days yet in his television career. Had he perhaps underestimated the painstaking preparation required to ensure total success in a TV series? Or, for that matter, the insatiable appetite the medium possessed for material? As Ronnie Barker would admit years later, 'Keeping laughter flowing is a tremendous challenge. The key ingredient is material. You have got to query and reject and demand material all the time. We could have taken easier options, worried less . . . but I doubt whether *The Two Ronnies* would have lasted more than six seasons.'

Furthermore, up to now Doddy had failed to evolve a successful style for television. It smacked too much of the stage. Some of his admirers even believed that he should have developed a double-act in the exuberant style of Morecambe and Wise, but the zany comic rejected such a notion. He felt confident than in time his television work would be acclaimed in the same way as his stage and radio performances. If he continued however to take on too much, it was impossible to see how he could concentrate enough on television to ensure a big success. At that time Forsyth, Hancock and Morecambe and Wise were very much committed to their television careers.

Not all the critics saw it James Green's way. T. C. Worsley in the *Financial Times* regarded Doddy as the cult figure of the North. He saw merit in the very things that left some of his fellow critics cold. He wrote: 'The Ken Dodd Show certainly got the new Northern programme off to a lively start. If I were a total Square, instead of a kind of Rhomboid, I should welcome the great cult success of Mr Dodd as a sign of returning sanity. For the whole pleasure of Mr Dodd's act is that he is an old-fashioned, stand-up comedian. He springs straight from the music-hall, and what could be more traditional than to end an act of quick-fire patter and puns with a real sloppy piece of syrup sung straight.'

Worsley went to pains to emphasise that in calling Doddy square, he was not being derogatory. As he explained, 'Far from it. I had, I admit, expected from the title yet another of those shows with an exhausted formula, like the Kathy Kirby Show, or the Danny Kaye Show, where the star pushes forward through the dancing boys and girls to do his first spot, then introduces a guest star with a lot of fulsome yak, barely gives the guest time to do a short number before barging in again and doing a double with him or her, with a lot of pushing to see who

135

can upstage the other, etc, etc. This is the best tradition of music-hall perpetuated on television.'

To Worsley, the Ken Dodd Show was different – it was shaped and planned for television. Half of it consisted of taped insets, spoof interviews, newsreels, sport commentaries, all making their points wittily, and above all, concisely. All in all he found it 'one of the shortest comedy hours I have ever seen on television.'

As viewers and critics discussed his TV show, Doddy was far too busy to join in any public debate. He rehearsed for a whole afternoon each week at the BBC's Paris Cinema Studio in Lower Regent Street and later in the day recorded *The Ken Dodd Show*, a radio series that was proving enjoyable with listeners. One morning he nearly missed rehearsals. It happened when a BBC secretary telephoned a hire firm for a car to take him to the studio, which was known as 'The Paris'.

During the trip the star sat in the back seat with his eyes on the radio script before him. Momentarily when he lifted his head, he saw they were about to drive into Buckingham Palace. The gates were already open. Suddenly, he shouted at the driver, 'Stop! What are you doing?'

The chauffeur kept his gaze on the road. 'Taking you to the Palace, like it says on the chit, sir.' Doddy could not resist a laugh. 'The Paris, not the Palace.' The embarrassed chauffeur turned the car and headed for Lower Regent Street. At least Doddy had a *real* excuse this time for being late for rehearsals.

At that time offers to go to work in America and Australia came his way, but he told Dave Forrester to postpone a decision for a while longer. With his diary full for a whole year, he was too busy to think of perhaps more lucrative work overseas. Although he had his hand on the popular pulse at home, it was not easy to imagine how his humour about jam-butty mines and Diddymen would be received in America. Australia was a different matter. Soon, Tony Hancock would be a big success there and it was quite conceivable that Doddy's frenetic approach would capture the imagination of the Aussies. His aim was still to promote laughter wherever that took him and in time he hoped to promote it abroad. At that time he was very patriotic, though he liked to describe Parliament as 'one of the last great music-halls left in the country'. Or quip, 'The British Navy – I was talking to him the other day.'

His repertoire of jokes was increasing. He described the TUC as 'The Ten Useless Charlies'. He still sprinkled his act with 'What a Beautiful Day' gags, such as: 'What a beautiful day for rushing into Woolworth's and shouting "Tesco's";' and, 'What a beautiful day for rushing into a maternity ward and shouting "It's your Fault for voting Labour".' He liked to dwell occasionally in a world of fantasy and imagination and it was from this rich source he sometimes drew his inspiration. As one observer put it, 'Doddy likes to take us in his act on a kind of mystery tour into a strange land in which the normal rules of logic are suspended and in which the language itself is capable of being twisted, altered and extended.'

But most of the time the star lived in a world of reality, reading scripts, planning engagements, endlessly discussing projects, and talking to Anita about her little black notebook, with its comments. It was impossible for him to get away from the world of comedy. People expected him to enliven their lives with humour. As the Squire of Knotty Ash, he had his obligations.

Early in February 1966 Ken Dodd was on his way to Birmingham when he learned that he had been named Show Business Personality of 1965 by the Variety Club of Great Britain. For a moment the thought of his role of Humpty-Dumpty in pantomime went right out of his head. 'I'm diddy-lated,' was his immediate reaction. And he added, 'I didn't expect an honour like this.'

That Wednesday afternoon he telephoned his parents in Knotty Ash with the 'fantastical news' and during the evening accepted the congratulations of friends and colleagues. At the final curtain in the Birmingham Hippodrome he was accorded a special round of applause. He was in good company. Robert Stephens was named best actor, and Dorothy Tutin best actress, while Benny Hill was chosen the TV personality for his *Benny Hill Show*. Doddy was getting the top award for his record-breaking season at the London Palladium, top hit parade disc *Tears*, which was well on the way to selling two million records, and his notable success in the Royal Variety Performance.

By now he was long accustomed to banquets, late night cabaret, and big civic occasions. But he admitted he was still overwhelmed by the sumptuous banquet at the Savoy Hotel that March afternoon. Once, however, he got on his feet to speak he broke the air of formality that permeated the banquet room and affected the large audience. No toastmaster when mentioning distinguished visitors has ever gone on to refer to undistinguished visitors, or when speaking of a young farmers' association has added – and some very old farmers as well. It was doubtful too whether the ancient Guild of Lodginghouse Keepers existed anywhere but in Doddy's mind.

Faced by such a gathering in the great banqueting room, the star confessed to a fine feeling of plumpishousness at receiving the award. Gleefully he recalled what his Little Diddy Granny declared when he started in show business: 'If all the agents in the world were laid out end to end – hurrah.' At the end of ten minutes' chuckles and laughter, Doddy referred to seeing a notice at the Admiralty that stated, 'Gone to inspect the Fleet – back in five minutes.'

After the laughter had subsided, he was serious for a moment as he recalled the wonderful year and admitted how proud he was to receive the award. 'I promise you I'll not overrun on this occasion,' he said with a hint of emotion in his voice. Among those to applaud him were

Anita Boutin and Mrs. Bessie Braddock. And in that same year he was further tickled by the unveiling of a wax model of himself at Madame Tussaud's. At the ceremony the star joked,' Good heavens, he's better looking than I am, better looking by about half-a-stone. Jolly good he is, even down to his little mole – very diddyfalarious.' Typically, he added, 'Will this one age now instead of me?'

Around that time he achieved another ambition – to present the popular radio programme *Housewives' Choice*. As he said, 'It's been my ambition for years to be host to British housewives. I regard it as an accolade – a sort of BBC good conduct medal.' Fearing that he would be late to rise in the morning, he travelled to London on the Sunday and thus ensured he would be punctual. He co-scripted the programmes with Eddie Braben but this did not rule out some ad-libs. Often he had listened to the programme and had his own views about it. 'Housewives are an intelligent audience. If they didn't have sense their husband wouldn't trust them with looking after the house, then they wouldn't be housewives, would they?'

Terry Warrick, a sharp-witted and wiry Londoner, was producer of *Housewives' Choice* and among the personalities who had presented the programme were Eamonn Andrews, Pete Murray and David Jacobs. At that time it had ten million listeners and was regarded as a very popular request programme. 'We received hundreds of cards every day requesting different music items,' Warrick recalls. 'Ken Dodd seemed eager to do the programme and I was pleased to have him. I had seen his show at the Palladium and to me he was a brilliant quick-fire comic who could be very funny.'

Early on Monday morning Doddy, accompanied by Anita Boutin, arrived at the small BBC studio. He was carrying a suitcase full of scripts and gags and when he opened it a few sheets of paper fell out. His producer looked on intrigued and soon he found him to be hyperactive and full of ideas. But he looked confident and composed and eager to get on with the programme which was due to begin at 9 o'clock. In contrast, Anita Boutin, who sat in one of the cubicles, was quiet and hardly spoke a word, which tended to surprise Warrick. 'I had been told that she liked to comment about shows and this sometimes irritated directors,' he recalls, 'but she made no comment to me. I could see that she and Ken were very close.'

It was plain to everyone after the first programmes that Doddy's *Housewives' Choice* was going to be different, and after the second morning's programme the head of the Gramophone Department, as well as one or two other BBC bosses, were alarmed by Doddy's behaviour. The comic was turning the programme into a comedy with lots of one-liners and funny introductory chat, which was a departure from the normally staid presentation. Terry Warrick was asked to talk to the star but he declined on the grounds that it would probably be futile.

'I think Ken's zany approach shocked some of them in Broadcasting House,' he says. 'Usually the personalities said a few words to introduce requests and left it at that. Most listeners preferred it that way; now a number of them complained to the BBC and said Ken Dodd had gone too far. I wasn't worried. I was more concerned by his demands which could be unreasonable. He wanted all kinds of weird sound effects and of course I could not supply them at a moment's notice. Otherwise, we got on well together.'

By the end of the week the audience figures had shot up by many thousands and Warrick felt vindicated in giving the comic his head. 'Although Ken played fewer records than most of the other presenters, his unique comedy style won over many listeners. Such was his success that the BBC invited him back to present bank holiday specials.' Off-stage, the producer found Doddy serious-minded and was surprised by his profound knowledge of the art of comedy. He had been told that the comedian had a reputation for being mean but he found this to be untrue. On the last day of *Housewives' Choice* Doddy presented him with two bottles of champagne, something new to him.

It was a hectic period in Doddy's career, yet he found time for the business side. The one-man Doddy industry was expanding. The Diddymen dolls were proving so successful that his firm was branching into other forms of merchandise such as Diddy clothes, slippers, ice-cream and jewellery. Two new records were in the pipeline, and he would soon begin a new series of six ITV shows called *Doddy's Music Box*.

It was a punishing programme and Doddy soon had to admit he was feeling exhausted. He needed a rest. He looked drawn and pale and friends warned him against pushing himself too hard. Colleagues suggested he should go to a healthy hydro near Liphook, Hampshire, where he would probably meet other tired stars looking for resuscitation. Previous guests at the hydro included Albert Finney, Jack Hawkins and John Mills.

Unlike other show business stars, Doddy did not play golf; in fact he exercised very little. Work had become his life and though he enjoyed every moment, it was taking its toll. He was now determined to get himself fit. At the hydro the daily routine included sauna baths, cycle exercises, rowing-machine work, and weight lifting. The menu . . . lots of lettuce, fruit juices, and grapes. Inevitably, the press heard about his self-imposed exile from Knotty Ash and photographers shot him in various stages of exercise.

When a *Liverpool Post* reporter visited the centre, he walked round the expansive grounds with the star. 'I'm feeling much better and more mentally alert,' confessed Doddy, whose colour had returned. And he laughed as he added, 'I've never been in bed before 3 a.m. for the past ten years. Now I go off to bed at about 7.30. I lie there

141

watching the telly and I'm sound asleep by 10 o'clock. This is the ideal holiday for anyone under pressure.'

It was one of the very few times he mentioned the word 'pressure', for he always liked to give the impression that he was taking work in his stride. But now he talked about running the machine down and that it needed lubrication. When he arrived he tipped the scales at 12 st. 4 lb. Already he had lost 11 lb. and he hoped to reduce further. Despite his exhaustion, he had not lost his sense of humour. As he quipped, 'When I went for a hair-cut the previous day, they put up the scaffolding in advance.'

Soon Ken was back sweating again in the only business he knew. And he quickly resumed his old routine of late-night conversations and morning lie-ins. At his age it was not easy to adapt to new ways. He was excited when Tom Sloan, head of BBC TV Light Entertainment, telephoned him to outline plans for a summer spectacular starring himself and the famous Bluebell Girls. Sloan had been delighted by the tremendous response to Doddy's Christmas show when it claimed an audience of twenty-one million. He was confident that the combination of Ken Dodd and the Bluebells would be a smash hit. The shows would go out live, each running forty-five minutes.

Doddy who was reputed to be getting £16,000 for the series, commented, 'I want to make it the greatest show on television.' The Bluebells, sixteen of them in all, would be making their first appearance in Britain. Launched in 1946 by Liverpool-born Margaret Kelly, who now trained the group in Paris, they had never been invited to Britain.

'Surprisingly, it's the first time anyone has asked us to appear over here,' remarked Miss Kelly. I can't understand it.' Tom Sloan regarded their engagement as a 'scoop'. Eventually what viewers did see was a spectacular with Doddy's costumes matching those of the Bluebells, and his comedy act was not overshadowed by the gorgeous girls. Critics regarded the show as a glamorous vehicle for the star and welcomed the girls to British screens as a decided asset, but they were undecided whether the show really did much to further Doddy's own television career.

Visually, the show looked lovely and Tom Sloan was pleased with the ratings. He had faith in Doddy and believed he fronted the show superbly well. He would have him back. Dave Forrester, who was as anxious as ever to surround Doddy with star support, decided to engage the Bluebell Girls at considerable cost for Doddy's next appearance at the London Palladium. After their success on TV everyone he knew was talking about the girls and he was sure they would dazzle Palladium audiences.

Although it was now 1967, it did not seem nearly two years to Doddy since he had last played the renowned variety theatre. He was thrilled to be going back there. The same could not be said about the attitude of the stage crew and technicians who had painful memories of his previous appearance when his shows overran nearly every night. They were determined to teach Doddy a lesson. One afternoon, the men collected in a nearby public-house and, using a Diddy-sized model of Kenneth Arthur Dodd as a target, began to stick pins and needles into it.

The pin-sticking ceremony was their way of showing the management that they did not like the way the star was allowed to overrun his act. He kept them late with the result that they had to fork out for taxis to get home – and invariably they missed their last pint at the pub. Scene designer, Ron Drain, who had made the Diddy-sized model, spoke for the men, 'We are all fed up to the teeth. When Doddy's here it's a foregone conclusion that we'll be late home. We decided to express our views in the hope that the management will take some notice.'

There was laughter as Nick Nicholas, one of the stage-hands, stuck a pin in the image, and exclaimed, 'Take that! That's for all the pints I've missed. I can tell you working with Ken Dodd is not easy. Several times I've had to stay in town. We work hard to finish at a reasonable time.'

That June, the Bluebell Girls electrified the Palladium audiences with their routines and dazzling costumes. Tall and elegant, their presentation was breathtaking. 'Bringing the Bluebells from Paris has certainly paid dividends,' summed up the *Guardian* critic. Armed with his tickling stick, Doddy joined the girls for dance routines. If anything, his performance surpassed that of 1965, with one critic describing it as 'sensational'. He still managed to overrun. Bill Platt said, 'We forgave him because the show was great. Backstage we were surrounded by all these stunning Bluebells and the atmosphere was magic.'

As before, Doddy received visitors to his dressing-room, talked endlessly, and said he felt the same thrill as the first time he played the Palladium. And old George Cooper, the stage-door keeper, was at hand if he wanted anything in a hurry. However, he was unable to help on the occasion Prime Minister Harold Wilson and his party came to the show and someone had mistakenly closed the door leading from the auditorium to No. 1 dressing-room. There was a moment of panic as stage-hands searched for the key. Eventually, Mr Wilson was led in at the interval through the orchestra pit and round to the dressing-room. Doddy apologised for the inconvenience, and the Prime Minister did not complain.

Usually Doddy ended his performance with *Happiness*, the song he had made his signature tune. At the Palladium he encouraged the audience to sing along with him, although aware that the backstage staff were waiting impatiently to close the theatre. But at no time did the management press him to end his act exactly on time, believing it would be an impossible request. Doddy did however try to end on better time. The trouble was the audience did not want him to go. It was Danny Kaye and Jack Benny all over again.

Doddy was an innovator. While most comedians of that time played golf for leisure, sunbathed or swam, Doddy was always thinking up new ideas. Some people claimed it was his funny way of keeping in the limelight. The star would deny the claim. In that July 1967, he planned the first Laughter Week in Britain, beginning on the tenth of the month. And he was in earnest about it. When some sceptics said it was a crazy idea and would not work, Doddy sat down and wrote to the *Morning Star*:

I have been asked to explain why I should want to launch National Laughter Week which begins today. Why not? I honestly believe that there is no bar, even in the midst of serious times, to encouraging people to enjoy a hearty laugh.

Laughter and happiness are the greatest of all the tonics and if a week of nonsense and fun can be organised on a national scale I'm sure that many lives could be brightened. After all, I believe that one of the best quotations I've ever heard is from Chamfort which goes, 'The most utterly lost of all days, is that on which you have not once laughed.'

So I am writing to ask your readers to join in the spirit of the week and make a special effort to be as good-humoured as possible. I'm not alone in this idea. Prince Philip has said, 'I'm in favour of anyone who brings laughter to the community and wish the week every success.'

The letter undoubtedly contained much of Doddy's long-held philosophy about laughter, especially happiness. In Liverpool he was known to visit sick friends regularly in hospital to cheer them. He considered he had a duty to try to brighten people's lives, on and off the stage. Growing up in a city where poverty and unemployment had sadly been the norm, he was aware of enough depression, yet on the other hand he had seen how people could be

145

cheered when they visited the Empire or Royal Court theatres for variety or pantomime. Despite modern cynicism, he was determined to promote happiness.

At that time he was seldom out of the news. When a Giles cartoon appeared in the press about gambling, the character looked like Doddy, long hair and teeth. It prompted the comic to write to the paper from his home in Knotty Ash:

> I was absolutely discumknockerated and full of a feeling of plumpiousness when I saw Giles' cartoon on gambling last Sunday (page 3). I wasn't going to say anything about that croupier, far right in the cartoon, until the phone calls started. All my fizzmelorious friends thought it depicted me.
>
> I don't know whether to be flattered or fantabusticated. It couldn't be me, of course, because I'm not a regular follower of fun with this kind of chips. I prefer the kind that come from Knotty Ash fish and chip factory situated three roads from the left past Pimple Park in Diddyland.
>
> I think Giles must have been watching *Doddy's Music Box* before he drew the cartoon and a little bit of me got into that long-haired character!

Giles wrote: 'Surely a case of any likeness to any living person being purely coincidental, I think this accompanying sketch of Sir Laurence Olivier is more like Ken Dodd than that croupier in last week's cartoon.'

By now Doddy had devised his own vocabulary and delighted in writing to the papers in a language of his own. His use of long, fancy words and phrases tickled his zany sense of fun and readers came to find it amusing. Someone suggested that he publish a Doddy Dictionary, and he promised to consider it. As always it was a question of finding the time.

CHAPTER 14

'Ken Had An Ability To Be Mad'

As Bobby Jaye was producing the *Late Night Extra* show for Terry Wogan in the late Sixties, the BBC was anxiously looking around for someone to replace Bill Worsley. Worsley, who was retiring, had from the start produced *The Ken Dodd Show*.

Jaye, outgoing and quick-witted, was informed that there were few experienced producers available to take over the popular radio series. Eventually, when he was offered the job, he telephoned his old radio colleague in Manchester, Jim Casey, for advice.

Casey had worked closely with Doddy in the North and remembered that after a recording session he was left with a lot on tape to edit as the comic overran. Consequently, he did not envy the task facing a new producer.

'Well,' asked Jaye, 'do you think I can manage it, Jim?'

Casey gave a short laugh. 'Emigrate, Bobby.'

It was the finality in Casey's tone that threw Bobby Jaye, but he tried to see the humorous side.

'I'm sure it will be fine, Jim,'

Jaye's enthusiasm for radio was remarkable. He began his career as a sound-effects boy on ITMA and later on decided that *The Goon Show* brought a new form of light entertainment to radio. It was zany, inventive and wildly imaginative. It created images as well as destroying them. It transcended traditional radio comedy and the Goons themselves were an inspired trio. As he began to produce *The Ken Dodd Show* at the BBC's Paris Cinema Studio in Lower Regent Street, he thought that Doddy caught the comedy mood of that time superbly. He was zany and capable of turning things upside down. He had an extraordinary ability to be mad. He decided there was a genius side to the man.

But there were problems. He soon wondered if, after all, Jim Casey was not correct. Doddy had lost his experienced script-writer, Eddie Braben. It was a serious loss. Braben had worked with the star during the previous ten years. It had given him a persona and he came to be greatly respected in the business. In addition, people came up to him in the street and remarked, 'That was a funny radio show, Eddie.' He wasn't vain but he was human and welcomed compliments like that from Liverpudlians.

'Eddie regarded Ken as a genius because of the way he worked his material,' says Bobby Jaye. 'Some people would go so far as to say he became his god. I suppose it was understandable. The same thing had happened with the Goons who looked upon Milligan as a genius and expected him to be brilliantly original.' In Jim Casey's view, Eddie Braben was becoming the best in the business. 'I thought that Ken was very lucky to have a script-writer like Eddie. He understood him, he knew the type of gags that suited his comedy line.'

Braben gave his excuse for breaking up the partnership: 'I am after more television work and more money. Of course I'm sad at the break after being with Ken so long. But he is committed so much to his dates in variety theatres and summer shows that half the year was gone and there was no time for telly so far as I was concerned.'

Dave Forrester managed both Doddy and Braben, and there were inevitable disagreements on policy – and money. The script-writer felt he was worth more than he was getting and was aware of what others like him were earning in the business. Furthermore, he saw no real future writing for Doddy who did not seem prepared to sacrifice his variety commitments for the more remunerative TV side.

Soon he signed up with Morecambe and Wise. His contract was reputed to be worth a five-figure sum. For the first time in his life he was in the big money league. 'I'll tell you something,' Braben said, 'writing for a solo comic like Ken Dodd is more difficult than writing for two men like Eric and Ernie.'

When he was asked if he would give Doddy a joke if he rang him up and was stuck for something funny to say, he replied frankly, 'No, I'm afraid not. We got on well together, but it's come to the end of the contract. That's that. This television series is so important to me I've got to give up everything else.'

The Ken Dodd Show was rehearsed – and recorded – on either Sundays or Wednesdays. On that afternoon the actors, Joe Manning Wilson, Talfryn Thomas, Michael McClain and Miriam Margolis were seeing the script for the first time, and sometimes in the rather humid atmosphere of the studio would go through it page by page, sharing out parts and experimenting with voices. Doddy would read a few lines and discussion followed and he might remark, 'What about playing that character in a Yorkshire accent?'

It was an unusual scene as he sat on the empty stage or stretched himself full length, with an elbow under his jaw, while the rest of the cast faced him in the front row of the stalls. The producer, with script in hand, sat a few seats behind the cast. 'We can't use that sketch about the Prime Minister,' someone might say. If considered in bad taste it would be dropped and another sketch substituted. At times, Doddy gave his advice and he was listened to attentively. It was always 'specific, practical and shrewd.'

After the departure of Eddie Braben, producer Bobby Jaye was forced to rely on a dozen different script-writers, the majority of them non-professionals. Doddy insisted that they be contracted to him and not to the BBC. Jaye recalls, 'I'd pay Ken a sum of money which he in turn paid to the various writers. These were people who submitted one-liners and sketches. Once, Ken said to me, "Bobby, I want you to meet this writer whose name is Malcolm." I asked the man if he was a pro writer and he replied, "No, no. I write one-liners in my spare time." When the producer showed some surprise, the man added, "I've a great sense of humour. I click with Ken." '

Jaye asked casually, 'What then do you do in real life?' 'I'm a male nurse in a mental hospital.'

The producer laughed. 'Is that where you met Ken?' To Jaye, it did not appear a good prognosis for the future. Occasionally during a recording session a few of the script-writers sat in the stalls in the hope of hearing Doddy perhaps say a nice word about a particular sketch or one-liner. Mostly they were disappointed, for the comic was more likely to quip, 'What a lot of rubbish!'

None the less, *The Ken Dodd Show* was proving very popular with listeners, mainly because of Doddy's star reputation and the expert team work of the experienced cast. To Bobby Jaye, some of the scripts were appalling and if found unworkable were passed over. However, the show gave Doddy the opportunity to try out every kind of comedy, straight sketches, stand-up patter, one-liners, weird fantasy and political satire.

Afternoon rehearsals did not always get off to a smooth start. It was not unusual for Doddy to arrive late on some flimsy excuse and did not seem to mind keeping the actors waiting. To Jaye, it was a frustrating experience, and it underlined the anarchic side of the comic. Yet he tended to forgive him because of his innate ability to create funny images for the listener – and he was, after all, the star of the show. He could say he was fond of him and there was warmth somewhere in his complex make-up. Moreover, he saw him as the first Northern comic to break down the divide between London and Liverpool and become fully accepted in the South. 'I could watch Ken do the same routine a dozen times,' said the producer. 'I admired the arrogance of the man as he told his audience, "By Jove, you *will* laugh tonight." And, of course, they always did laugh at his act.'

The atmosphere during the four-hour rehearsal was invariably jokey, although more than one observer sensed a mild undercurrent of tension between Doddy and the cast, but the actors by their professionalism camouflaged their feelings and got on with the show. All the time Bobby Jaye sat in the third row of the stalls, script propped up on his knees in front of him, occasionally putting an imaginary cross through material he knew would never be recorded. Shortly before 7 o'clock the cast took a break. On resuming, after about twenty minutes, they did a quick run-through of the bits involving sound-effects. By 8 o'clock the audience were already queueing to get in. Eventually when all the five hundred seats were filled the audience ranged in age from ten to seventy-five. Some had come by coach from as far as Brighton.

Usually Bobby Jaye did the warm-up and read out the names of the parties who were in; then the cast was introduced, one by one, until Doddy bounded on stage waving a colourful tickling stick, his hair ruffled, his teeth showing. Immediately he unleashed a succession of one-liners and in no time at all the audience was beside itself with laughter. 'He's a comic genius,' remarked Bobby Jaye, as he listened in the wings. He had heard a few of the gags before, but he still laughed.

At 8.30 the show itself started. The opening and close of the show were recorded first because the orchestra could not be left sitting around, otherwise as Doddy went on and on they would be clocking up overtime. The audience had already been told of the procedure, and they did not worry unduly. It was Doddy they had come to see. His opening spot was supposed to last three minutes but continued on gaily for twenty-five minutes. The audience loved every minute, but producer Bobby Jaye shook his head. He saw already a massive editing job before him.

Similarly, a few of the sketches overran and tended to leave some of the audience feeling exhausted. Describing the scene, one observer noted, 'What is significant is the way Dodd in all of them managed to blend the familiar and the unfamiliar, corn with the cob, mother-in-law jokes with surrealist and inspired. The audience fell about at the comic's standards, "Do you know the way to Biggle-swick? It's quite easy as long as you keep your legs apart".'

It had been an extraordinary free show for the fans. By the time it was ended at ten o'clock Bobby Jaye had a monumental problem – reducing ninety minutes on tape to around twenty-five. For him it meant burning the mid-night oil as he tried to piece together a show that millions of listeners would hopefully find funny. However, if he considered the show above the ordinary he would say so to Doddy before he left the theatre and walked outside to join the cast for drinks at the Captain's Cabin. Even then Jaye knew that the star had a reputation for being 'careful with money' and he was inclined to agree. But that was not his worry as he sipped beer; he was already thinking of the hours of work on the tapes. 'Dodd's impossible,' he'd sigh with frustration. But so far there was little he could do to change him. The star addressed him as 'Commander' and Jaye called him 'Ken'. He decided it would take a good deal to damage their relationship, although at times it was under severe strain.

After a drink with the cast in the Captain's Cabin, Doddy and Anita set out by car for Liverpool. It grieved the star at that time to find the city's Royal Court Theatre closed and maybe doomed. Imbued with a strong crusading spirit, he decided to do something about its future. He was convinced that people were returning to theatres and it was imperative that they remain open. The Grand Theatre, Blackpool was another under threat of closure.

He blamed some theatre managements for the bad reputation live theatre had had over the years. Cheap shows, lack of publicity, big companies who owned theatres, but whose interest lay elsewhere, and a general lack of get up and go – all were contributory factors. There were still, however, people who showed faith in the theatre. At that time Nottingham had spent £4 million on a new theatre.

He decided to be producer and performer to save the Royal Court Theatre. In that year, 1970, whenever he went past it he felt sad. As he recalls, 'I couldn't bear to see a fine theatre standing empty. The old posters outside were curling off and torn. The place had a desolate look.'

That June he telephoned impresario Bernard Delfont's office and asked for an appointment. Later, they had discussions in London and Delfont suggested that Doddy should see the owners of the theatre, Howard and Wyndham Ltd, to find out if they would lease it for twelve weeks. They agreed and an agreement was signed between Delfont, Dave Forrester and Doddy. The trio would meet all the costs of the show, pay the salaries of artistes, theatre staff, everybody. Doddy himself agreed to handle publicity and advertising, delivering the ad proofs, paying the bills.

His gesture caught the imagination of the Liverpool public. Inside a few months a £1,000 advance booking a day was pouring into the box-office. Doddy engaged Dickie Hurran to direct the variety spectacular and Dave Forrester ensured a strong supporting cast. By the time the doors opened more than £50,000 had been taken in advance booking. Doddy announced he was prepared to assist in saving any theatre in Britain threatened with closure. The success of his dual role made him think about further excursions into production.

He was grateful to Merseyside audiences. They were the best in the country in his estimation because they encouraged local talent. As he said, 'I could not have got where I am without their encouragement. It is not the same in other parts of the country. I can recall many occasions when artistes appearing here in local shows have been applauded and cheered and generally given the equivalent of a "Kop roar". Whereas show folk from other places of the country to whom I have talked have revealed that their home friends and fans have often been more inclined to criticise and "knock" their early efforts.'

It was one of the reasons why Doddy was so determined that the Royal Court Theatre should stay open. The great comic tradition in the city could only be maintained by the availability of live theatres to provide an opportunity for potential talent.

Despite his wealth, Ken was still very attached to Knotty Ash. He considered Doddy Towers his castle. 'I could not really conceive of living anywhere else,' he reflected. 'Knotty Ash is my key. Just as a singer has a particular key in which he can sing comfortably and give of his best, so I want to feel in tune with where I am and what I am doing. I like to be where I feel most at home – and that place is Knotty Ash.'

Apart from owning an extra car or two, he avoided the trappings of success. He was aware that people talked about his earnings and occasionally, when quizzed by the press, he referred to the subject, though with some caution. As when he said, 'Even if I do earn £5,000 a week I'm still an enthusiastic amateur. I hate the thought of doing it for money, but I suppose I measure my success in monetary terms with a dirty great 3 foot ruler like anybody else. I don't like taking home £5,000 a week when some poor chap working hard all week in a car factory only takes home £15. I'd like to take just a third of my wage and give the rest to stop theatres from having to close down. Theatres are happy places. The trouble is I occasionally have to sign cheques for £50,000 to the little diddy man from the Income Tax.'

The tax-man figured at that time more than once in his utterances. 'Tax,' he declared, 'isn't the only price a comedian has to pay for being a professional. You have to be hard. You have to go on stage and tell jokes even when your heart is broken.' He was remembering the recent death of his mother, and the night she died. He admitted he was grief-stricken. 'I thought I'd never be able to tell another joke, but I had to go out and face the audience. It stems from a colossal desire to be loved and we all have it – me and Laurence Olivier and Harold Wilson.'

Doddy was going back that summer to a changed Blackpool. The Costa del Sol was by then attracting many of the people who would otherwise be spending their holidays at the resort. Yet the day-trippers and 'week-enders' crowded the Golden Mile and packed the theatres, though these were fewer in number than in the Fifties, when Doddy played the Central Pier.

He was now the top star in Blackpool and was already on the way to creating a box-office record at the 3,000-seater Opera House. Magician Cyril Critchlow went along to see the comic and came away overwhelmed by his performance. 'He was unrecognizable from the young man I first saw at the Central Pier. He was composed, bubbling with confidence and at the top of his form. Many of his gags were hilariously funny. To me, he had no equal as a stand-up comic.'

To Frank Carson, Doddy's frenetic act was an undoubted success. 'Blackpool loved him. He could go on for hours and he was improving with age. It was astonishing really the way he refused to spare himself. His quick-fire style was perfect for holiday crowds who wanted laughs.'

'Doddy's machine-gun delivery was the key to his success,' recalls tenor Josef Locke, who by now had paid his tax debts to the British Inland Revenue and was able to work in England again. Seeing Doddy in the show convinced him that he was still the funniest man he ever saw on the stage. 'The Opera House audience just wouldn't let him go.'

The *Guardian* sent along Robin Thornber to review the show:

Doddy's Laughter Spectacular is just that: the most expensive, the most hilarious, the one with a real live waterfall on the stage at the end of the first half. Dodd himself is Blackpool at its best – it's his ninth season here since 1955. An aristocrat of true vulgarity, he knows exactly what people want and gives them a little bit more. He does it by taking the same corny gags that the rest of them use, but teasing out the logic to its zany limit and out the other side; it's the only act in Blackpool that stretches the imagination or strikes true chords. The tickling stick's still there but now it's yards long, a Scarfean phallus nodding over the stalls, 'Are there any honeymoon couples here?' he asks. 'Good-morning.'

From time to time comedians at the resort complained that other comics were stealing their jokes. It was something that tended to anger Doddy. 'I spend thousands of pounds a year on ideas and materials, and this poaching is very annoying. It became so bad that one comic put advertisements in the local paper. He warned that he would take legal action 'against any other comedian who used his material'. He claimed he saw a young man in the front row of the stalls writing down everything and was even marking the jokes 'poor' or 'big laugh'.

Jimmy Tarbuck, a popular star with Blackpool audiences, commented, 'Poaching has been getting worse. I have never stolen a joke directly. But I can't claim that every joke out of Liverpool is mine. I am disgusted by the poaching, but although they steal my act they can't steal my face!'

As ever, Doddy relaxed during that warm summer season in 1970 by staying up late and pursuing his favourite pastime – talking. People found him an entertaining conversationalist. He was still fascinated by the psychology of humour. As he would say, 'Humour is not funny. I've spent fifteen years of investigation in the libraries trying to find out what humour is, but no one knows. I sometimes think I would like to found a University of Humour. It's just as important as music or poetry and it's central to everybody. Take Harold Wilson; if he'd been to the University of Knotty Ash and studied under the Professor of Giggleology he'd never have made that awful joke about the BBC. Everybody should learn humour, especially the clergy and politicians.'

Doddy found Blackpool audiences 'very responsive'. He had studied the reaction of audiences and liked to expound on them: 'An audience is like an animal, a warm blob of affection which loves you and grows warm if you treat it well, and smothers you and eats you and if you don't entertain it. You have to stroke it and tickle its muscles. I've played to plenty of hostile audiences but I don't worry until they all stand up and start coming towards you. When I say at the end, "Do you give in?" I'm really asking, do you acknowledge me? Have I succeeded in entertaining you? It's a cry of triumph. I want them all to walk out of the theatre saying to one another, "By Jove, that was a smashing evening." '

On another occasion he recalled his most terrifying evening in the theatre. It was on the stage in Bristol and he was singing *Love is Like a Violin*. One single spotlight was trained on his face, with the rest of the theatre in complete darkness. Suddenly he could sense someone standing alongside him on the stage. As he sang he turned his head slightly and saw a man with horrible staring eyes. He just stood there swaying and glaring at him.

'I thought, this is it!' he told the *Yorkshire Post*. 'My number's up. He's got either a gun or a knife hidden away somewhere. While I was thinking this, the stage-hands had gathered in the wings ready for action and as the last note of the song died away, the spotlight faded, and for a moment the entire theatre was in darkness. Out dashed the stage-hands. I threw myself one way and the man lunged another. He eluded the stage-hands, dashed across the stage, down the steps and out of the first exit. We never saw him again.'

Meanwhile, breaking the box-office record at the Opera House afforded him immense satisfaction. Ever since he first arrived at the resort as a raw young comic he wanted one day to top the bill there. Now, he would say, 'It's a wonderful feeling when you strike three thousand funny notes at once and the theatre rocks with laughter. You feel ten feet tall. Being a humorist is the greatest profession in the world.'

CHAPTER 15

'Oh, Yes, There are Butterflies'

Over the years Doddy had gained the reputation for being careful with his money. So had Bob Hope, who had the habit of borrowing the odd dollar to tip caddies or waiters and then 'forgetting' to repay. And the late Max Miller, for all his tremendous sex appeal, was said to be mean. Yet Doddy has been known in his native Liverpool to send bottles of champagne to friends as a token of his loyalty. 'Doddy remembers me at Christmas,' says one showbiz writer.

If the star was as careful with money, or as fond of it, as some people claimed, it was doubtful if he would have been persuaded to play a Shakespearean role at the Liverpool Playhouse in November 1971. Eventually, when he did agree to play Malvolio in *Twelfth Night*, it meant the loss of thousands of pounds, for the fee for this straight acting part was, in the words of a local theatre critic, 'peanuts'.

It was nothing new for comedians to take on Shakespearean roles. George Robey's Falstaff years before won critical praise, and Frankie Howerd played Bottom. Later, when Ronnie Barker performed the same role, he remarked, 'I wasn't very good as I find Shakespeare's clowns almost impossible to play. You can only get laughs with his comics by doing things that aren't in the play-physical business and gimmicks, in other words.'

Doddy's opportunity to join the 'straight' theatre came about after Antony Tuckey, artistic director of the Liverpool Repertory Company, saw the comic on stage in variety and pantomime. He decided he was one of the great artistes of the twentieth century. To some people, his words might seem an exaggeration, but Tuckey was adamant. He approached the comic and invited him to play Malvolio. Doddy thought hard about the implications involved. It was a brand-new field for him and there was a risk in tackling something so new, yet he was tickled by the invitation. 'When I received it I was thrilled because they thought I could do it. In a short while, I proceeded to cancel or postpone my other engagements to take the part.'

In another way, he regarded it as an adventure and a chance to widen his experience. 'If I want to be an Olympic runner I've got to sprint a bit first.' The production would mark the diamond jubilee of the Liverpool Playhouse. Doddy regarded the opportunity as a challenge. He quipped, 'This is the Theatre's diamond jubilee year, and the artistic director obviously wants to give Merseyside audiences something they will never forget!'

He said that like many other comics he had a secret ambition to play Hamlet, but he would really be content with Malvolio or even 'Omelette'. There would be no adlibs he promised. When he was asked if he thought he was like Malvolio in any way, he nodded, 'I don't think I'm like him. Perhaps people see a Malvolio in me. No, I don't have a – what's the line? – a distempered appetite.'

The news that Knotty Ash's legendary stand-up comic was about to put away his tickling stick for a mitre aroused unusual interest, not only in Liverpool but as far as Fleet Street. Erudite critics were already planning to make the trip to see first-hand the metamorphosis in Arthur Kenneth Dodd. Soon he was badgered for interviews and he tried bravely to cope with the requests. Anthony Tuckey thought it wise at that stage to invite the press to meet Doddy and the cast.

'How much are you being paid?' someone unwisely asked the comic. Before he could reply, a member of the company snapped, 'The same as the rest of us.' At the press conference he strode in wearing brilliant yellow tights and cradling a bust of Shakespeare, calling him, 'The best script-writer I've ever had. And his fees are so modest.'

In more subdued mood, he confessed to being 'very, very excited about his straight-acting part'. But he advised Antony Tuckey to keep a strict watch on him to cut out adlibbing. When he was asked his view of Malvolio, he said, 'I see him as a man who gives orders, lays down the law and can't admit he's ever in the wrong – a sort of Shakespearean Bill Shankly.'

Driving down from Knotty Ash to Liverpool Playhouse for rehearsals, he sometimes memorised Malvolio's lines:

Madam, yond young fellow swears he will speak with you. I told him you were sick: he takes on him to understand so much, and therefore comes to speak with you. I told him you were asleep: he seems to have a foreknowledge of that too, and therefore comes to speak with you. What is to be said to him, lady? he's fortified against any denial.

At the outset, such lines seemed to him strange, even stilted, but as rehearsals progressed he found them easy to grasp. None the less, he was apprehensive. 'Oh, yes, there are butterflies,' he admitted. 'It's like a child starting a new school.' But he reassured himself by seeing the amusing side. He wondered, though, how he would cope with the scene at the beginning of the play where Malvolio is on stage for seven minutes without speaking. He joked, 'I have the legs for the part, and the author's fees are so modest.'

161

He fitted into the rehearsals like a glove. He listened in silence to Antony Tuckey's directions and only occasionally asked for further explanation about the character. 'We treated Ken like any other member of the cast,' recalled Brian Coburn who was playing Sir Toby Belch. It was the way the comic wanted it. There was only one concession allowed Doddy. His photograph in the programme was larger than the others. He was unsmiling, even serious-looking. Shakespeare would not have complained. The words in small print under the photograph read: 'KEN DODD – Malvolio. The most talked-about, the most successful 'Live Theatre' comedian in modern times; professor of tickleology at Knotty Ash University and creator of the Diddy Men; Top-of-the Pops; Ken will demonstrate his versatility and complete professionalism during *Twelfth Night* . . .

It promised to be an auspicious occasion for the Liverpool Playhouse. The theatre was first opened on 11 November, 1911, and to mark that historic event John Masefield wrote a poem, the first four lines of which read:

> *Here in this house, tonight, our city makes*
> *Something which must not fail for all our sakes,*
> *For we begin what men have been told too blind*
> *To build elsewhere, a temple for the mind.*

On this first night, Tuesday, 16 November, there was an unmistakable buzz in the theatre, not all of it by any means caused by Doddy's presence. True, there was undoubted interest in his appearance, as shown by the presence of Fleet Street critics, but Liverpudlians were also celebrating the jubilee of the oldest repertory theatre in Britain.

Among the audience was Henry Cotton, vice-chairman of the Board of Directors, and an avid theatre-goer. 'For us all it was a very exciting occasion,' he recalls. 'It was considered an inspired stroke on Antony Tuckey's part to engage Ken Dodd. I had always admired him as a standup comic, now like everyone else I wondered if he was up to the challenge posed by Malvolio. Antony Tuckey assured us he was. I remember earlier we had discussed the part and I was a little surprised when Ken's name was suggested. He agreed to play it after some consideration on his part.'

Today, Henry Cotton is in charge of the archives at the Liverpool Playhouse and, in the course of discussion, produced the *Twelfth Night* programme. 'I think it was a very big step on Ken's part to take on Malvolio. From early on I agreed with the director that he wanted to do it. Although I prefer Shakespeare's tragedies, I believe that *Twelfth Night* was the right diamond jubilee choice. And, by now, Antony Tuckey was recognised as a convincing director of Shakespeare's plays and he was excited about Ken Dodd's participation in the production.'

'If music be the food of love, play on', are the memorable opening lines of the play, but they are not spoken by Malvolio but by Orsino, Duke of Illyria. It was almost seven minutes before Malvolio uttered a word. Or when Orsino asks what he thinks of the Clown, and Malvolio replies, 'Yes; and shall do, till the pangs of death shall shake him. Infirmity, that decays the wise, doth ever make the better fool.'

The funny thing was that Doddy had been on stage for nearly all of the seven minutes without many of the audience recognising him. Not surprisingly, for the wild hair was plastered down and was parted, and the famous teeth seemed to be hidden. He stood on the stage motionless and in neatly fitting costume. The restless vitality of the 'mad loon' everyone knew was frozen into the solemn killjoy.

To Henry Cotton, it was an accomplished piece of acting and underlined the discipline Doddy brought to the part. Obviously the comic had taken the advice of his director, who told him, 'For the first half of the play I don't want you to get a laugh. Let the play do the work. You just be Malvolio. Try to soak yourself into the character of the man and let the play take its course. In the second part, I'll let you have your head a bit.'

The critic Michael Billington had expressed some reservations when he first read that Doddy was to play Malvolio since, in his opinion, great clowns rarely made great actors. But that night at the Liverpool Playhouse he thought that the experiment worked well because of Doddy's own strenuous self-discipline and partly because Malvolio is a character who is allowed the licence of direct address to the audience. In the final analysis, he felt it worked like a dream.

At the final curtain there was prolonged applause for the cast and director and it was clear that Doddy was anxious to be accepted as 'just another member of the cast'. He gave no indication that he wanted to sing *Happiness*. He bowed and smiled and never stepped outside the character of Malvolio.

That night there were many young people in the audience, mainly because *Twelfth Night* was on the college curriculum. They were asked their views later about Doddy's performance. 'He was excellent,' said one fifteen-year-old girl, and another student added, 'Doddy was so much better than I thought he would be.' The students on the whole reckoned he adapted to the play very well.

Doreen Tanner of the *Liverpool Post* regarded his performance as a 'fresh triumph'. Doddy's acting she described as 'as an intelligent piece of half-comic, half-sad acting as anyone could wish to see. He hadn't put a foot wrong – except on purpose. And after praising Antony Tuckey's stylish production, she stated that 'Ken Dodd fits superbly into this scheme of things: the comedy, the expert timing of his (relatively) few jokes, one can take for granted. But he coped well with the serious moments – even up to the genuine pathos in Malvolio's last miserable cry for revenge.'

Miss Tanner concluded: 'Perhaps also he was not only witty in himself but inspired the rest of the cast to comic brilliance. But out of an excellent production, the fact is that one is going to remember the Malvolio. And not just the laughs either. Ken Dodd created an entirely plausible character, with just the right measure of absurdity and pathos, until it was possible to forget who was actually lurking under Malvolio's massive beaver hat.'

In the late Fifties, John Barber was one of the few Fleet Street journalists to take notice of Doddy, and to predict that he would have a successful career as a comedian. When he heard that he was to tackle the role of Malvolio, he was fascinated and immediately decided to make the trip to Liverpool. He was now with the *Daily Telegraph* and was recognised as one of the leading theatre critics of the day.

In the course of his review, Barber wrote, 'Of course, Ken Dodd is funny – as when his bouncy strut gets entangled with his pompous stick or when he dallies before picking up the letter that undoes him. And he wins a splendid laugh when Olivia, thinking him ill, anxiously inquires: 'Wilt thou go to bed, Malvolio?'' '

In his view, the high point came, not when Ken Dodd was cross-gartered, but when he turned on for the first time the requested smile for his lady – a toothless grin that melted slowly into the ecstatic radiance of the Professor of Tickleology himself. All praise, too, for his attack and enunciation: he gave Malvolio a super-proper voice of a clarity that was a lesson to the rest of the soft-spoken, tentative cast.

The critic concluded: 'Mr Dodd will no doubt work on his Malvolio. The fact remains that a comedian's job is to make fun of his own personality: result, a hilarious caricature. A comic actor's job is to interpret a character conceived by someone else: result, a living person. This Malvolio was by no means the rich, ridiculously overweening personality we look for. It is a restrained sketch of the man, put across with expertise and decorated with some capital incidental lunacies. For the rest Antony Tuckey's production suffers from an ugly and unobtrusive set which makes Illyria look Moorish and remains unchanged for different houses and even the seashore.'

To Michael Billington, Doddy seemed much truer to the Shakespearean ideal than almost anyone else in a rather lifeless production that looked as if it were set in an advertisement for Fry's Turkish Delight. Nevertheless, the production enjoyed a most successful run and after a few weeks Doddy was asked to go with the play to Oxford and then the West End. But he decided to say no to the offer for fear of being trapped in a long run. It would have meant a further loss of earnings from variety and cabaret shows. His success in *Twelfth Night* however fired his ambition to do other straight roles.

When *Charley's Aunt* was suggested to him, he turned it down because 'it would be too great a strain on him to try to correct his Northern speech-patterns'. Instead, he talked of *Billy Liar* and parts in Molière and Sheridan plays. As he said, 'I'd like to do them if I could cut me "errs" and "verrs" – the gerl with the ferr herr!' Henry Cotton made the point that the Liverpool Playhouse wanted the star to do more straight parts and *Hobson's Choice* was mentioned, but in the long run it was a question of Ken finding the time. They knew he had other commitments.

'He was very good to the Playhouse,' added Cotton, 'and very generous too. He must have earned his smallest performing fee for years, as Malvolio. But I think he derived great personal satisfaction and proved to himself that he was able to tackle a straight part.'

During the run of *Twelfth Night* Doddy welcomed friends and visitors to his dressing-room. It was noticeable that a few former Liverpool Playhouse actors returned for the performance, among them Sir Michael Redgrave. His verdict on the production was important to the company: 'It is well worth seeing; both for Ken Dodd's performance and for the play as a whole.'

Redgrave had been with the company in the Thirties and his last role with them was Malvolio in 1936. Now he was delighted to meet Doddy in his dressing-room and chat about the past as well as the present. He told the comic, 'Don't worry, Ken. I was very bad as Malvolio and you couldn't be worse. I did enjoy your performance; you got inside the part.' Doddy liked meeting famous actors of the legitimate theatre, if only to get their views of modern theatre. He listened enthralled as Redgrave recalled famous names associated with the Liverpool Playhouse.

To Henry Cotton, the Playhouse had a proud cast and had proved an excellent training ground for actors, a number of whom had become big London names. Antony Tuckey was already thinking of inviting Doddy to play Bottom in *A Midsummer Night's Dream*. As far as he was concerned, the comic had proved an exemplary actor in *Twelfth Night*.

Back in the solitude of his home in Thomas Road, Knotty Ash, Doddy was tickled pink by what the critics said about him. But he was never one to be carried away, and that was true even in his triumphant Palladium days. He had really no intention of putting away his tickling stick for good. 'By Jove, what would the Diddymen think?' he asked himself as he mapped out future variety engagements in Blackpool and Liverpool. When he was asked what next, he replied good-humouredly, 'Perhaps *Romeo and Juliet* – with me in one pair of tights.' He showered praise on Antony Tuckey and the rest of the cast. 'They were all marvellous people and made me feel accepted as a member of the Playhouse company.'

What tickled him most of all was the way the audience enjoyed the play. As he said, 'It is essentially a happy play with one or two chances for a comedian to let go. It's a bit like a Christmas show, with laughter and romance as the ingredients.'

When someone suggested that he go to Stratford-upon-Avon for a summer season instead of to the Opera House in Blackpool, Doddy was amused. 'By Jove, it sounds a nice idea,' he reflected. 'Can the Diddymen come along?' It was his way of saying that despite the adulation he would stick with his friends. The Squire of Knotty Ash knew his place.

Years later a story was told that Doddy was both flattered and mystified by being chosen as Malvolio and asked Antony Tuckey, why him? The director was supposed to have hedged somewhat and said he'd give the answer in due course. When the comic asked again, Tuckey replied, 'It has always appeared to me that Malvolio was a jumped-up peasant with delusions of grandeur.'

Doddy grinned, and said, 'Thank you very much. I'm glad I asked.'

In the autumn of that same year, 1971, Doddy was among the various celebrities who agreed to give their opinions about Christianity. In fact, he was never slow to voice opinions provided the interviewers did not pry into his private affairs.

For instance, he felt that the move towards freedom and a permissive society was something that must be treated carefully. As he explained, 'It's often been said that everything that is enjoyable is either bad for you or makes you fat. It's quite true. Things like alcohol, sex and money are wonderful things, but they are things that demand skill. They are things that must be taken gradually and handled with extreme care. I believe that if you make a pig of yourself, then you must expect to be treated like a pig. I must say, though, that I'm glad all the terrible cobwebs, the shadows, the monsters about sex hanging about since Victorian days have been chased away. The agony that young men and women used to go through –

thinking that they would be struck by lightning or go blind or something.'

He emphasised that freedom brought with it responsibility. And with a permissive society people had a greater responsibility to others – and to themselves. If he could have a wish, he would want to have a more open mind. Also to have a greater intelligence and understanding. 'But I do wish that everyone would drop their guard and be friendlier,' he urged. 'If leaders of nations and every human being could just drop their guard and have respect for others, then the world would be a happier place. It takes more courage to go up to a man and say, 'Why can't we be friends', than it does to shout abuse at him from the other side of the street.'

Doddy had never been shy to recall his own upbringing, nor his mother's faith in God. He described his religious upbringing as 'cosy' and it had left its mark. He thought strictness and a lot of weird dogma were wrong. They could alienate children and frighten them with tales of retribution and fear. 'I'm quite sure that half the atheists in the world are atheistic because their religious upbringing was too strict and dogmatic,' he declared.

Being an inveterate optimist, he thought that people were never going to destroy the Christian faith because of the greatness of Jesus Christ. Christian beliefs – and there were humanist ones too – in things like integrity, honesty, and kindness helped people to live a better and a happier life.

To Doddy, one's religion was a private matter and he never saw himself as an American-style evangelist. Yet he was never ashamed to talk about his belief in God, just as he was not ashamed to recall the austerity of his boyhood. The same could not be said about some other comedians who had moved away from Liverpool.

CHAPTER 16

'My Ambition is To Do a One-Man Show'

'With this show I'm jumping in where angels – and devils – fear to tread,' proclaimed Doddy in March 1973, a week before he was scheduled to open at the Liverpool Play-house in his first one-man show, *Ha-Ha*.

'Why do I do it? I've a lifelong ambition to do a one-man show. It's probably the most creative thing an artiste can do. I'm trying to be the complete entertainer.'

The show, ambitious in the extreme, called for endless stamina, craft and all Doddy's stage experience. 'This is an attempt to be as creative as possible,' he explained, 'without anything else getting between me and the audience.'

Significantly, at the same theatre a few years before, Michael MacLiammoir had delighted Playhouse audiences with his elegant solo show on Oscar Wilde. Doddy was now concerned in case theatre-goers thought he was going to be too serious. He promised that the show would not be full of analysis or his theories on comedy. 'People want to laugh, not to see how it's done,' he said. 'We're hoping to gather people who just want to come and have a belly laugh. I'll spend a little time saying what my theories are.'

No one could accuse the comic of doing the show to enhance his millionaire status. As with *Twelfth Night*, his box-office earnings would be modest compared with his returns from pantomime or his Blackpool Shows. *Ha-Ha* was something he had desperately wanted to do ever since he succeeded in making an impact as Malvolio. Furthermore, he regarded a solo show as part of his education and a worthwhile challenge. 'Laughter is a word like music,' he reflected. 'It can mean so many things, a whole spectrum. There's a power of joy you only get in children. They only laugh because they're happy. Humour drags us back to childishness.' It was true, as some critics pointed out, his humour had this touch of innocence, despite its naughty innuendoes. It was happy, unmalicious. More than once he stated, 'I never frighten people. I want to be what I call a "yow wow" comic, to play comedy at full pelt, very exaggerated. The new relaxed technique doesn't work for me. I'm a full-steam-ahead comic.'

He was not sparing himself. Friends wondered how he maintained such a hectic pace. All Doddy would say was, 'I don't know actually.' Blessed with boundless energy, he found time to do radio, stage and TV shows, but by now he had given up – temporarily at least – full-season summer shows. His enthusiasm, his personal crusade for laughter, was as vital as when he started to entertain around Liverpool. When asked about recreation he murmured rather vaguely about racing, reading and football.

A love of football was ingrained in him since boyhood. Now he loved to joke about it: 'In Liverpool we have two of the greatest football teams in the world – Liverpool and Liverpool Reserves. Yes, that's my game: football. I've been a red-hot Liverpudlian ever since the day my uncle made me wear a little red jersey when I was a boy. Then he hung me in the rear window of the family car. I've lived the game ever since, and never cease to wonder why they don't give me Sir Alf Ramsey's job. I would very quickly select a team that would beat any in the world. I would choose it from Liverpool and Everton (heck, I nearly forgot that they came from God's city, too).'

Doddy predicted that *his* team would win the World Cup, the America's Cup, the Kentucky Derby, too. And Pot Black would be a cinch with all those Reds lying about! And his own qualifications? 'Well, I was the best inside right they ever had at Holt High School in Liverpool, and I once played for St Freda's School for Forward Gentlewomen – until they found me out. That was tattyphilarious and filled me with plumptiousness, but alas, after touring the country on my firewood round and scouting for Liverpool, I decided to change my career. Everyone acknowledged that in the realms of football management I had great potential.'

To Doddy, the Liverpool manager Bill Shankly was king. He was his favourite manager in football. Everything about Shankly – his Scottish accent, sharp asides and personal dynamism – intrigued him. Sometimes he attended training sessions at Anfield, the home of the Liverpool team, and talked tactics with Shankly. 'When I put forward my daring plans to beat opposing defences, Bill really concentrated. To such an extent that he had often been known to fall off his chair – fast asleep!'

But eventually the comic opted for a career in show business and had to give up all his sporting activities . . . well, almost! 'The chief reason for my early retirement,' he recalls, 'was that I was afraid I would damage my God-given asset – my teeth. Even today I am the only one in our family who can eat tomatoes through the strings of a tennis racket.'

Soon he found less and less time to pop down to Anfield to join Liverpool players in training sessions, and a Saturday league match was virtually out. However, he was careful not to give the wrong impression to his fans: he wasn't getting above himself or 'going all intellectual'. He reassured himself by recalling how they had warmed to his performance in *Twelfth Night*. They knew he was ambitious and wanted to do new things, climb new mountains. 'I cannot stand still,' he would say. 'I must find new challenges.'

When he first conceived his one-man show around Christmas-time he wanted to make it theoretical, scholarly and inventive. He reckoned that his audiences would be interested in what a laugh was, so he began to sketch out the history of laughter. As he worked on it in spare moments while playing in *Robinson Crusoe* at the Nottingham Empire, doubts began to fill his mind. Was he after all becoming much too theoretical? The only way to find out was to try out the script on audiences. He booked a civic theatre somewhere in the North-west like Knutsford or Macclesfield and invited people in to see the show. He was in for a shock. As he said later, 'After doing the third one, I realised with horrific certainty that these people just didn't want to know. They came along because they wanted to see Ken Dodd. Then they got the idea he was going to use types of comedy as a vehicle and they were even a little bit interested in the theory that the caveman was the first man to make himself laugh by hitting another man over the head with a gigantic club – which is Stephen Leacock's theory that all humour is based on aggression and superiority.'

Doddy found they were mildly interested in that theory and considered it somewhat funny, though not hilariously so. He brought out a huge club and said that even in those days they had clubs for women. But he quickly realised they did not want to know about Schopenhauer's theory of that. For the most part the audience sat in the stalls, baffled, wondering if the Liverpool comic was going out of his mind. Some grew restless but as far as Doddy could recall none of the audience laughed at him.

'I realised then that if I was going to have a show that was entertaining it would also have to be funny,' he concluded, before he left the theatre. 'So I had to draw back from that very quickly and make the items more funny than educational. I found that to be entertaining about humour, you had to make people laugh.'

At that time he confided in the critic Michael Billington that it had been a close shave, for without the try-outs he would probably have kept to his original line based on the analysis of humour. He now knew this would prove disastrous. Gradually he grew more confident that the show would work, though he was still far from certain. It was unknown ground for him, but he was encouraged by friends to go ahead and meet the challenge.

He was forty-two and had been in show business nineteen years, having been drawn to it, he says, by a desire for eccentricity. 'I have always wanted to be an eccentric.' Was he taking on too much? One thing was certain, few other comics in Britain would have attempted it. Doddy's success so far had been built on a broad-based career founded on solid family entertainment, one that evolved year by year and was flexible enough to include playing Malvolio.

He had by now achieved most of his ambitions. He wasn't afraid of a failure or two. His enthusiasm for his work was as keen as ever and he was intent on learning more about comedy. He still bought books on the subject – he had a room full of them – and in his view humour was a valuable and often underrated gift. He admitted thrashing an audience boneless with laughter was very hard work and if an audience did not want to use their imagination there was nothing one could do.

The nervousness as he approached the Playhouse with *Ha-Ha* was real. He knew it was going to be one of the high points – or perhaps low points – of his entire career. Some Fleet Street critics had already intimated their intention of reviewing the show. In Liverpool, expectations were high. Antony Tuckey, who had directed *Twelfth Night*, believed Doddy would make a very good shot at ensuring that his first one-man show was a success. Likewise, Henry Cotton, a director at the Liverpool Playhouse

– he had seen four performances of *Twelfth Night* – was confident that Doddy could pull it off.

If John Fisher had been asked, he would probably have agreed that nothing was beyond Kenneth Arthur Dodd. That autumn his book on comedians, *Funny Way to be a Hero* had been published by Frederick Muller and in dealing with Doddy, he commented, ' More than any other performer he proves that laughter is contagious, as it ricochets on its zigzag journey through an audience with the casually devastating effect of a stray spark in a box of fireworks. His method is such that the chuckles raised in the first few minutes accelerate by the end into one tumultuous roar of laughter.'

To Fisher, Doddy was a great stage comedian. He was able to remove all barriers between audience and performer. As he observed, 'It is in this final relationship with his audience that his essential spirit becomes more obvious. He is the modern equivalent of the Puck or Robin Goodfellow of medieval times, not only in the way he jumps and skips about the stage, but in that he is at once mischievous and innocent. His misdeeds never become more than jests or pranks, whether putting sunglasses on a hen destined to spend three weeks trying to hatch out a black-pudding or suggesting to the audience that they should all march down to the Chinese Embassy and squirt rice pudding through the letter-box.'

Fisher's admiration for Doddy was encouraging in the context of the comic's impending one-man show. He talked of his 'sheer electric vitality', a useful asset in any solo performance. Always he waxed enthusiastic about his stage shows. 'To experience a performance by Doddy is as telling a means of revivification for a jaded, spiritually dead public as any visit to the fair.' But it was the comedian's unique penchant for establishing a firm rapport with his audience that would most count in his exacting solo show. Alone on stage, he would have to be at his most accomplished to achieve the kind of success that had

175

sometimes eluded not a few gifted actors. Much would depend on the quality of his material, but in this respect the show afforded him wide scope to experiment.

Radio producer Jim Casey believed that Doddy was versatile enough to surprise his admirers. 'The fact is that Doddy is riveting on stage,' he said. 'Not since Max Miller have I seen anyone who can hold an audience as a stand-up comic on his own like Ken. For me he is better than Miller because I've never known another comic to get as many laughs. True, other comics have got longer laughs in different ways, but none of them get as many laughs. Ken destroys an audience; they become putty in his hands, and they will laugh at anything he does.'

Years before Casey had performed on the same bill as Doddy at the Glasgow Empire, recognised as the grave-yard for English comics. 'For the first five or six minutes,' he recalled, 'Ken wasn't getting the laughs, then he suddenly began to burlesque *On the Road to Mandalay* and he had the audience with him. From then on he destroyed them. His attack, and delivery, were brilliant and if one gag failed he had another one ready.'

If Doddy had known at that time the steadfast faith others had in his ability to succeed with his one-man show, he'd probably have been less worried than he was. Dick Condon, general manager of the Theatre Royal, Norwich, was a theatre man who had infinite confidence in the comedian, so much so that a few months before, he had invited him to break new ground.

Condon had decided to hold a series of Sunday night variety shows at the Theatre Royal; he discussed his plan with Dave Forrester, Doddy's agent, who immediately agreed and intimated that the comedian would be delighted to do the shows. Condon went ahead and inserted advertisements in the local newspapers and inside a few days advance booking was brisk. However, when he entered his office at the theatre his assistant manager, David Sandford, was talking to a stranger.

As Condon came into the room Sandford said to the man, 'There's the boss.'

The man left his briefcase on the table and said seriously to the manager, 'I'm from the Lord's Day Observance Society and I've come about the Ken Dodd shows you have advertised. Well, you can't present them.'

Condon was taken aback. At first he had taken the man to be an insurance agent and he had not heard of the Lord's Day Observance Society. He looked at the other and said, 'What am I to tell the two full houses who have bought their tickets?' The man said it was not his business to worry about them. He was anxious that Ken Dodd did not go on.

Condon: 'Are you going to tell those people, or am I?'

Man: 'You're not taking me seriously. I am going to the police.'

Condon saw no more of the man and did not think it necessary to contact Dave Forrester. The auguries were good for the new series, despite the fact that Norwich could be a graveyard for comedians. Some years before, Eric Morecambe and Ernie Wise had died a death at the Theatre Royal and vowed not to return. When eventually Dick Condon invited them back, they returned rather reluctantly, and on the second occasion they enjoyed a big success.

When it came to comedy and comedians East Anglia lacked the tradition of Liverpool. People did not laugh at the same things as Liverpudlians; some of the people in fact lacked a sense of humour. As Dick Condon would say, 'Liverpool is the cradle of comics. They are not just comics but entertainers. They come out of Liverpool thick and fast.'

As usual, Doddy dominated the variety bill. The people of Norwich responded rapturously to him. There were no protests outside the theatre from the Lord's Day Observance Society, and it was soon obvious that the experiment of presenting Sunday shows in the city had paid off handsomely. Not unexpectedly, Doddy overran, but no one left their seats. His jokes about Knotty Ash and his Diddy uncle were as much appreciated by the audience as his wisecracks about nudity: 'Come on – let's take all our clothes off and parade past the Town Hall. We'll show 'em.'

When the audience was exhausted from laughing he suddenly gave them an irrelevant limerick, or even an unfinished one. When the small orchestra started up, Doddy sang *Tears* and followed with *The River*. To Dick Condon he was a revelation. 'What impressed me was the way he didn't spare himself. He gave both houses full value for money. He had this wonderful ability to see things that were funny, which other people passed over because they were less perceptive. After that first Sunday, the shows took off and we had packed houses every week.'

The musicians complained that they missed their late-night drinks because the shows overran. Doddy, in exhilarating form, went on and on and by the time he led the sing-a-long with *Happiness* it was after midnight. The spontaneous applause of the theatre audience acted like a heady drug on him. Anita Boutin was not present to see his latest triumph. Most Sunday nights she preferred to stay at home in Liverpool with her relatives or friends. She probably knew too that Ken would be in conversation for hours into the night – usually it was daylight before he got back to Knotty Ash.

Dick Condon found their late-night discussions stimulating. As he recalled, 'I was always amazed how Ken could be so fresh after performing two nightly shows. Sometimes we had a meal in the theatre restaurant or a few glasses of champagne. I considered him a comic genius on stage, and off-stage he had the intelligence and perception of Dave Allen. Normally I didn't stay up late talking to performers but with Ken and Dave it was a joy.'

He talked to the comic about theatre, art and life itself. It was Doddy's great interest in life that fascinated him. 'Sometimes, too, we talked about his native Liverpool and Ken showed genuine concern about poverty and the neglect of certain areas of the city. He had this warm interest in people. I think his talent stems from his sharp observance of the people around him.'

Since a few of the Sunday night shows were now ending at 12.20, Dick Condon decided to retitle the 'show suppers' as 'after-show breakfasts' and the funny thing was that late-nighters dined at the theatre restaurant and asked for breakfast. Doddy was tickled by the turn of events and how Norwich was responding to Doddyism. By now he regarded the Theatre Royal as the flagship for other provincial theatres. It was making money and at the same time serving the people of East Anglia extremely well.

To Dick Condon the best way to keep theatres open is by putting bums on seats. Doddy agreed. Although the general manager paid Doddy a 'high fee' for his Sunday night performances he had no hesitation in doing so. 'Ken was worth every penny he was paid,' he says. 'Few other entertainers were as generous with their time on stage. And he has a unique ability to entertain.'

Back in Liverpool, meanwhile, Doddy was ready for his one-man show. There was an auspicious opening on 3 April 1973. Before he went on stage the comedian was nervous and appeared restless in his dressing-room. The evening attracted radio and stage producers, actors and comedians, and many of his friends. As was the case with *Twelfth Night*, there was a buzz in the Playhouse.

'Before the curtain rose,' recalls Henry Cotton, 'there was this exciting air of expectancy, as though the audience did not know exactly what to expect. For me, it was an incredible solo performance. Ken threw all kinds of items into the show. There was a scene from *Twelfth Night* and impersonations of legendary comics. He analysed what made people laugh, but he did so in an entertaining way.'

To Jim Casey, the performance was brilliant. 'At the time I could not think of any other comic who could attempt it without bringing on someone else to fill out the three hours or have something to break it up. It was a phenomenal achievement on his part to do it solo.' Eric Midwinter, who was researching a book on comedians to be published in the late Seventies, remembers, 'This Celebration of Humour began at 7.30 and there was the usual interval. At 11.40 I had to leave, aching and fatigued, in order to catch my last bus.'

Michael Billington, critic of the *Guardian*, had missed few of Doddy's big moments in the theatre. He used to say himself that he had a confession to make: 'I had a passion for stand-up comedy. As an adolescent I haunted the halls and even now carry round pin-bright memories of the incomparable Maxs (Miller and Wall), of the lugubrious Jimmy Wheeler, of Tommy Trinder, Jewel and Warriss (best of all double acts) and of a little-remembered duo called Morris and Cowley.'

He was particularly glad, he said, to have got the fag-end of the music-hall since at that time they were breeding a new race of mini-comics who either spent all their time imitating other people (without making any impression) or who danced a bit, sang a bit, gagged a bit and who had all the pungent flavour of cellophane-wrapped processed cheese.

But for Billington the scene was not all gloom. Doddy was an exception. That week he had joined the audience at the Liverpool Playhouse for *Ha-Ha* and came away convinced that it was the funniest evening he had spent inside a theatre since he saw *Beyond the Fringe* at the Edinburgh Festival in 1960. And partly for the same reason: that its sole aim was to make people laugh. There were no dancing girls in laddered fishnet or dancing boys in bum-clinging trousers, no garish starlit backcloths, no tonsil-baring vocalists, no tumblers, trapeze artistes or vent acts.

All they had was Ken Dodd colonising the stage for over three hours, as if qualifying for the *Guinness Book of Records* with the longest comedy act ever. Ostensibly the intention was to explore the nature of laughter; in reality what the audience got was a king-sized Dodd-feast. A few days later Billington wrote: 'The show begins with those wayward teeth spotlit in what looks like a conscious parody of Billie Whitelaw in Beckett; and it goes on to run the gamut of Doddy jokes. There are old jokes ("Tonight we have the famous lady from Belgium, Ann Twerp, the well-known contortionist Willie Snapit, the fearless lion-tamer Claud Bottom"), blue jokes ("King Midas. Everything he touched turned to gold – it could be very embarrassing"), and literary jokes (Malvolio – the sort of man who used to stand up in a strip club and shout, "What time do the jugglers come on?")'

Doddy avoided too much theorising and for that the audience was grateful. He did quote Freud's opinion that a laugh was a conservation of psychic energy, but as he pointed out, amid laughter, the trouble with Freud was that he never played the Glasgow Empire second house on a Friday night. Yet the show managed to reveal a good deal about the nature of comedy.

Michael Billington, in his summing up, decided that *Ha-Ha* provided a brilliant demonstration of comic technique. 'It reminds us, for instance, how much mileage can be got out of props and costumes. One of my favourite moments comes when Dodd brings on a giant Sally Ally drum and proceeds to beat out 'Come and Join Us', 'Go to Sleep My Baby' and 'Silent Night' before asking the audience, "Give in?" And his wardrobe is like something dreamed up by a colour-blind tailor on a weekend bender: a black cape with a lining striped like a liquorice allsort,

a maroon maxi allegedly made out of twenty-eight moggies, a mustard-yellow coat and a titfer that is eminently
phallacious.'

Surprisingly, the booking at the box-office was slow in
the first three days, but as the majority of the critics
praised Doddy's performance the show soon became a
sell-out. It was predicted that it would break all records
at the Playhouse. Predictably, the comedian said, 'I'm
absolutely thrilled and delighted with this success. I hope
to take the show to other cities and eventually to London's
West End.'

But as was the case with *Twelfth Night*, he could not
find the time to present it elsewhere. Perhaps the show
itself was too demanding for a long run, although it was
felt at the time that it could be pruned. For Doddy, it
was another mountain successfully climbed. Few people
referred to the review by Merete Bates, in the course of
which she stated: Ken Dodd has, at cost, perfected his
professionalism. It is not enough. In his personal striving
he is also too calculating. Self-conscious, even self-
absorbed. On stage, alone, for too long, his limitations
grow monotonous.'

When Doddy himself was asked if he considered *Ha-
Ha* a success, he replied, 'I can only answer by saying,
"Did the audience laugh?" '

The only other question that remained was where the
comic would go from here. What was left for him? Somehow he had an inkling what it might be.

CHAPTER 17

'This Has Got To Stop, Ken'

Nothing had changed at the BBC's Paris Cinema Studio in Lower Regent Street for the rehearsal and recording of *The Ken Dodd Show*. To the annoyance of producer Bobby Jaye and the cast, Doddy still continued to arrive late at the studio, and the recording overran by sixty minutes. It was not unusual for Jaye to end up with ninety minutes on tape when in actual fact he required only a third of that for the programme.

There was no denying however that *The Ken Dodd Show* was as popular as ever with listeners. At that time it was *the* most popular comedy on radio, despite the fact that it was produced at the rather cheap cost of £2,000. As one observer pointed out, 'With that kind of budget it is possible to experiment, try out ideas to see if one can get the joker.'

In spite of the obvious difficulties, everyone connected with the show worked full out, although Bobby Jaye noticed a facet of Doddy's performance that had escaped others. It was his view that Doddy was insecure when he first stepped on stage to face the studio audience. As he recalled, 'At that moment it was the equivalent of the blank white canvas of the painter. I suspected he asked himself, "What joke shall I tell them? If I tell them that one will they laugh?" Until he got their laughs and applause he looked unsure, lacking in total confidence, which was curious for such a clever comic. However once the audience responded he was in full flight and they loved him. He is truly a genius with an audience.'

There was something else that concerned the producer. While Doddy had immense appreciation for the talented actors in the show, he did not always get on with them. 'I don't think he knew how to treat them,' says Jaye. 'The fact is none of them were comedians so there existed a slight antagonism in his attitude towards them. Yet, in another way, he loved working with them in the show. It was I suppose a bit paradoxical. For their part, the actors regarded Ken as a comic genius while accepting he could be difficult.'

The scene at rehearsals remained unchanged. Bobby Jaye occupied a seat in the third or fourth row of the stalls and the actors sat a few rows in front of him, while Doddy sat on the stage, or lay sprawled across it with his arm resting firmly under his chin. For hours they worked on voices, ideas and, in the case of the comedian, on patter and one-liners. If a sketch was considered inadequate it would be discarded, although occasionally not before Doddy had remarked, 'I'd like to try it again, Bob.'

Usually the studio was full for the recording of the show, with the audience made up of both young and old people. At 8.30 the recording itself began with Doddy entertaining the audience with funny one-liners. There were a number of 'What a Beautiful Day' gags followed by some wild sketches. The opening spot, which should have run for three minutes, had gone on to twenty-five minutes. There was nothing that producer Bobby Jaye could do about it, except listen to the laughter of the audience. Once again he admired the comic's sheer arrogance as he said to the audience, 'By Jove, you *will* laugh.' Sometimes even Jaye himself could not refrain from laughing at the more zany humour.

He had to admit, though, it had been a frustrating day at rehearsals and he now realised that the recording would go on and on. He was determined to do something about it, if only for the actors' sake. After the audience had filed out of the cinema, he talked to the actors for a while, then decided to go to Doddy's dressing-room. Feeling somewhat agitated, he climbed the stone steps to the room and inside found the comedian facing the mirror with a sandwich in his hand. At that moment Anita Boutin was about to hand him a can of lager. Sometimes when the recording had gone particularly well, Jaye came to the dressing-room to compliment the star, but tonight he simply said, 'Ken, this has got to stop.'

Doddy finished eating his sandwich and, without taking his gaze from the mirror, remarked, 'What's that, Bob?'

Jaye: 'I'm saying that next week I want a script of thirty-five pages and not seventy-five pages. And, next week, you'll arrive on time.'

Doddy: (casually) 'Yes, Bob, yes, Bob.'

Jaye was relieved. He thought: that went down well. He was fond of Ken and felt nothing could destroy their friendship, but he was determined to try to make him see things his way. Suddenly Doddy turned his face from the mirror and said, 'There is but one thing, Bob.'

Jaye: 'Yes, Ken, what's that?'

Doddy: 'Remember . . . you need me more than I need you.'

Jaye: (smiling for the first time). 'It's not a new line, Ken, but it's well delivered.'

Jaye knew that the star was right. There was no show without him. The actors relied on him. Once or twice he had mentioned Doddy's behaviour to Anita Boutin and she promised to talk to Ken about it. 'I'm sure she did her best to get him to come to rehearsals on time,' Jaye recalls, 'but the fact is he didn't change. Ken was single-minded, even stubborn. I always felt he loved Anita and the feeling was reciprocated, yet he remained his own man and did things his way.'

Despite his brief confrontation in the dressing-room, Bobby Jaye joined the rest of the cast in the Captain's Cabin for drinks and shortly afterwards was joined by Ken and Anita. The producer was gregarious and popular, though he was sometimes amused by the retinue of unpaid helpers that Doddy attracted around him. 'They were people who were totally enmeshed in show business,' Jaye recalls. 'They liked to be with him, listening to his views on comedy, treating him like the star he undoubtedly was. For his part, Ken seemed to enjoy their company even though it must have been trying at times for Anita.'

The unflappable Michael McClain, who was one of the key actors in *The Ken Dodd Show*, had unbounded admiration for the Liverpool comedian, despite the fact that occasionally at rehearsals he gave him a hard time. Not long after joining the cast he became friendly with Doddy. Unlike most of his colleagues on the show, be believed he knew the comic very well off-stage. 'I found his personality warm and his conversation intelligent. He possessed an original mind as far as comedy was concerned, but he didn't try to be funny all the time. I avoided talking politics with Ken because he tended to go on and on about the merits of the Conservatives.'

McClain had seen his shows at the Palladium and visited his dressing-room. As a stand-up comic, he considered him the best on the variety scene and he marvelled at his superb control over his audience. The actor did not agree with the critics that Doddy fell below that standard as a television performer. He had played in a number of sketches with him and found him very convincing. 'I remember he once portrayed a South American dictator and was made up accordingly. He kept up the accent effortlessly and never stepped out of character. I think he was underrated as a TV performer.'

Like Bobby Jaye, he felt that the star was wise to stay put in his native Knotty Ash and not come South as other

Liverpool comics had done. 'Ken was very much at home in Liverpool,' says McClain, 'and wouldn't have been happy living in London. Of course he enjoyed playing the Palladium and loved every minute of his success there, but at heart he is a true Liverpudlian and his own people were there and he likes being among them.'

As the doors of the Captain's Cabin closed the actors and their friends gathered on the pavement and continued to talk show business. Doddy seemed to be talking to everyone at the same time and, curiously for such an hour, expounded on his latest theories on comedy. After midnight a corporation cart arrived on the scene and someone remarked to Doddy, 'Here are the scripts for next week's programme. 'It was by now a ritual gag cracked after every recording. Bobby Jaye could be forgiven for not seeing the humour in it. Doubtless he was thinking of the hours of editing that lay ahead of him.

Nearby Talfryn Thomas was telling someone how he enjoyed working with Ken Dodd and that he gave the cast scope to excel in the sketches. Jo Manning Wilson and Gretchen Franklin were in earnest conversation about a new show in the West End, while all the time Doddy was trying to break away from his friends who surrounded him on the footpath. Eventually the exuberant star, accompanied by a somewhat impatient Anita Boutin, climbed into a chauffeur-driven car and set out for Liverpool. Anita, who looked tired, sat quietly beside him. It was a scene that listeners to *The Ken Dodd Show* could never have imagined.

With so much on his mind, it was doubtful whether Doddy gave as much as a second thought to Bobby Jaye's problems about over-written scripts or some inadequate sketches. Mostly he was thinking ahead to his next project. Ever since he had presented his one-man show at the Liverpool Playhouse he had given serious thought to getting his name into the *Guinness Book of Records*. It was, he sometimes reflected, a crazy notion, but as usual he was encouraged to try it by his friends and media people. He envisaged it as a laugh-in and hoped to beat Sammy Davis Jnr's unofficial world record of two and a half hours of non-stop jokes.

The *Marathon Mirthquake* would take place at Liverpool's Royal Court Theatre on 5th June, 1974. Doddy was excited about the prospect of achieving 'immortality' in the *Guinness Book of Records*, and announced, 'The man from Guinness will be present and a couple of nurses will sit in the stalls to make sure the audience and I survive. What's more, I will be attached to a heart machine which will bleep away throughout the performance to see how delightfully stressful I am when I am at it.'

Puzzled newsmen asked him why he wanted to keep people laughing for over three hours. Doddy grinned and remarked, 'If people like Dick Crawshaw can wear their feet off walking around Aintree for charity, I felt the least I could do was try my own marathon thing. Since walking is not up my street, the obvious thing to do was to tell jokes.'

Everything the star attempted seemed to catch the imagination of Liverpudlians. Everyone talked about his latest venture, as though he wanted to climb Everest. Remembering his one-man show and how enjoyable it had been, many local people expressed a wish to be participants at Doddy's latest record-breaking bid. They would be admitted free to the theatre, although any contributions they made would be donated to charity. Doddy said, 'I will be donating a hundred gleeful guineas to be shared between charities.'

In preparation for the event, the comedian spent the previous night in his study at Knotty Ash swotting from a pile of notebooks containing gags he had accumulated over twenty years. Alone on stage, apart from his tickling stick and a few odds and ends, he hoped to deliver what he sub-titled Doddy's Penny Lecture. A minimum three hours of non-stop jokes.

From shortly after noon on this sunny June day the crowds began to file into the Royal Court Theatre. They included more than one thousand pensioners. Loud-speakers were set up outside the theatre to broadcast the fun to bus queues and passers-by. It promised to be a unique occasion. No one seemed to doubt the star's ability to create a new official record. After the success of his solo show they felt anything was possible where Doddy was concerned. Independent checkers were already in the theatre with stop-watches; they would count the number of jokes. The nation-wide appeal of the event was guaran-teed, for Doddy's attempt would be linked up with the Jimmy Young radio show.

As if the record bid was not enough in itself, Doddy decided to hold a lengthy press conference beforehand. Would his voice be tired even before the show began? Show business writer Philip Key of the *Liverpool Post* joined his colleagues at the Royal Court and sipped a drink before Doddy appeared. He was twenty minutes late. He summed up, 'This is an educational show – when you go out you'll say, "Well, that taught me a lesson".'

To Key, the comic was a phenomenon and was confi-dent that he could create a new record. At that moment the manager of the theatre, David Liddy, was anxious to get the show underway, but Doddy remained for a while talking to some elderly men and women in an adjoining bar. Philip Key found some trouble in finding a seat in the packed stalls and eventually grabbed one next to a lady from Liverpool Corporation.

To loud applause, Doddy walked on stage at 1.19 p.m. He called on a newspaper friend to join him and the man removed the comic's coat, 'made from the skins of twenty-eight moggies', leaving him resplendent in a blinding can-ary-yellow suit. Doddy quipped, 'The only trouble is every time the budgie sees me he grabs me with his beak and bangs my hand against his bell.' He then told the good-humoured audience, 'We've got artistes from the four corners of the labour exchange – and some of the finest musicians out on bail.'

Philip Key noted, 'His next laugh came when be began "Er . . . er . . . u," as if he'd forgotten his lines. The audience roared. Then into a song, *Make 'Em Laugh*, and straight into his usual "How Tickled I Ham" routine.' Soon the photographers were busy popping flashbulbs at him, and he was cracking back, 'Three different poses – 4s 6d.' He asked another cameraman, 'Doing a lap of honour?' He broke into a song and was about to start another when a man came on stage carrying a telephone. Jimmy Young was getting into the act by telephoning him during the show. Doddy explained what he was doing – getting the names of some of the Liverpool firms sponsoring him over the air – and then Young asked him, 'So you're telling jokes – will you tell us one then?'

Doddy, with only a split second's thought, went into a long one about a holiday in Blackpool. The phone call over, he told the audience, 'You're now entitled to an audience fee of ten shillings – I don't know how you're going to share that around.' Throughout the show the audience changed continually. And all the time Ted Martin from the *Guinness Book* was sitting in the stalls while the independent checkers kept an eye on their stop-watches.

There was no stopping the comedian: 'We've got a chap from Switzerland who will be sitting on his tickling stick and yodelling.' And: 'And we've got the ugliest stripper in the world. Last time she appeared, she had them shouting in the aisle, "Get 'em on!" ' Then: 'This watch is fantastic. It goes underwater. It tells what time you drown.'

Philip Key noted that he had been sitting in his seat for nearly two hours. He was, on his own admission, quite exhausted from laughing. And in that time the comic hardly repeated a single joke. As ever, Key admired his command of the stage and his effortless technique and above all his ability to project verbal into visual. Always the visual comic, he found no trouble in holding the audience's attention through the lengthy show, nor did his breath-taking tempo ever drop. The gags cascaded forth at the rate of ten a minute, each one, as someone remarked, 'encroaching upon its predecessor.' To Key, there was another ingredient – the sheer warmth that Doddy radiated from the stage. Although he had seen his performance on many occasions it was this marvellous rapport that made the biggest impact on him.

By now he must have related a few hundred jokes at machine-gun speed. But he continued as though his life depended on it: 'You can always tell a bloke who comes from Liverpool – he has a policeman on either side of him.' And: 'Oh what a lovely day for opening your windows at 5 a.m. and climbing in.' Or: 'There was this docker nicknamed Diesel – because he lifted goods saying, "Diese'll do for the wife".' After singing *Tears* and *Love Is Like a Violin* he proclaimed, 'I'm not cheating by filling in time by singing – if you know my voice it's a big joke.' All the time the loudspeakers broadcast the fun to crowds outside the theatre.

The star was never once lost for a joke. He talked about his days in his black pudding plantations and kept on cracking more of those racy jokes. As someone remarked, 'He was digging deep down in his joke-mine and coming up with ten a minute.' It was doubtful if Anita Boutin could have coped with so many jokes, not that she tried on this occasion to mark her black notebook. With joke piling on joke it would be an impossible task. Like everyone else she was content to listen and laugh.

Two hours in and the star resorted to a script for the first time, which seemed justified, as it was a particular monologue once given by Billy Bennett. Doddy had used it eighteen months previously in his solo show and Eric

Midwinter had observed, 'Ken Dodd affectionately and splendidly presents the topsy-turveydom of the Bennett monologue.' Leaving aside the script, he turned to the audience, 'The ceiling of this theatre is a copy of the Sistine Chapel – done in whitewash'.

With three hours up, he announced he had done it – and the theatre rocked with applause. To make it official, Ted Martin said, 'This is a world record and will go into the *Guinness Book of Records*.' In fact, the official time was 3 hours and 6 minutes. Astonishingly, Doddy had told 1,500 jokes. When someone asked later how he remembered them all, he said, 'It was easy – and I've still got a whole thumbful left.'

As the news was flashed round the world, Doddy returned to his No. 1 dressing-room, perspiring but intensely happy. He told his waiting friends, 'I feel absolutely goalified. I am discumknockerated. And I feel absolutely plumptious'. Amazingly, he looked as though he could go back on stage for another three hours. More than 4,500 people had flocked in and out of the theatre to see the marathon show.

Joe Riley, the *Liverpool Echo* showbiz columnist, noted, 'It was the performance of a lifetime for a man who has been making millions laugh for twenty years.' Riley, like Philip Key, went to the dressing-room to congratulate the star, who drank a glass of champagne and to everybody's amazement was still telling jokes. And he said he was tickled that the show raised £1,000 for charity. Doddy's parting line was, 'I could have gone on for hours more but I had to make room for the play on stage tonight.'

There was no let-up for the comedian. His diary was filled with appointments, rehearsals and performances. It seemed he dared not contemplate a foreign holiday. His week read something like this:

Saturday: Had to be up early today to drive from Knotty Ash to Manchester. I was making a personal appearance at a record shop in Albert Square to sign copies of my new record *I Found You Just in Time*. It's been out since Christmas and hasn't done too badly- it's bubbling along. Stayed on in Manchester for my show at the Opera House (plug, plug).

Sunday: Drove myself to London to record my regular Radio Two show that goes out today. Since they brought in the 50 mph speed limit it takes a lot longer to drive there – at least four hours. Don't do the journey non-stop, but stop off for a cup of tea on the way. Stay overnight in London.

Monday: Show never the same each night. There's a lot of adlibbing, and new topical jokes. On the electricity crisis I suggested a new way to keep warm: 'Take your wife to a wife-swapping party – swop her for a bag of coal.'

Tuesday: Up in the morning, but not first thing. I don't usually get up until just after lunchtime, for it's usually the early hours before I get to bed, two or three o'clock. It's often when I get up that I get the ideas for jokes, sometimes while I am shaving or getting dressed. I have 'special thinks', too.

Wednesday: Train strike today. Notice there is a lot of extra traffic about when I drive to Manchester and it takes me a little longer than usual. But I know all the back ways now, there's no great problem. At the theatre, I have a bit of luck. I have a script that has to get to London and I was not very happy about posting it because of the strike. But a music publisher has driven up from London to have discussions about my next record and he can take it back with him.

Thursday: Script-writing today. I have the script of my weekly radio show to do and also a script for a television appearance shortly. It's been a busy week, but it's not always like that. I usually like to have a couple of afternoons off in a week.

It was proving a plumptious year for the Squire of Knotty Ash. Apart from the success of his marathon show, his BBC Television series, produced by Michael Hurll, was an exciting venture and together they were trying out new ideas. And coming up was his Palladium season. After all his engagements in the North of England, playing the Palladium always seemed to him a welcome diversion. He looked forward to visiting the home of variety and knew it was a prestige engagement which reflected his current popularity.He would be occupying the No.1 dressing-room for three weeks. It was always a thrill for him to be handed the key by old George Cooper, the stage-door keeper. He was sure of a welcome from George who never worried how big or small one's name – the welcome was always the same. With the advance booking heavy, Doddy was reassured and Dave Forrester looked as confident as ever about the show.

However, the Palladium backstage hands worried that Doddy would overrun, yet no one dared to visit No. 1 dressing-room to tell the star of the show that he must finish on time. By now Kenneth Arthur Dodd was a law unto himself – even at the Palladium. And once more, he bowled over the critics who were mystified by his indefatigable zest and endless stamina. The critic who asked. 'How does he do it?' was speaking for his colleagues.

'Well, Doddy's energy is joyously unflagging,' he told his readers, 'and those demonic eyes are two discs of anarchy in a face that, without them and those teeth cantilevered from the upper jaw, would be in danger of classical beauty. And the whole body works; with lovely dexterity he mimes a woman in clogs kicking her husband out of bed. But it is the words that are the essence. He imparts no social or moral message; just delirious images of incongruity; ears sprouting from armpits, Darbys and Joans celebrating increased pensions by streaking around in gangs, dressed only in bits of Thermogene and digging up other people's bowling greens.'

Nothing was sacrosanct as far as the comic was concerned. He touched on trade unions, Arthur Scargill, Neville Chamberlain, and even gave a minute's synopsis of the plot of *Carmen*, and a tribute to Tito Gobbi. One London critic observed, 'Without the tragic undertone of Edward Lear or the minute characterisation of Dan Leno, Dodd is, in fact, a superb exponent of that line of nonsense that stretches back to the Middle Ages. His Jam Butty Mines and Broken Biscuit Repair Works belong to the fourteenth century *Land of Cockaigne*, where the churches have black puddings for bell ropes. Spreading plumptiousness with his multi-coloured tickling stick, he is a reincarnation of the Doctor in the old mummers' play, come from Itty Titty to restore the hero with Alicumpane. And he is himself a tonic.'

As usual, Doddy's No. 1 dressing-room was like a railway station. After the performance, it was crowded with friends and media people and not a few comedians. Anita Boutin fussed about him and had a can of lager ready for him as he arrived perspiring after the final curtain. The star always reserved a special welcome for showbiz columnists from Liverpool and he would usually say to them, 'Thank you for coming.'

During the run of the show Joe Riley, of the *Echo*, visited him, having sat through the performance. Doddy told him, 'It's been fantastic really. Mind you, this is only a rehearsal for Liverpool.' The room was full of cards and messages and telegrams. To Riley, the star had not changed. He was as talkative and affable as ever. He never tried to get above himself. It was something that continued to puzzle the Fleet Street columnists who expected Ken Dodd to begin to *act* like a big star. In Riley's view, his latest Palladium performance was a complete one, and one for the fastidious theatre-goer. It was probably more successful than either of Doddy's previous Palladium seasons. It was certainly more polished. To Bobby Jaye, it was extremely funny, a riot of laughter. Once again he won over the cockneys; it was something that tickled Doddy enormously.

Yet, as Joe Riley sat with him in his dressing-room, he found him more concerned about his big Christmas show scheduled for Liverpool. 'Merseyside is a mountain of mirth,' he mused. 'There's a special kind of humour and they all know how to enjoy themselves.' With Doddy, it was always the next show that mattered, which tended to underline his restlessness as an artist. However, he must have been happy with the line from the *Guardian* critic, 'Doddy's Palladium season has won him the kind of critical plaudits to which he has become accustomed.'

CHAPTER 18

'Ken is Grief-Stricken'

Doddy's wonderful world of laughter dramatically turned to anguish in July 1975. Anita Boutin, he was told, was seriously ill. Doctors at Clatterbridge Hospital on the Wirral had diagnosed a brain tumour and this evidently meant long months of cancer treatment. In his heart the sensitive comic hoped she would respond to the treatment, but he was warned by Anita's doctor that it would need a miracle.

As ever, Anita was courageous. 'You must carry on as usual, Ken,' she begged him. 'The doctors and hospital staff will look after me.' Doddy knew it wasn't going to be easy for him. 'It's very hard to go out on stage and make people laugh,' he confided to a few close friends, 'when all you want to do is to cry inside.'

In the ensuing weeks and months he grew more introspective and preferred to keep his big worry to himself. As he entertained audiences and sent them wild with laughter, they had no idea that it was an increasing effort on his part. Deliberately he took engagements near Liverpool so that he could return on the same night to be at Anita's bedside. Unfailingly, she enquired about his performance or his radio and TV commitments, as though anxious not to worry him about her own illness.

Watching her suffer, Doddy's heart was heavy. Memories of their happy days together flooded back. It was Anita who, in the first place, had encouraged him to become a comedian when he himself was convinced that his forte was singing. 'Forget the opera stage,' she would tell me. 'You're a funny man, Ken, not an opera singer.' She taught him how to take the good times with the bad and gave him the confidence needed to face discerning audiences. In her efforts to bring a scientific approach to comedy, she filled countless notebooks with scribbled notes in her strange shorthand about how Ken's gags were received. They had been lifelong partners and apparently more happy than a lot of people who were married.

Bill Boutin, Anita's brother, saw that the news of her illness had shattered the comic. 'Ken had always thought the world of Nita,' he said. 'Now the strain on him was going to be intolerable, but he was devoted to my sister and I knew he would comfort her as long as her illness lasted.' Doddy's sister, June, who was very fond of Anita, felt for Ken. 'We all knew without him telling us what he was going through.'

Anita, who was undergoing radiotherapy, was in and out of Clatterbridge Hospital. Whenever Doddy was asked about her he would nod and say, 'She's improving.' However, his audiences continued to be left in the dark about his secret heartbreak; it was the way he wanted it to be. As June Dodd would say, 'Ken always tried to keep her illness to himself – even from us. He never wanted to cry on people's shoulders.'

Doddy's agent, Jack Oatley, knew that the star always put a brave face on and even when he got bad news from the hospital he tried to bear it and give his audience the best show in the world. 'I knew that Ken lived for Anita,' Oatley recalls. 'They were terribly devoted. They had been together for a long time and she was very supportive. And she was very well liked in the business.'

Because Doddy preferred to stay around Liverpool as much as possible during Anita's illness, the BBC decided to record his radio show in the city. Producer Bobby Jaye and the cast stayed overnight. 'We could see that Ken was taking Anita's illness badly,' recalls Jaye, 'and we really had no other option but to record the show in Liverpool. I think he appreciated the gesture.'

Michael McClain had come to know Anita Boutin quite well and like Bobby Jaye felt she had always wanted to be Mrs Ken Dodd. 'This fact was plain to us all for a long time,' he says, 'and in view of their close relationship it was understandable. I regarded Anita as a talented woman in her own right. She once wrote the lyrics for one of Ken's songs. She was kind as well as perceptive. She was good for Ken.'

Talfryn Thomas, one of the anchor men on *The Ken Dodd Show*, now tried to cheer up the star. He knew what Anita's devotion meant to Doddy and he was aware of the agony he was going through. Coming to Liverpool, though, reminded him of one particular sketch he had done on Ken's radio show and, though exaggerated, it summed up his early life in Knotty Ash.

Talf: I say Ken, what sort of an upbringing did you have?
Ken: We were poor, but we made the best of it. We could never afford much food, in fact me brother was so thin, me Dad used to keep him in a flute . . . but he was happy . . . They were hard times but they taught us the value of things . . . I always remember the day me Dad found half-a dozen cockroaches in me bed . . . he belted me earhole and said, 'No pets allowed.' But I was happy . . .
Talf: I had patches on everything I wore – me jacket, me trousers, me cap – even me underpants . . . I once walked by mistake into a fancy dress ball and won first prize as a quilt . . . but I was happy . . .
Ken: I used to feel so ashamed walking down our cobbled street with me Grannie in her clogs and straw bonnet . . . I mean, she could've put some other clothes on as well . . . but we were happy . . .

To Talfryn Thomas, there was a sensitive side to Ken Dodd as well as an eccentric and rebellious side. It pained him to see him unhappy, remembering as he did their happy days together.

One evening, producer Jim Casey and his wife Joan called to the hospital to see Anita and were disappointed to be told that she was not seeing anybody. Eventually they were allowed into her ward. 'Joan knew Anita very well,' said Casey, 'and was anxious to talk to her. We sat by her bed for a while and talked quietly about things, but she seemed more concerned about Ken and his career and hoped he was not overwhelmed by her illness. I think she was very brave. She lived for Ken and it was nice to know that she had seen his great successes at the London Palladium. Anita believed totally in his genius.'

On their way out of the ward the Caseys talked to the nurses, who told them that Doddy called every night and stayed until morning. He would sit by her bedside and hold her hand and tell her about little things in the business. Although she was ill, and often tired, she would listen. Sometimes she would sleep, but when she woke she would find him there and immediately he would take her hand in his. At times Doddy remembered that Anita had been a nurse and she used to joke, 'I moved from the sad side of life to Ken's mad, zany world – and I love every minute.'

As the months dragged on, Anita's condition did not improve. Doddy, fearing the worst, decided not to do a summer show. Back in the hospital, Anita had several more sessions of radium treatment, but they had failed to halt the growth of the tumour, diagnosed nearly ten months before. The strain was now beginning to tell on Ken. For years he had grown used to having her travelling with him to shows outside Liverpool, but that had not been the case for more than a year. Carrying his secret with him was the worst part of his personal anguish, yet he knew he must continue to work if only to try to forget for a little while Anita's agony.

Most nights, as the final curtain came down, he wanted to dash from the theatre to be at her bedside. He was living, he felt, in an unreal world, one most comedians feared, for it seemed absurd to be making people laugh as one was going through one's own private torment. Occasionally comics had talked to Doddy about it and reminded him that most of them faced the same dilemma in their careers. He had a job to do and in time he agreed it was best he should continue with his engagements, otherwise the whole thing would get on top of him. Anyway, it was what Anita wanted and he dared not go against her.

June came. Each night he travelled back to Liverpool from Darlington, where he was playing variety. He felt she now needed him more than ever. 'It's taken its toll on Ken mentally and physically,' said Jack Oatley. At the end of the month Doddy was told that Anita was dying. Any faint hope he had of her pulling through seemed at that moment to fade. Worse still, Anita knew she was dying but accepted it with exemplary resignation. 'The show must go on, Ken,' she continued to tell him as he sat by her bedside until dawn. He decided to cancel the Thursday night show and instead joined his own family and the Boutins at Anita's bedside. At 1 o'clock in the morning she died – his fiancée for twenty-two years. She was aged forty-three and her passing was peaceful.

For days afterwards Doddy was too upset to talk to anyone. He retreated into himself at his home in Knotty Ash which he shared with father, Arthur Dodd, who was by now nearly eighty. 'Ken is grief-stricken,' said June Dodd. 'He has taken Nita's death very badly. It must have been a terrible strain for him to go on stage and be his usual self, knowing he was going to lose the only woman he has ever loved. But it was Anita helped him to keep going. That was the kind of wonderful, courageous girl she was. The whole family loved her.'

Jack Oatley eventually got through to the star on the phone. 'I know Ken,' he said later. 'He'll just cut himself off and work it out that way. I don't think he will speak to anyone for some time. I think he might feel that it's all over as far as show business goes now, but I'm certain he won't in the end. He loves it too much.'

To his admirers in Manchester and Blackpool and elsewhere, the news was a shock. Doddy had kept his secret strictly to himself for a whole year and they now wondered how he had managed to go on in the final weeks of Anita's illness knowing that she was going to die. In theatres all over the North of England staffs had come to know Anita Boutin as the woman with the notebooks in the wings. Dick Condon, general manager of the Theatre Royal, Norwich, wondered if Doddy would continue with his career, but remembering his passionate love of the theatre he had no doubt that the comic would bounce back on stage.

In London, radio producer Bobby Jaye heard the news with a sense of sorrow. Although he and Doddy had had their differences, he was always able to enjoy a drink with both Ken and Anita, or visit the comic's dressing-room to tell him that the radio show had gone particularly well. Anita, he knew, was close to Ken and understood his eccentric ways – and she loved him deeply. He would miss her fussing around him off-stage, handing him a can of lager in the dressing-room, or ensuring that he had all his props with him. She had devoted her life to him. 'My only regret is that they hadn't married,' reflected Jaye, 'but that, I'm sure, was Ken's decision.'

Gradually Doddy came to terms with Anita's death. Six days after her passing he said he would not be giving up show business. As he explained, 'Anita wasn't a quitter, so I'm certainly not going to be one. She was a lovely and wonderful person, very much my partner in show business and the architect of my success, helping me and making my decisions. I know the way she fought a very good fight and was still helping me when she was terribly ill.'

To the comic, Anita had been an inspiration. 'While she was with me, she inspired me to be a successful entertainer, and I hope her memory will continue to inspire me.' He planned to take a short rest, but he would be back. 'My job is to bring happiness. There's enough unhappiness in the world without me adding to it. There are many people who have suffered similar grief to me.'

Doddy received countless messages of sympathy from his fans all over the country, some of them exceedingly touching. The tragedy of the comedian losing the woman he loved gripped the public's imagination. What pleased him most of all were the letters and notes urging him to carry on promoting happiness. It was one of the few occasions when he could say that tears were his consolation.

A congregation, comprising mourners, fans, friends and show business people, filled St John's Church, Knotty Ash, on that sunny July morning to bid farewell to Anita Boutin. At the same church some years earlier a service had been held for Doddy's mother, Sarah Dodd. Now, as the Reverend H.B. Siviter began to address the congregation he directed his words to the comedian who was sitting silently some seats away: 'How true is the saying that behind every great man there stands an equally great woman. As you know, I used to talk to your mother, Ken, a number of times during her lifetime and she, too, played a vitally important role in your life. In one sense you have been richly blessed in having behind you two ladies who understood you, who helped you, who loved you.'

For a brief moment the vicar paused, then raising his voice ever so slightly, he went on, 'The greatest way you can show your love for their memory is by rising over this great sorrow and going out in your profession, showing that their lives have not been in vain and that the love they have shown has helped you climb the ladder of success.'

Dressed in a dark suit, Doddy listened, his eyes focused directly ahead. For him, it was an intensely solemn occasion, one far removed from that other stage where Anita had helped him to attain stardom. Yet the solemnity touched him and the memory of Anita stayed with him throughout every moment of the service. An extra hearse was needed to take the floral tributes from the church to Anfield cemetery, where she would be buried.

Hundreds of people, including reporters and cameramen, made their way to the cemetery. All eyes were on Doddy, as though everyone present wanted to know how he was taking the bereavement. Cameras clicked and for a moment it looked as if the press were intent on turning the sad event into a show business occasion. To Bobby Jaye, who was standing a good distance away, it seemed the cameramen were making it all an unedifying spectacle. 'I think this was one time they should have let Ken alone with his grief. I didn't like what I saw.'

In most people's minds the long love story between Ken and Anita was over. That morning in the graveyard, a few people expressed regret that the pair had not married. It did not seem nearly enough that they should have remained partners and lovers, when marriage appeared the only logical climax. The real reason, according to close friends, was because Doddy was Church of England and Anita was Roman Catholic. In show business circles that was considered an inadequate excuse.

When he was asked about the vicar's advice to him to resume his career, Doddy remarked, 'The vicar is right. It will be in keeping with Anita's wishes for me to get back on stage. I know it will take me some time to get my courage together, but I'll be back.'

Within a few weeks he was throwing his full weight behind his personal crusade to save theatres. First, it was the beleaguered Royal Court Theatre in Liverpool which had been closed for a year. It hoped to have its doors opened that September in 1978 with a gala variety show starring Doddy, who said it was essential that positive steps were taken to ensure the future of the Royal 'one of the finest theatres in the country'.

At that time he was further committed to keeping the Grand Theatre in Blackpool in operation and gave his full support to the Friends of the Grand who were dedicated to preserving the impressive Victorian building. He joined in their fund-raising which had a target of £350,000. This would enable them to buy the Grand from EMI and make it a full-time theatre again. If they were successful, Doddy said he would hire the theatre for its first summer-season show.

It was a constant worry to him that some of the country's most historic theatres were threatened with closure, perhaps to be replaced by towering office blocks. At that time he was playing variety at the Palace Theatre, Manchester, and one afternoon he held an urgent press conference. There was a danger that the Palace would close for good.

From the empty stage he waved the emblem he called his tatty diddling stick towards the tiers of seats soaring towards the chandeliers and gilt-encrusted ceiling, and declared, 'Can you imagine England's second city allowing this marvellous theatre to close? The greats have trodden these boards – Charlie Chaplin, Dan Leno, Vesta Tilley, Gracie Fields, Danny Kaye, Frank Sinatra, Judy Garland . . . it's not just a building, it's part of our heritage, an essential amenity.'

The problem was that the eighty-six-year-old theatre was not paying its way, as was the case with a number of other provincial theatres. Now Doddy offered to finance his own Christmas show to the extent of £100,000.

205

What concerned him most was the prevailing apathy – that people would allow theatres like the Palace, with its long tradition, to die. It seemed utterly preposterous.

'You need love to make a success in show business,' the comic said, with more than usual conviction. 'Real love of the theatre. Today's managements sitting in London think they can run halls in the provinces. They can't.'

It was a question of extreme urgency, he added. Action was needed to save theatres. He wanted to see a Theatre Rescue operation launched. He would put in some of his own money. They were fighting some theatre-owners who wanted to put these buildings to what they termed, 'better use'. That afternoon, Doddy was holding auditions for his chorus and as he gazed wistfully at the bustling rehearsal room where a line of pretty girls were going through their paces, he commented, 'What a terrible thing if one day there were no theatres left – only those tiddly little halls up and down the country. And all because nobody cares.'

One of the problems was of course that a big theatre was recognised as a very wasteful thing. Few owners made a fortune out of them and unless subsidised, would continue to find it hard to survive in an entertainment climate geared to TV, video rental shops and discos. Yet Doddy was able to point to the Theatre Royal, Norwich, which was a commercial success because of its sophisticated management, and there were a few others as well. If people were enthusiastic enough they could hold on to their theatres. They had got to appreciate that if live shows were reduced so would the quality of the performers they got on their TV screens. Commercial managements must have courage. Local authorities could assist them and put some money into theatrical projects.

Behind Doddy's one-man crusade was a deep-rooted feeling of the debt he owed to provincial theatres. Without them he would, he knew, still be a salesman in Knotty

Ash. Now he was determined to repay that debt and it
was also one of the reasons he devoted so much of his
time to playing the provinces. And now he had the satisfaction of seeing his £100,000 investment paying dividends at the Palace Theatre. From the middle of December
he had packed every one of the 2,200 seats with his spectacular *Laughter Show*.

As usual, showbiz columnists went along to the star's
dressing-room to talk to him about his latest stage success.
What awaited them was a mixture of chaos and fun.
Doddy was as hard to pin down as a slippery eel; not that
he didn't like publicity – it was a question of his time –
he never had enough of it. Joe Steeples was a newspaper
friend of Doddy's and as he stepped inside the dressing-
room he could hardly believe what met his eyes. 'Going
into the room was like stepping into a wardrobe just after
Hurricane Hetty had blown through. The tiny space was
littered with a débris of mad costumes, suitcases full of
raggedy scripts, crates, silly hats, dirty glasses, piles of
footwear, and one dishevelled comedian.'

Doddy was wearing an orange fur coat that looked like
a reject from War On Want. In his left hand was the
redoubtable tickling stick and his long black hair stuck out
in all directions, or as Steeples said, 'like a wheatfield after
a fire'. The comic sat for a moment amid the weird props
and reflected seriously, 'How dare people say live entertainment is dead. How dare they. When you watch a
theatre show, you just don't watch it, you're in it. As far
as I'm concerned, a live audience is the most important
part of entertainment. You can't clown away in a vacuum.
You can't tell jokes to yourself.'

Steeples followed the comic out of the dressing-room
and watched him perform from the wings. Although he
had seen his act on numerous occasions, he still found it
madly funny. Now, with tickling stick in hand, the comic
told the audience, 'How tickled I am, Missus, to be
appearing in this magnificent hut, decorated in the elegant

style of Cadbury's rococo.' As the laughter subsided he plunged into his What-A-Beautiful-Day routine and three minutes of inspired lunacy.

'*What a beautiful day for going out and buying the wife an unrideable mule . . . What a beautiful day for bumping into Raquel Welch . . . slowly.*'

Doddy hurried back to the dressing-room and changed into a policeman's uniform and at the same time tried to answer Steeple's questions, which was not at all easy since the comic was offering a cup of tea and a glass of lager all at once. 'Laughing has great therapeutic value,' Doddy philosophised. 'When you go out of my theatre, you should feel all the better for it.'

They talked for a little while about Anita Boutin, and Doddy said in a quiet voice, 'I owe everything to her. She was my partner, and we had a deep lasting relationship.' But he would not reveal why they had never married. 'That's a private thing, too personal to talk about.'

Suddenly, he stood up amidst the costumes and the raggedy scripts and announced with a smile that revealed his shining, protruding teeth, 'Yes, I'm happy. Very happy. Particularly when I'm out there on that stage. It's a beautiful experience to go out and make people laugh. Just to hear a belly laugh makes me go all oogle-oogle-oogle.'

At that moment, he hastened out of the dressing-room and ran on to the stage to announce the appearance of that great Russian stripper, Eva Vestoff. Joe Steeples stayed behind, looking at the room of débris with the comedian's tea and lager still untasted. As he walked away, he heard the thunder of applause in the auditorium. Steeples was convinced more than ever that Doddy was an extraordinary Liverpudlian.

Soon two hundred academics would probably say the same thing. For the star had been invited to a gathering of psychologists at Cardiff University, the only working comic among the distinguished group. He was not in the least overawed by the honour. 'I shall be giving a working comedian's point of view to people who have been studying it from the academic angle,' he said. 'And I'll be wearing the cap and gown of Knotty Ash University – singlet and socks. You have to have a signed document to say you've got clean ones on.'

Among the delegates would be Dr Tony Chapman, lecturer in social psychology, Cardiff, the conference organiser. 'I have an immense respect for Ken Dodd because he appeals to all ages,' Chapman said. His respect was probably tinged with envy. As a student of humour for six years, Dr Chapman still could not tell jokes. As he explained, 'I can't remember them properly. I'm a big disappointment at parties.'

Like Doddy, however, he believed humour was communication. 'Communicating happiness is part of it. But I think its most important function is a more subtle form of communication.' Doddy promised to bring along some of the log-books of audience reaction to his performances kept night after night, which recorded in minute detail the response to every joke in every town he had played. Each entry also showed the date, season, whether first or second house, time on and time off, the size and mood of the audience, and even the weather outside. From this he had built an encyclopaedic geography of British laughter.

As a practical man among theorists, he was slightly defensive about his own view of humour. 'Some very high IQs will be discussing humour and laughter,' he said, 'and while it's very easy to say that it's a serious business, I don't altogether agree. It's not a gloomy subject. I see it as the communication of happiness.'

As if to show at that time that he fitted the role of versatile genius, Doddy had written a book about his favourite butties (or sandwiches). 'This is the first book I've ever written, so I decided it had to be a tome of great intellect. The jam butty was the first great butty. It was invented in Liverpool and the jam butty mines are now famous in all parts of the world.'

He recalled that, as a boy growing up in Knotty Ash, the jam butty was very close to his heart. 'It bridged that gap from the time you came out of school until your dad came home and you all had tea together. It filled that vacant space in your tum.' He proceeded to give the recipe for this popular butty.

His own favourite butty was cheese and onion – 'but you have to pick your friends carefully!' He made no secret of his enduring love of butties. 'When I was in training for my marathon mirthquake at the Royal Court Theatre, I trained on a diet of butties. They included "corn"flake butties and shredded "wit"butties. But during the recent bread strike, we were in dire straits – with no bread, we just had to eat toast.'

Eventually the comic's butty book was published and sold as quickly as butties in Liverpool and Knotty Ash. Doddy was rather thrilled to be described as an author. In time he would have competition from Jimmy Tarbuck and Tom O'Connor.

CHAPTER 19

'I'm old enough to remember Poland'

A court jester to No. 10 Downing Street?

Preposterous, you might say. But for years the wise-cracking Bob Hope, who had campaigned for presidential hopefuls in the United States, came to be accepted as court jester to the White House. Unlike America's star entertainers, the British, with a few exceptions, tended to keep their politics to themselves. Although Doddy was a self-styled court jester, his brief did not extend as far as No. 10.

Presumably if there had been a court jester to No. 10 in that year, 1979, it would probably have been Kenneth Arthur Dodd from Knotty Ash; certainly not Benny Hill nor Jim Davidson. Doddy's credentials were impeccable. He could not remember when he was not a Conservative and he showed undisguised admiration for Margaret Thatcher. However, no one could ever accuse him of being partisan on stage. He had entertained Tory and Labour politicians, and once at the Opera House in Blackpool told the audience that Arthur Scargill was being deported. As the cheers subsided, he added, 'The bad news is that Mark Thatcher is driving him to the airport'.

'The Labour Party believe in share and share alike,' he quipped. 'The trouble is they always want their share first.' And: 'Denis Healey refuses to leave Downing Street until they find him another council house. But he can

211

always go back to stealing bread off the ducks!' None the less, he could be serious about political issues. He had been unhappy with Britain under Labour. As he said, 'As an entertainer I get a glimpse of what goes on behind the scenes. What appalls me is the wastage of time and money. An artiste lives on applause. So do the ordinary people. They want to be applauded. But under the Socialists they have no encouragement as they are taxed so heavily and bullied. How can you expect people to work hard for a goal when the Chancellor said he would squeeze until the pips squeaked.'

Dangerous thinking no doubt for an entertainer whose audiences comprised Tories, Labourites and Liberals. But it was not that alone that forced him to nail his colours to the mast prior to the 1979 election. It was simply his own vision of the Britain of the future. 'I saw that in the event of the election going the same way as the previous one, it could be the last election we would ever have in this country. I saw people who would seize power and completely destroy our way of life. It terrified me. My God, we're going to become an Eastern bloc state. I once crossed Checkpoint Charlie into East Berlin. Just for a couple of hours. But it looked as if the whole place had been taken over by the Co-op.'

He was too young to participate in World War II, but he remembers living through the Liverpool blitz in May 1941 as German planes dropped 2,000 bombs and started 1,200 fires on Merseyside. In one of the raids the Liverpool Corn Exchange was razed, and the following morning the members met to transact their business in the street. That was typical of the indomitable spirit of Liverpool. The blitz left an indelible impression on young Dodd. He was old enough, too, to remember tanks in Hungary. As he says, 'I'm old enough to remember Czechoslovakia and I'm old enough to remember Poland. It's not the place of the entertainer to get embroiled in party politics, but as a private citizen of the United Kingdom, I felt that this time I had to stand up and be counted.'

None the less, it was a bold step for Doddy to take, particularly in a city not noted for its love of the Tory Party. Some of his professional colleagues regarded his excursion into politics as 'a somewhat silly thing to do', and believed he would be better employed leaving it to the professionals. Doddy however went to pains to draw a distinction between Conservatives and Tories. 'I don't go around shooting foxes and pheasants like the landed gentry,' he asserted. 'I'm a Conservative and believe in the freedom of the individual to choose their destiny and be rewarded for their talent.' There was another reason. The comic was convinced that Margaret Thatcher would in time give the country back its pride. He was uncertain about socialism. 'I'm told it was Clemenceau who said, "If a man is not a Socialist when he is twenty he has no heart; if he is a Socialist when he's thirty, he has no brain".'

Of course he did not altogether believe that. But he feared at that time that a section of the Labour Party in Liverpool was in danger of being hi-jacked by extremist elements within the party. Mindful of the dangers ahead, he canvassed in a local by-election for the Conservative candidate. He felt the party was best equipped to deal with the powerful trade unions. As he said, 'I've spoken to lorry drivers who all think Britain is the greatest country in the world and want it to be kept that way. They are prepared to co-operate with any government, but think that a judicial system to look at their wage levels would be the best idea and the Conservatives would introduce something like that. At the present time I feel that many honest trade unionists are being led by the vociferous minority. In my own actors' union it's the left-wing element that are causing all the trouble.'

Some Labour supporters claimed that Doddy could afford to be a Conservative because he was rich and famous; others felt Thatcherism appealed to his vision of an American-style Britain where the wealthy would prosper. But Doddy argued that it was the spectre of a left-wing takeover of the country that prompted him to take to the streets of Liverpool sporting the Tory Party colours and a blue tickling stick.

He was not the only entertainer that year to stand up and be counted. The Tories could also rely on Cyril Fletcher with his odes, and Les Dawson. The Liberals had backing from Derek Nimmo, Nicholas Parsons, Honor Blackman and pop singer Steve Hartley. And the Labour showbiz supporters included Donald Pleasence and John Thaw, who was playing Inspector Regan in *The Sweeney*, Robert Morley, Dame Peggy Ashcroft and Sheila Hancock. Surprisingly, the most politically-minded of the lot, Mike Yarwood, did not get involved like Doddy: he was too busy at that time impersonating Harold Wilson and Edward Heath. More than anyone else, Yarwood was aware of how sensitive political supporters could be and for that reason steered clear of direct involvement. As he recalls, 'The complaints I most regularly received were political. If correspondents convinced me that a particular routine or joke was in bad taste, then I withdrew that sequence.'

Doddy did not think show business personalities upset their public by taking part in politics, but he was not at all certain. 'In the 1960s, politics were good for a joke,' he said, 'but the way the country is going in the Seventies when I look round, it is no longer a joke.' In a few weeks he would find out the grim truth.

One May morning, as he canvassed with the Tory campaign team in Speke market, the entourage were kicked, punched and kneed. The campaigners also had their posters ripped from their van while hecklers shouted them down with loudhailers only feet from their faces. 'By Jove, they mean business,' Doddy was heard to say above the bedlam. It was the ugly side of politics and the star was not tickled one bit. But he managed to keep his temper, even his sense of humour despite the provocation. It was strange, he thought, coming from his own people – the people who make up his variety audiences in Liverpool theatres.

'Mr Dodd was subjected to the most vicious abuse I have seen in fifteen years of election campaigning,' commented a Conservative spokesman. 'He is a man who has no need to take sides, but, because he feels strongly, and has chosen to do so, why he should have to suffer such personal attacks is difficult to understand.'

Undeterred by the violent scenes, Doddy continued to campaign for the party candidate, although later he and his campaigners were pelted with eggs. He was now becoming unsure if he would repeat his efforts for the general election. Yet he was convinced that left-wing parties wanted to annihilate the freedom of choice on education, religion and housing. 'If we don't get a Conservative government this time,' he said, 'Britain could be another Soviet satellite in the next year.' Eventually, when Mrs Thatcher came to be Prime Minister, he was asked about her. 'People think she is a straight Tory and aloof. It's not so. She is a down-to-earth Conservative and working-class lady. I've met all three leaders and she's the most impressive.'

Doddy was not interested in being court jester at No. 10, nor any kind of public relations officer for Mrs Thatcher. Mike Yarwood was once amused when he met Harold Wilson in Blackpool and got the impression that he had been a sort of PRO for the Prime Minister. Mr Wilson told him that some of his best impersonations had been as good as party political broadcasts for him. Doddy avoided close encounters with politicians and felt no obligation to satirise them in his stage act. But he did admire the strength of character of Margaret Thatcher. He could not see how such admiration could affect his professional career in his native Liverpool.

That spring, 1979, he was busy fund-raising for charity, in particular for cancer research. Since the death from cancer of Anita Boutin he had involved himself more and more in charitable causes. He was relieved to find that his excursion into politics was only a nine days' wonder and his popularity did not suffer. Occasionally the question arose in discussion, or debate, about the rivalry between Liverpool comics. Was it true or imaginary?

Radio producer Jim Casey has always felt that a rivalry does exist. 'It's a friendly rivalry in my opinion and is in no way nasty. I think most of the others concede that Ken Dodd is the governor. Ken was the first big star of the modern era to follow Scouse comics such as Arthur Askey and Ted Ray, but the truth is he turned out bigger than either of them.'

To Casey, Doddy was never jealous of his colleagues or rivals. As he said, 'He is too big for that. Occasionally I've known him to be angry when other comics pinched his jokes. For years they have pinched his best gags, and when you consider he has to pay for them, it is not funny. But he has remained number one comic in Liverpool for a long time. This is undisputed. My father Jimmy James, who admired Ken's talent, once defined a great comic to me as a man who says things funny and not a man who merely says funny things. Ken says things funny. Jimmy Tarbuck says funny things.'

Doddy has been known to help younger comedians with his shrewd advice and encouragement. One of them was Tom O'Connor, the ex-Bootle headmaster who made his début at Newton British Legion Club in Wigan for the grand sum of £5. But when he first tried comedy in the act he made the mistake of telling out and out jokes. 'You die very quickly if you start telling old jokes that the audience already know,' he says.

Later, he discussed his problem with Doddy. 'Ken put me right. He pointed out that I was getting bigger laughs from the run-up to my gags than from the actual punchlines . . . and he told me about people, and observing life. Really life can be very funny. It took off from there. Doddy's advice proved invaluable.'

O'Connor admired the way Doddy performed *with* an audience, the way he 'beat' them into submission. 'Like Doddy, I'm a Scouser at heart,' he would say. He had made a study of Scouse comedy and written about it. A sample: 'Excuse me, conductor, do you stop at the Adelphi? What! On my wages?' And: 'There's rats on this ship, we want vermin money.' . . . 'Am I all right for the museum?' 'Yes, but I wouldn't leave it too long if I were you, mate!'

Philip Key, of the *Liverpool Post*, dropped into the Royal Court Theatre more than once that season to see Doddy performing in his own variety show. He had grown to like enormously the comic's zany approach to comedy. Off-stage he felt no strain talking to the star. 'He is one of those people the psychiatrist would probably dub a workaholic – constantly busy with his career,' Key decided. So busy was Doddy that the columnist could only catch up with him while he was working – and that was back stage in the theatre during the interval of the first house. It was one of the very few moments that Doddy could take a rest. Even so, through their half-hour meeting Doddy remained standing, and busying himself with callers, costumes and drinks for his visitors. However, he looked pleased with himself. The show was on an extended run and he saw it as another example of the need to keep theatres alive.

He stopped for a moment in the middle of the room, and told Key, 'I think people are returning to the theatre and discovering its magic all over again. They don't want to stay in every night watching television.' Privately, he blamed a lot of theatre managements for the bad reputation theatre had had over the years. They presented cheap shows and some of them were big companies whose real interest lay elsewhere. It was one of the reasons why at that time he preferred to produce his own shows.

To Key, the star was genuine in his concern for the live theatre, but he could see he was very busy. There was a summer season coming up at Scarborough, records, and probably a new radio series. Whenever Doddy talked about songs and lyrics he sounded enthusiastic. He had high hopes for his new release, *Give Me Your Love*. 'I think it's a good song,' he mused. 'It's a while, you know, since I recorded and I know my fans want to hear me again. *Tears* did very well for me – that was a double gold record. Of course everything was going for it: it was a ballad and it was released at a time when there was a lot of music with a heavy beat. I think a ballad came as a welcome change and a bit of a relief. I was thrilled I can tell you.'

When they talked about holidays and if the star intended taking a break, Doddy it seemed to Key almost took pride in saying, 'Throughout my career – it must now span twenty-four years – I've only had one day off through illness – and that one day I had pneumonia! The next day I went back to the theatre. The stage door man just said, "Good-evening" as if nothing had happened. And so did everyone else. No sympathy at all. But that's one of the great traditions – the show must go on. I agree with it.'

He knew it also made show business people unique. He wouldn't have it any other way, despite the pressure on him from friends to take a holiday and cut back his heavy workload. 'I'm only really happy when I'm working,' he continued to say – and of course it was true.

Key was not alone in being baffled by the comedian's simple life-style. When he visited his home in Knotty Ash he invariably came away with the impression that it was not exactly the kind of place in which you would expect a star of show business to live. Key recalls, 'Doddy's front room was often cluttered with plastic Diddymen on the fire-place, pictures of him in the roles of various music-hall stars on the wall, and various records and magazines around. Yet it's the sort of place where you'd like to think someone like Doddy would live. Because he remains a people's comic.'

Key was inclined to compare the star with Arthur Askey who, despite his seventy-eight years, was still working hard. Doddy was a mere fifty-one – and told Philip Key that he couldn't see the day he would stop. As he reflected, 'I'd like to keep working until I'm ninety-eight – just to beat Askey.'

In early October, he was preparing for his return to the London Palladium, or, as he dubbed it, the Temple of Tickleology. Bob Hope had said, 'For an entertainer there's no better stage or better audience than the Palladium. I intend to keep coming back as long as they'll have me.' In Doddy's case it was six years since he had played there and it seemed much too long an absence. By now he had acquired a big London public and it was somewhat of a disappointment that he had not played the Palladium more often. Like Bob Hope, he loved the atmosphere of the place. It was unique. In the main foyer pictures of most of the stars who entertained there hung on the walls and were a constant delight for visitors. The theatre had a glamour all its own, or as Mike Yarwood used to say, 'The Palladium is a prestige engagement because it's the premier variety theatre in the world.'

As far as the showbiz columnists were concerned, Doddy was back in town. It was fifteen years since he had made his sensational début at the Palladium and now they vividly remembered his performance, even one funny one-liner, 'My sister was engaged to an Eskimo but she broke it off.' They described the comic as unique. One warned his paper's readers, 'Mr Dodd triumphs by pummelling his audience into submission with an onslaught of gags, puns, quips and voyages into the surreal and frankly sexual avenues of his rich imagination. It is a rare and wonderful thing to be caught up in the fever of insanity Mr Dodd produces on stage. Television gives no clue to the singular theatricality of the occasion. He is a phenomenon.'

The star looked relaxed as he talked to the press a few days before opening night. He exuded confidence as he stood on the famous Palladium stage. 'Nice to be back,' he said with a laugh. 'By Jove, it's been a long time. We've got some fresh ideas, new material, new songs. Lots of gags, wheezes, funnies and japes. No one's getting out until they have enjoyed themselves. It's going to be a no-holds-barred.'

Because of his emphasis on phallic symbols, some of the press tended to liken Doddy to Max Miller. Both were the master of innuendo, the incarnation of British music-hall, but sex was not the enduring theme of Doddy's comedy, nor did he take the same risks as Miller. More-over, no one could describe Kenneth Arthur Dodd as that 'Cheeky Chappie'. At that time what Doddy possessed in abundance was exuberance and sheer enthusiasm. His incredible success as a stand-up comic depended to some small degree on these ingredients.

Now as he stood on the empty stage of the Palladium, surrounded by journalists and photographers, he knew he was celebrating more than twenty-five years as a pro-fessional entertainer. In conversation he liked to draw comparisons between live theatre and television: 'When I go on stage I have the time of my life. That's the difference with live theatre . . . TV is great but you don't get the feedback. It's up to the skill of the entertainer to pick material to suit the audience. Everyone has a capacity for laughter. The public is the catalyst who can release it.'

Not surprisingly, he was asked about the sexual conno-tations. His act had by now been described as a fertility rite, as full of phallic symbolism as a cucumber patch. 'Ah,' Doddy said with a shrug, 'sex? Oh yes, lots of that. If God invented anything better he kept it to himself.

What a great sport it is. I celebrate being alive and that includes all the joys from music to pleasures of the – er – flesh. It's a wonderful thing.'

Undeniably, Doddy remained a puzzle to some of the more perceptive Fleet Street journalists. They agreed that he was an original from the British music-hall tradition, yet he held an almost isolated place in the entertainment establishment. He guarded his privacy and was not an obvious showbiz socialiser, although the comic claimed his friends were mainly in the business. Unlike most other comics, he often acted as his own impresario and was reputed to have an acute business brain.

To most of them gathered on the stage of the Palladium, he had not changed. The buck teeth, saucer eyes and fly-away hair were still part of his comic's equipment, but he looked as much businessman as comedian in his executive striped suit and correct collar and tie.

Compared with some of his former Palladium seasons, the present one was a mere two weeks, yet it was reassuring to him that every seat was booked in advance. Incredibly, the reception was as ecstatic as ever. As he bounded on stage, waving his tickling stick, he smiled gleefully and in no time at all had seduced his audience – all 2,500 of them – with a cadenza of one-liners and his usual 'What a Beautiful Day' gags: 'What a Beautiful Day for extending the hand of friendship across the Channel – if you can find a man with arms twenty-two miles long.'

Once more he was unashamedly the salesman, ever on the offensive. Someone observed, 'Doddy loves the laughter he generates.' It was true. Tonight, as he waved his tickling stick towards the people in the stalls and boxes, the laughter was contagious. Was there now a danger that he might miscalculate his audience? As John Fisher pointed out in *Funny Way To Be a Hero*: 'Sadly however there is always present in a Ken Dodd performance an uneasy hint that one day the ultimate orgasm will be achieved, the audience go so far in the direction of exhaustion that they succumb to hysterics, sulks, even chaos. One recalls how the Danny Kaye myth lost so much of its potency during his third Palladium season. Convinced that the audience, which he already held in the palm of his hand, would become even more compliant, he sat on the edge of the stage and asked them to follow his actions, clapping their hands, touching their elbows in unison. It seemed a fair enough request to make, but he had miscalculated.'

Doddy did not take such a risk. At the crucial point when he had his audience on the verge of exhaustion, he suddenly changed the mood as he sang one of his popular balads; or left the stage to somebody else. It was the same with his entire act; unlike Max Miller he never worked on a knife-edge. On this occasion there was no Harold Wilson to visit his dressing-room, but Prime Minister Margaret Thatcher dropped round to say 'Hello'. Although he over-ran most nights, it was not for any great length and the backstage hands did not complain or have a management spokesman visit his No. 1 dressing-room to convey their annoyance.

As usual, he took longer than an hour to unwind after each performance. Showbiz stars and friends crowded the dressing-room and sometimes he did not leave the theatre until after midnight. Conversation was, as always, his way of relaxing. He sipped a beer and talked about a variety of subjects, often about his forthcoming engage-ments, as if to him the Palladium was just another date. It was true, for the comic treated every provincial engage-ment as though it was at the Temple of Tickleology.

There was no denying that his latest success at the Palladium afforded him immense satisfaction. It proved to him that after twenty-five years in the business he had held his popularity. He might not have been the cult figure of other years, but his creative approach to comedy was still appealing to the masses. He was tickled no end and felt he might after all go on until he was a hundred

years old and put his name in the *Guinness Book of Records*
for the second time. 'What a beautiful thought, he
reflected. 'By Jove, it's worth a bash.'

Back in Knotty Ash they took Doddy's latest triumph
almost for granted; they were now more interested in the
rumours about a new woman in his life. Since the death
of Anita Boutin three years before, his name had not been
seriously linked with any other woman. Though he was
over fifty his love-life was still of interest to the people of
Knotty Ash.

At that time Doddy was guarded in his attitude and
when eventually his name was linked with singer Sybil
Jones, he was upset. When confronted in his dressing-
room by a reporter to confirm or deny this rumour, he
looked startled. 'It would be embarrassing for me if anything like this appeared in the papers,' he said. 'You
know how these things can get all blown up. We're in
pantomime together, that's all.'

It seemed a rather ridiculous line to adopt for the star
comic who could scarcely hope to keep his love-life secret
for long. Typically, he tried to pass it over. That Christmas
he was starring in *Dick Whittington* at Birmingham's Alexandra Theatre and Sybil Jones, dark-haired and attractive,
was playing the Good Fairy. A former Bluebell Girl, she
was aged forty-five and had known Ken for a number of
years. At one time she used to work at Manchester Airport
and left to become a Bluebell Girl in Paris. Her ambition
had always been to go on stage and eventually she played
guitar, sang folk numbers and did impressions.

And her friends, who called her Anna, counted Doddy
a 'very lucky man' to have a friend like her. She spoke
four languages and had a friendly disposition. Now, off-
stage at the Birmingham Alexandra Theatre, the cast
noticed that Ken and Sybil were inseparable and evidently
in love. The panto's leading lady, Sally Smith, recalls,
'Every night when Ken left the theatre to go home to

Liverpool, Sybie went with him.' Another member of the cast remarked, 'I was warned on the first day of rehearsals to watch what I said about Ken Dodd because his girlfriend was in the show. They are always together, but they don't mix with the rest of us.'

As in the case of Anita Boutin, Miss Jones now attended to the comic in his dressing-room, even drove him to the pantomime and usually they lunched together. The fact that his secret was out annoyed Doddy. It was the kind of publicity he disliked. Sybie Jones said, 'We're just good friends and have been for a long time.' Once, when Doddy was an hour late for a panto photo-session, she paced the stage anxiously and kept asking where he was. When he eventually arrived he fussed around his Good Fairy and adjusted her headgear before they went in front of the camera. And as they posed for pictures, they frequently gazed into each other's eyes.

It was noticeable that Sybie Jones said nothing to Doddy about his late arrival, which suggested that she, too, was incapable of changing the comic. By now she had come to accept his eccentric ways. Members of the cast, though, were often irritated when the star kept them waiting. Some of them found him enigmatic, even aloof. 'Unlike other leading actors, Ken does not mix much with the cast,' explained a theatre employee, adding, 'While the rest of them go to the nearby pub at lunchtime Ken and Sybie are known to go off on their own. It's nice that he's found someone again.'

Never once was the question of marriage mentioned. In Knotty Ash the people were understandably philosophical about the romance and after their experience with Ken and Anita they dared not ask him if he intended to marry. Nor did the local press think it wise to confront him. To them, he was still a very private person and they knew nothing would change that. But he did confide in a few friends that he loved Sybie.

There was no reason to doubt him. Together they

enjoyed each other's company. Sybie, like Ken, was fond of music and her stage act included Country and Western songs. She was intelligent and supportive and was reckoned to be good for his career. And she liked to think she understood him.

On the other hand, Doddy made no secret of the fact that he liked women, particularly the company of clever women. Throughout his career he had entertained them in his dressing-room and after shows invariably went to the stage door to sign their programmes. He doubted if he could live without a woman.

However, his view of marriage had not changed. As he said, 'I believe that marriage does something to certain couples; they stop working at their relationship. If you're living with someone, the knowledge that they can just walk out means you don't take one another for granted.'

It was clear that the Squire of Knotty Ash had no intention of rushing into marriage. It wasn't that he was now too busy – few would accept that excuse any more – rather that he liked better the idea of a happy liaison. Sybie Jones preferred not to be drawn on the question.

CHAPTER 20

'Show Business is a Lovely Game'

Looking overdressed in a neat, well-fitting suit, bright shirt and tie, Doddy sat facing chat-show host Michael Parkinson in a compact television studio. It was the early Eighties and the comedian had been invited on *Parkinson* and accepted the invitation without hesitation. Friendly comedians are most popular in Yorkshire, his own research had shown, and Parkinson was a Yorkshireman to his fingertips. Parky liked to remember being taken to see his first music-hall show in Barnsley. 'I was soon drunk on the smell of Barnsley bitter and Woodbines,' he recalls, 'hypnotised by the lights and the beefy chorus girls in their darned tights.'

Doddy prodded his tickling stick into Parkinson's face, ran it over his nose, and withdrew it with the deft touch of a matador. As Parkinson recalled in his book *The Best of Parkinson* (Pavilion Books, 1982), Dodd then began to tell a joke about a man cruising down the M1 in a gleaming Jaguar at 60 miles an hour, when on his outside he saw a cloud of dust overtaking him doing at around 70 mph. Jolted from his lethargy by what he thought was a chicken in the middle of the dust cloud, he eased up behind the chicken. It was a chicken all right, but no ordinary one. He was sure it had three legs.

Suddenly the bird picked up pace and sped off at 75 mph. The Jaguar driver followed, hard on the heels of the mysterious chicken. Without any warning the chicken veered off the motorway on to a small country side road. The Jaguar driver followed, now doing 90 mph and on the edge of his seat with excitement. The next thing the chicken disappeared round a bend into a nearby farmyard. In went the Jaguar in hot pursuit. Ahead, the driver saw a frail old man with a walking stick inching his way across the farmyard. The driver frantically slammed on the brakes of his car and skidded uncontrollably to a halt, missing the other by inches. He jumped out of the car and asked the old man, 'Did you see a chicken come in here?'

Farmer: 'Yes' (in a West Country accent).

Driver: 'Did this chicken have three legs, by any chance?'

Farmer: 'It did.'

Driver: 'What is a three-legged chicken doing here?'

Farmer: 'I breed three-legged chickens.'

Driver: 'Why?'

Farmer: 'Well, I like a leg, the wife likes a leg and the son, he likes a leg.'

Driver: 'Well, what do they taste like?'

Farmer: 'I dunno . . . we've never caught one . . .'

The casually dressed Parkinson laughed; he suspected that Doddy was in one of his irrepressible moods. For a moment the comedian pushed the tickling stick in front of his face and the chat show host pulled back his head. By now Parkinson's name was a byword in the TV chat scene. He had chatted up such celebrities as David Niven, Sammy Davis Jnr, Peter Ustinov, Dr Henry Kissinger and Christian Barnard. With his easy, friendly style, he managed to make stars feel they were not being threatened. He had a clear definition of the exact nature of his role.

'I've always believed that the ideal chat show is like a successful dinner party,' he says, 'where the viewer pulls up a chair and looks over my right shoulder at someone they've always wanted to meet. And the interviewer, as the perfect host at a dinner party, has but one task – to bring out the best in his guests and not treat them like a captive audience for a display of his own wit and opinions.'

By now Doddy had been the subject of not a few such shows. Shortly before, he had made quite an impression in the *South Bank Show* when he talked to the smooth Melvyn Bragg. Filmed in the manager's office at the Palace Theatre, Manchester, Doddy talked about his ideas and theories on comedy and these were illustrated by scenes from his show during an evening performance in the theatre. Viewers saw the star as he chatted with Bragg at length about his campaign for the live theatre. He did his Shakespearean bit from *Twelfth Night* in a hat that he had worn at the Liverpool Playhouse when he played Malvolio. It had been made out of real beaver fur and they gave it to him as a keepsake.

Doddy felt uninhibited on chat shows and enjoyed himself immensely, although he was noticeably wary when confronted with questions about his private life. The producer of *Parkinson* was the energetic John Fisher who, on his own admission, liked working with the comedian. As he says, 'Doddy is reluctant to map out any performance in advance. He is a skilled jazz improviser. He plays an audience like an instrument.'

Like other interviewers, Parkinson found it occasionally difficult to pin down Doddy, who sometimes liked to go off at a different tangent. When he commented on his features, his teeth in particular, the comic could not resist prodding his host with the tickling stick as he replied, 'I do find it rather difficult as a comedian having these perfect features! I did think of having my teeth straightened once, but let's face it, there wouldn't have been anything left to laugh at. I think a comic has to learn very early on to let people laugh at him as well as with him and he has to take it all in his stride. I really don't mind.'

Parkinson was showing a genuine interest in his life of

comedy and Doddy's own background. Remembering his own younger days, he would say, 'I grew to love, everlastingly, the men who made me laugh. Being a Yorkshireman, I became addicted to these comedians whose humour grew out of the grimness of Northern industrialised society. Case-hardened comics, epitomised by the greatest of them all, the incomparable Jimmy James.'

Now, in the studio, they talked quietly about seaside variety and immediately Doddy recalled his Blackpool days. 'I have just done a season there and they always start all these conferences in Blackpool when I'm there. As a resort, it is a very upmarket place, I mean they get a much better class of seaside hooligan there; in Eastbourne and Bournemouth they get Mods and Rockers, in Blackpool they get the TUC! Anyway, Mrs Thatcher was gracious enough to come and see my show and actually did laugh all the way through it. It's all right telling jokes about people as long as you don't attack the dogma, and one joke I tell is about Sir Geoffrey Howe – how he wants to get us out of this mess as soon as possible because he's got another one waiting for us. I've been telling that gag now for twenty years at Blackpool, so it shows how long we've been in a mess!'

Parkinson , who is reckoned to be one of the 'nice guys' of television, did not try to score points off the comic. He listened as Doddy told more Northern jokes and he laughed softly at some of the more funny ones. Doddy told him about his Giggle Map and how at the outset of his career in Liverpool he had kept notebooks on what jokes went down well and over the years it had developed into this Giggle Map that informed him what sort of gags people liked in different parts of the country.

'Take Yorkshire, for instance,' said the comic, 'they're a very odd lot! They have one trait, which is their strength as well as their weakness – they are stubborn and very gritty. One joke I tell is about this old lady who went to a stonemason and asked him to engrave her husband's name on a memorial stone, as he had just died. He asked her if he should put R.I.P. on it so she said O.K. but put T.I.C. after it. He asked her why and she said that her husband had spent all the club money, all the money that they had saved in the teapot – he had drunk it all down in the Dog and Duck; "So put R.I.P. – Rest in Peace and then T.I.C. – Till I Come!" '

Doddy talked about his native Liverpool and Knotty Ash where he had been a salesman. He reminded his host that he was by now twenty-six years in show business, and added proudly, 'It's a lovely game, it's a business where we get paid for trying to bring happiness, you know, getting their chuckle-muscles working.'

The comic's appearance on the show was hailed by one Sunday newspaper critic as 'memorable' and he went on to write, 'Doddy firmly declined to be stampeded by his host into a comparison of the grimness of present-day life with the bad old days.' When asked later about the question, Doddy said, 'I think you've got to live in today's world. You can't always be looking over your shoulder at the troubles of the past. The fact is that the good old days are today.'

In that year, 1981, Doddy decided to do a new series in Manchester. His producer would be Jim Casey who had produced his first radio shows in the late Fifties. 'I was fond of Ken as a person and we got on well together,' says Casey, 'but when I worked in the 1969 series with him it was fairly traumatic for he persisted in arriving late which left little time for rehearsal.'

The new series would be recorded in the Playhouse Theatre, Manchester, with an audience and orchestra. The cast included Talfryn Thomas, Peter Wheeler and Marlene Sidaway, and the show was broadcast on Radio 2. In Jim Casey's view, Doddy had gained in confidence and was a more accomplished radio performer, although he was still a bit of a fluffer because of the speed at which he said his lines, but it didn't worry him as he knew he could always say them again.

Rehearsals began in the early afternoon and the audience was admitted three hours later. Working with people was not, the producer knew, Doddy's forte; however on his own he was a tremendous force. And he projected well on radio. Another problem quickly surfaced: the producer usually ended up with as much as a hundred minutes on tape which had to be boiled down to under a third of the length. Jim Casey revealed later that he once spent twenty-four hours editing six shows. 'It was painstaking, even exhausting work,' he says. 'I'd take a line from show five and insert it in show two and so on to make the whole thing work.'

As Bobby Jaye had discovered some years before, there was little a producer could do to change the comedian. Jim Casey recalls, 'There was really no point getting worked up. You knew he was going to be late for rehearsals, that he would overrun at recording sessions. Once when his contract specified that rehearsals would start at 12 o'clock I changed it in his case to 10.30 and he arrived just around noon. Months later he found out and as my wife Joan and I were going into a cinema in Liverpool he shouted after me, "You So-and-So, Jim". I knew it was a silly way to run a railway but it was better than having a blazing row every Sunday.'

Unlike Les Dawson, who created strong characters in his radio series, Doddy always performed as Ken Dodd and never tried to create colourful Knotty Ash characters. As Jim Casey pointed out, 'Ken talked about people in Knotty Ash but that was all. Ken was always the man with the same voice on radio, with the same kind of delivery. In other words, he didn't act. He performed as Ken Dodd.'

The producer had produced the Jimmy Clitheroe Show for years on radio, and scripted Les Dawson, but in his view Doddy was unique. Certainly he wasn't sympathetic when he found that Jim Casey had to work for long hours editing the radio series. The producer said, 'Because Ken worked almost round the clock, he could not see why others did not. Once he telephoned Eddie Braben at one o'clock in the morning from a Northern theatre and referred to a sketch he had written for him. When Eddie, who was in bed, said, "You've got it then, Ken?" the comic replied, "Yes, yes. But I want two more, Eddie." Braben was curious. "You don't mean tonight, do you?" Doddy said, "Yes . . . tonight . . . I'll pick them up on my way home through Liverpool." Braben was speechless as he heard Doddy joke, "There's no business like show business . . .".'

Losing Braben as his script writer was, in Casey's opinion, a big loss to Doddy. 'Eddie and Ken were a perfect combination. Eddie was a very creative writer and knew Ken backwards and the kind of gags that suited him. They had this tremendous rapport which used to remind me of my own rapport with my father when I was writing for him, or, in more recent years, Les Dawson.'

The present radio series had a number of people writing sketches and gags and it was considered a popular success. Doddy invariably said the opening lines, which on one occasion read:

That's what this show's all about, gaffer. We're going to be different, we're going to be outrageous. We're going to talk about things you shouldn't talk about. Things that'll shock you. But we're going to do it in a more sophisticated, mature, honest way. Subjects like: thingy and whatsit. And when two people . . . you know. Thing. But we're going to do it openly. And not be embarrassed. Because, let's face it, Missus, let's face it – everyone's got a whatsit, so we're not going to be embarrassed about it, and make up silly names, because we're ashamed to use the real word. We're not going to say whatsit – we're going to say belly button.

Despite Doddy's success on radio, Jim Casey felt that both radio and television were a compromise as far as the star was concerned – his real love was the stage. Furthermore, no one had succeeded in making him a megastar on TV. In fact, it was generally agreed that he had not up to then won the same fame on TV as he had achieved on stage and radio. 'You put Ken in television sketches,' says Casey, 'and you find there are other comics who do better sketches. You try to get him to play other characters and again other comedians can play these characters better than Ken. But none of them can beat him as a stand-up comic in front of an audience, so the only solution is to photograph his stage performance. In America it has come off with Sammy Davis Junior. It is difficult and may not come off, but in Ken's case I think it could be a success.'

Would Doddy perhaps do as a double act? The producer was emphatic. 'No, it wouldn't work because Ken is essentially a one-man band. To do radio and television he had to sacrifice some of his genius.'

That month, Doddy's name was in the news again when he received an OBE in the New Year Honours List. The people of Knotty Ash were delighted, so were his admirers in Liverpool. Doddy told the world, 'I feel full of plumptiousness and I am discumknockerated. In other words, it is a lovely feeling.' Tributes were paid to his charitable services, which included work for cancer research charities.

The honour wasn't totally unexpected. He was after all Mrs Thatcher's favourite comic: even Harold Wilson conceded that. And his politics at that time leaned towards Toryism, much to the dismay of the dockers along the Pier Head in Liverpool. It was no laughing matter to them that Doddy made the Tories laugh. And his parents? Had they not voted for the Labour Party all their lives.

Would he make the Palace ceremony on time? Inevitably, the question was asked in show business circles. To ensure that he would, the comic drove from Liverpool to London and stayed overnight in a hotel. That February morning in 1982 he rose early, and thought, 'What a day for visiting the Palace, and receiving an OBE from the Queen.'

For Doddy, it was a great occasion. He was nervous and somewhat uneasy. Top-hatted and wearing morning dress, he looked smart, even elegant. His hair was tidy, his teeth looked under control, and there was pride in his darting eyes. He revealed that he had left his tickling stick in his car. 'I was tempted to surprise Her Majesty, but my courage has failed me,' he quipped. 'It is just as well.' It was probably also as well that he did not drive up to the Palace in a replica of the car he owned when he first became a professional entertainer. For painted along each side was the slogan, 'Ken Dodd – The Comedian Who is Different . . .' The car turned heads everywhere because the word 'different' had been painted upside down.

He was now taking a few days' break from his stage and radio work. Apart from show business commitments, he was patron of Clatterbridge Cancer Trust, the Pat Seed Fund, the North Staffordshire Scanner Fund and various theatre trusts.

Outside Buckingham Palace, he told a reporter that he was petrified at the prospect of meeting the Queen, but he was tickled by the honour. Eventually, as he stood before the Queen to receive the OBE, he looked serious and genuinely moved by the occasion. Among the other recipients were Dan Air hostess Elizabeth Coen and Captain Jonathan Dalrymple-Smith, heroes of the Shetland air crash in July 1979.

A more relaxed Doddy remarked afterwards, 'Oh, yes, I was on time for Her Majesty. I mean, no one is allowed to be late for the Queen.' For years he had made no secret of his extreme patriotism. Whenever he was asked about it, he invariably replied, 'Yes, I am a patriotic man. I love my country. I love England. I think it is the best country in the world. No country is quite like it in the rest of the world. I am a very proud man to have got the OBE.'

But he had his eccentric side. Every year the compilers of *Who's Who* asked the comic to notify them of his date of birth and just as regularly he ignored their request. 'I don't want to be a veteran,' he said, claiming to feel thirty-five. 'I'm a young man and I'm in love with show business.' In the thirty years since his Nottingham début, he had missed only one night through illness. 'Mind you,' he quipped, 'I've been on with bronchitis, enteritis, Montezuma's Revenge and a sprained ankle. Funny thing is, the moment I hear the music I feel like a racehorse when the tapes go up. All of a sudden, the pain goes and my mind focuses on just one thing.'

He admitted he was in love with Sybie Jones, although he dismissed speculation about a possible marriage. The folks of Knotty Ash had agreed a decade before that he was not the marrying kind and their belief was reaffirmed when the comic repeatedly told the media, 'I'm in love with show business.'

In 1984 Doddy celebrated his thirtieth year in showbiz. It was a landmark in his career. He spent that summer making a grand tour of seaside resorts, travelling as usual with his dog Doodle, a large black poodle. And he was still driving himself to venues in a Ford Granada Estate with a bundle of stage costumes in the back seat. Sometimes he made the theatre with only a minute to spare. 'It is true that I have come straight from the car to the stage on occasions,' he confessed. 'But I think time is a tyrant. It has to be obeyed, but it tries to rule us with a rod of iron. I object to that and when people say my shows overrun I say, "What is wrong with giving an audience a bonus?" '

He had a lot of imagination, he said, a slight touch of anarchy, and the sort of mind which wanted to turn the world upside down. In many ways he didn't want change for the sake of change, but because he was subjected to so much change – places, people, situations – he wanted a rock to cling to. As he said, 'I like solidarity around me and I know I have to have it.'

He was now considered a workaholic and when asked why, after thirty years in the business he still worked non-stop, his reply was simple, 'I am still stage-struck. There is nothing that can equal making people laugh.' He regretted, though that there were so few really funny people around the entertainment scene. As he explained, 'Benny Hill's jokes are either denigrating about ugly women or put beautiful women in embarrassing situations. Then you've got the people whose material is sensational and vulgar, like Billy Connolly and Jim Davidson. I don't believe that's very clever, either.'

Certainly it was hard to imagine Doddy's act punctuated with direct-to-audience shouts like 'Any poofs in tonight?' Or him saying off-stage, 'I get fun out of the old right-wing stuff on stage because it's the really wrong thing to say, isn't it? Like you go out with a girl who is a veggie and drives a Citroën and when the waiter comes along you order "freshly clubbed seal".' By now there was a distinct danger of comedians being divided into *Us* and *Them*: the Ken Dodds as opposed to the Jim Davidsons.

The alternative comedians' philosophy seemed to be encapsulated in the words of George Orwell: 'The aim of a joke is not to degrade the human being but to remind him that he is already degraded.' At times open hostility was noticeable between the *Us* and *Them*, as though the former were telling the latter, 'You're letting down the business. You're degrading comedy by your vulgarities.' *Them* would probably tell *Us*: You're envious of our success. You're behind the times. You're living in the Forties and Fifties.'

Doddy's reply to that would probably be, 'Rubbish.

You're not creative.' It had become an unedifying scene. After thirty years in the business, he had few real regrets. Occasionally he talked about foreign travel and admitted he had not gone abroad on holiday until the early Seventies. Now he says, 'I wish I'd known at eighteen the thrill and excitement of travelling. I think everybody should travel. It should be compulsory. It's only when you go abroad you realise what a wonderful country this is. Now I could live anywhere in the world, but I'd never leave Knotty Ash. I still live in the house where I was born.'

It wasn't nostalgia that made him reflect on his past, rather a sense of belonging, an urge to recapture the happiness of his early years. 'My childhood was very happy,' he says. 'I spent most of my time in the fields and woods around Knotty Ash digging holes, swinging from trees and lighting fires.'

He agreed he learned by his mistakes. And on his office desk he has the inscription 'The man who never made a mistake never made anything.' He was still hooked on show business and saw himself as a travelling salesman for comedy. As he said, 'I travel 55,000 miles a year by car between shows. To keep the shows fresh I put in about six new gags a night.'

He had still a lot of travelling to do before he had fulfilled his ambition of playing all the country's theatres.

CHAPTER 21

'I Shall Try to Be Honest'

On a humid July day in 1987 Doddy arrived at Broadcasting House, Portland Place, and was met by producer Michael Ember who accompanied him to a studio in the basement. Awaiting him was Dr Anthony Clare, presenter of the Radio Four series *In the Psychiatrist's Chair*. The two men shook hands and chatted for a while before the start of the recording session.

Dr Clare, determined and urbane, had been interviewing celebrities for the series since 1982 and liked to say, 'I don't choose people I don't want to interview.' Spike Milligan figured on the first series and admitted to the psychiatrist that he was a manic-depressive. 'I had no difficulty with him,' recalls Dr Clare. 'I understood his humour; it was infectious, punning, rhyming.'

Later he talked to controversial cricket star Geoffrey Boycott, and it was, on his own admission, 'confrontational', the direct opposite of Dame Janet Baker's which turned out to be gentle and revealing about her life as a singer. He had never seen Doddy on stage, although he had seen his television shows and heard his radio programmes. Since he had decided to talk to him, he had read up a great deal about his career and discussed him with BBC producers who had worked with him.

Now, as he sat at the circular table in the studio with the star sitting at an angle to him, there were a few things that particularly interested him about Kenneth Arthur Dodd, who had once been described to him as the Squire of Knotty Ash. He felt that other things he was expecting would surface in the course of the interview.

To most people who knew him, particularly the press, Doddy's presence in the studio would be viewed as a surprise. Regarded as a 'very private person' off-stage, he had refused up till then to discuss his love-life, except to say that he had not married due to lack of time. Now, here he was, prepared to face an experienced psychiatrist and broadcaster who would undoubtedly ask some personal questions. Where had he invested his money? Was he as wealthy as people believed he was? Had he serious regrets about his career?

The irony of the situation would not be lost on the citizens of Knotty Ash who occasionally wondered what the private Doddy was really like. The Liverpool press corps, who had always been loyal to him, might be forgiven for asking why he had not given them the interview before he decided to face a psychiatrist. However, it would hardly affect their good relations with the star.

When first invited on the programme, Doddy did not show any reluctance to accept, which in itself seemed in his case a volte-face. He was even cheerful as he faced Dr Clare, who had already gained a reputation for conducting searching and incisive interviews. His style was forceful, his attack direct. At the outset he asked the comedian how he felt talking about himself. Doddy replied unhesitatingly that he was delighted, or, to coin a phrase, he was full of plumptiousness and feeling, in fact, completely discomknockerated because of the invitation. He wondered what he would say and how he should approach the interview. A lot of people were frank, very blunt, and tried to be really honest. At other times one's mind was ticking over and you said you knew this would sound good if you said it, so he decided to try a mixture of both, 'I shall try to be honest,' he told himself.

Dr Clare would say that the aim of the programme was explicit. 'It's an interview with someone who is a psychiatrist and therefore is interested in motives and influences and early experience, as well as attitudes and feelings. I treat the person I interview as a subject and not as a patient.' Up to then he had interviewed about forty people and enjoyed the exercise.

When he asked Doddy, for instance, if he accepted the general view that he was a private person, the star said it was true. At the same time he admitted he sometimes liked to show off and he had opinions about which he was quite prepared to stand on his little soap-box and let fly. They discussed the psychology of humour, but as Dr Clare said later, he was not all that interested in the comedian's theories on the subject. 'I found that when people talked theoretically about acting or politics, it was a way of keeping me at bay. I sensed that Doddy wanted to theorise.'

He listened as the comic traced his life in Knotty Ash up to the time he joined the professional ranks. As he said, 'When I became a pro I wanted to know more about humour and what made people laugh. I visited libraries and looked up the word laughter: comedy, comedian, comic, clown. I had been the sort of boy who used to read avidly, particularly adventure books. I wanted life to be an adventure. I wanted to be an explorer, a pioneer.'

He was relaxed as he reminisced about his happy child-hood, and his parents. The funniest man he ever knew, he said, was Arthur Dodd, his father; he was a brilliant clown and knew great stories. 'I still tell stories now, jokes that he told me.' When he was asked what he was like at the age of eight, he replied that he was 'quite shy and quite meek'. He believed, though, that everyone was born with a spirit of play in them, but that as various pressures arose and you grew older, people tended to inhibit that spirit of play. They might be school-teachers or rates officers. But like most people who were comedy-minded, discipline came very hard, very difficult to accept.

Dr Clare: 'In your case, what sort of discipline?'

Doddy: 'I don't take kindly to it, although I know a lot of it is for my good. Even at school I'm afraid I was always in trouble.'

Dr Clare: 'Were you? How would this show up in your personal characteristics? Does it mean that you're less constrained by things like this?'

Doddy: 'Ah, that was very tactful of you (laugh). Oh, I thought you'd heard about me. I'm not the most punctual person in the world.'

The interview was assuming a certain pattern. Dr Clare had exposed one of the star's failings – lack of punctuality. For a time the conversation became dull as they discussed Freud's theory of humour and this prompted Doddy to say, 'I think a lot of the problem when philosophers and psychologists and psychiatrists try to explain humour is that they will treat it as one formula, whereas you wouldn't expect to explain music with one pat formula.'

Dr Clare asked if he reacted like most other people in the event of a personal bereavement or an emotional set-back? The star's voice softened as he replied, 'I remember when my mother passed away I was dreading it, but it was totally different to what one would expect.' When he was asked in what way, he said, 'I knew that I was being helped because I didn't fall into this tremendous trough of despair. I didn't go to pieces. I felt some strength come from somewhere.'

In the course of his research, Dr Clare had come across references to Doddy's religious beliefs, and it was an aspect of his life which he regarded as interesting. Was he a spiritual person? What influence had religion on his life?

Dr Clare: 'You say your strength came from somewhere . . . I mean, where do you draw your strength from?'

241

Doddy: 'I don't know. I don't know where this strength came from. I have an idea but . . .'

Dr Clare: 'You're referring to some kind of religious source of support?'

Doddy: 'I think so, yes.'

At this point a slightly mysterious air was introduced into the conversation. Dr Clare asked, 'How religious are you? Are you a very religious man?'

Doddy's answer seemed frank, 'Yes, I think so. I try to have a conversation with my Maker. I find it difficult to find some religious service relevant to our world of 1987. I find them a little bit medieval and therefore make up my own conversations. And I pray.'

There was a hint of emotion in his voice when he answered Dr Clare's next question. 'When your mother died, was that source of support even stronger than anything that went before?'

'It was very strong, and I was able to go on and do my next show. I remember it was a very good show. It was so good that at the end I was really moved to tears. And in taking the applause I was crying with – I don't know, perhaps relief, joy. I knew the audience was there with me.'

Dr Clare: 'So you're saying in a sense that on stage, doing what you do, you were able to in someway – not exercise – but express your grief?'

Doddy: 'No, I think I was helped. Yes, I think I was helped directly.'

Dr Clare: 'Directly helped?'

Doddy: 'Yes, I'm not a spiritualist.'

Dr Clare: 'This would be an assistance from God Himself or . . . ?'

Doddy: 'I don't know.'

Since the series began, Dr Clare had been asked if he found an aura of stardom or an aura of power around some of the people he interviewed. The question tended to amuse him. As he joked, 'The basement in Broadcasting House is a great leveller.' And he added, 'I did not feel in Ken Dodd's case any aura of stardom mainly because I wasn't looking for it. It was different in the case of Sir Michael Tippett, the grand old man of British music. I suppose there was something about him. The dignity of age was one thing.'

The question of stardom in Doddy's case was relevant. By now it was clear that international stardom and the resultant fame had somehow eluded him, although he would say, 'I really set out to be an international star, oh yes.' It was never enough, it seemed in his mind, to be recognised as England's undisputed Clown Prince of Comedy; he wanted to be accepted overseas, in films, as a TV comic, as a stand-up comic of universal appeal.

Liverpool Echo journalist Joe Riley, an admirer of Doddy's talent, felt that the comedian's stage act would not travel to America, for instance, simply because it wasn't exportable. And someone else argued, 'How could they be expected to unravel the mysteries of chuckle-muscles, tickling sticks and diddymen?' However, theatre manager, Dick Condon believes that Doddy's humour is universal. 'I think that if he had seriously gone after international fame he would have achieved it. Perhaps he should have tried his luck in America and Australia in the Sixties when he was at the height of his career.' Eric Midwinter said there was a glitter about Doddy that could well have appealed to international audiences.

In the late Seventies, the critic Michael Billington wondered where the 'great man' would go from there and thought it was anybody's guess. He was confident, though, it was forward because of the shrewd way Doddy had managed his career. Yet, while he could visualise him at the top of his profession for another twenty years, he did not refer to his success in an international context. In fact, he never discussed that important aspect of the star's career, except to say, 'Comedy to him is not simply a profession, it is a reflex instinct, a necessity, a burning unassuageable passion. And while he talks of having more time to devote to such hobbies as painting and breeding dogs, he admitted he envied comics like Benny and Hope who managed to make two or three salient characteristics last a lifetime. None the less, one cannot easily see him slowing down the tempo either of his life or his act. He is too manic, too fervent, too irresistibly funny.'

It could be argued that Doddy became so engrossed in the British comedy scene that he had neither the time nor the energy to concentrate solely on achieving an international breakthrough. Nor was it clear whether he had the supreme confidence needed to emulate a Benny or Hope. No matter how hard he tried on TV, he still gave the impression that theatre was his forte, and was perhaps his only love. Unlike Bob Hope, he had not attracted major film companies, so was not given the opportunity to achieve screen fame. Up to now even his television series did not seem to be 'exportable'. It was the reverse in the case of Hancock, who, as Harry Secombe claims, was never completely happy in the variety theatre. 'The strain of doing the same performance night after night and trying to invest it with an apparent spontaneity was more than Tony could bear,' Secombe said. 'His timing and delivery were never better than when he was doing something fresh – creating and not re-creating. That was why he took to TV so well.'

Not that the Americans had entirely ignored Doddy's talent. Once, after his appearance in a Royal Variety Show, a New York critic described him as a 'surrealistic monologist'. Doddy was tickled. He knew it was not the type of description that would ever sell tickets for a show in Las Vegas. Whimsy, rather than surrealism, he thinks is the line he walks.

This morning, talking to Dr Clare, he did not express any

Hair-raising news:
Ken Dodd is declared the Show Business Personality of 1965.
(Press Association)

The Show Business Personality of the Year (1965)
with fellow award winners *(from left to right)*
Michael Miles, Benny Hill, Dorothy Tutin and Hughie Green.
(Press Association)

Ken with Bluebell girls Gillian Elwins *(left)* and Paula Harvey.
The Bluebells formed part of his 1967 Palladium show.
(Press Association)

As Malvolio in *Twelfth Night*.
The critics were impressed.
(Liverpool Daily Post & Echo)

Dodd is tickled by a fan lett
from Margaret Thatcher congratulating hi
on his 1978 Christmas Show at Liverpool
re-opened Royal Court theatr
(Liverpool Daily Post & Ech

Prime Minister Thatcher (with her own tickling stick)
meets Dodd during his season at
the Palladium in the early 1980s.
(Press Association)

Top – The new love in
his life, showgirl
Sybil Jones.
(Liverpool Daily Post & Echo)

Right – Taking swimming
lessons in Bournemouth
from cross-channel
swimmer Bill Pickering.
(Press Association)

Left – Something to
smile about:
with tickling stick and
his OBE, awarded in 1982.
(Express Newspapers)

Ken remains cheerful after the preliminary court
hearing into alleged tax evasion in 1988.
(Liverpool Daily Post & Echo)

real regret about missing out on international fame and the psychiatrist did not pursue the matter. He did suggest to the star that in his view the life of a stand-up comic was a strikingly solitary one, to which Doddy replied with infectious enthusiasm, 'Being a comedian is a wonderful experience. I don't know what it is, but there certainly is some kind of magic that happens and transforms you from being a very ordinary person like me. On stage, I feel twenty-feet tall because the audience are all laughing away and their eyes are shining and they want to applaud. I really feel great. It's a wonderful experience.'

When asked if it was the best experience, he replied that he could not be sure as life was full of joyful experiences. 'I mean you can get a high in your life just walking through a garden and seeing all the beautiful flowers, and particularly if it has just been raining and it can actually make you almost kneel in ecstasy.'

In the quietness of the studio the conversation seemed easy, natural. Doddy was fluent and spoke briskly. Suddenly, he remarked, 'I wish I had a lot more confidence. I wish I wasn't so terrified sometimes when I did a big show like the Royal Variety Show; that really separates the men from the boys, and I'm one of the boys.'

It was true. Fellow stars had often noted Doddy's nervous approach to the show and tried to soothe him. They noticed how he freely perspired, causing him to change his shirt more than once before he went on stage. Sometimes this nervousness was exacerbated on stage when something went wrong. At one particular Royal Variety Show he was obliged to follow a sketch that had cast a chill over the proceedings. Soon, he discovered to his dismay, he was getting no feedback from the audience whatsoever. As he told Michael Billington, 'All of a sudden a rod of steel entered my body and I thought, "You b—s. How dare you do this to me. I've been nearly twenty years in this profession, I've given my life to this profession. You're not going to do it." I brought every bit of courage from every corner of my body and every bit of skill I had acquired in Blackpool and Bournemouth and Scarborough and I thought, I'll beat you or you'll have to come and shoot me before I get off.'

To the *Guardian* critic, it was the difference between the comic of real genius and the mere coasting joke-vendor. To Harry Secombe it was an attribute every comic needed. 'He must have a certain mental toughness, a quick wit, the ability to shrug off a bad reception, and at the same time possess the sensitivity to be aware immediately of the mood of his audience. Two options are open to him – either he gives them what he wants or he provides them with what they want.'

Off-stage it was another matter with Doddy. He was prepared to discuss most subjects and this morning with Dr Clare he listened carefully as the psychiatrist reminded him that once he had talked about 'man's delight in women, women's contempt for men'. He said he was intrigued by the remark as it seemed to suggest Don McGill postcards and so on.

Doddy explained that man's delight with ladies was a wonderful thing. 'I mean ladies are so beautiful and so marvellous and wonderful.' Dr Clare , who has a sceptical side to his nature, did not seem at that moment impressed by superlatives.

Dr Clare: 'Why did you never marry one?'

It was the kind of question that begged an answer. Again, in his research, the psychiatrist had come across references to the women in Doddy's life and the people who tried to find the answers as to why the star never married.

Doddy: 'To be honest with you, I was, as you know, engaged for a long time, but I know it sounds amazing but we were too busy to wed. Every television series that came along, every stage show, posed for us a fresh set of emotional challenges.'

Dr Clare: 'You're talking about your fiancée, Anita Boutin. Did she want to get married?'

Doddy: 'Yes, yes. It was quite normal, you know, but I mean everything was normal but (laugh) . . .'

Dr Clare: 'You never did?'

Doddy: 'We were always too busy.'

Dr Clare: 'Your engagement – it lasted for a long time?'

Doddy: 'Oh, quite a while, quite a long time.'

Clearly, Dr Clare was not entirely satisfied with the star's explanation about not finding time for marriage. There was a hint of frustration in his voice, as if he felt he was not getting the complete answer. But he listened politely as Doddy continued, 'Many a lady saying caustic things about her husband can still love him – as many wives do – but they can't help firing off an occasional salvo now and again.

Dr Clare: 'Was that something that worried you?'

Doddy: 'Oh, I noticed.'

Dr Clare: 'I mean were you worried that that's what would become of a relationship?'

Doddy: 'Oh, no. I deserve to be hammered now and again. We're terrible to ladies, it's a man's world, isn't it?'

Dr Clare: 'I don't know. I'm asking you.'

Obviously, Doddy was enjoying himself talking about women and agreed that at times they got on his nerves because they had this natural ability to give you hell if they wanted something, even a shelf put up or a garden dug. 'By Jove, they know all the weak spots.'

He had still not answered Dr Clare's question about why he had not married. Maybe the psychiatrist intended to answer it for him later.

CHAPTER 22

'He is a very secretive man'

It was noticeable that the longer the interview lasted in the warm confines of the basement studio, the more restive Doddy seemed to become. The atmosphere inhibited his flamboyant style, giving the impression that he was introspective, even humourless. The Squire of Knotty Ash could be forgiven for thinking he had wandered into the wrong studio. What would his fans think of this inquisition?

Dr Anthony Clare and Kenneth Arthur Dodd had little in common. Politically, the doctor had become disenchanted with Mrs Thatcher's 'predictable' Britain; Doddy, on the other hand, retained his admiration for the Prime Minister. He had in his possession a fan letter, on 10 Downing Street paper, congratulating him on his achievement in re-opening Liverpool's Royal Court Theatre and noting his 'entreprenurial initiative' and adding that Liverpool was one of the first champions of free enterprise.

Dr Clare enjoyed success as a media psychiatrist, Doddy was happiest dispensing humour as a tonic. Dr Clare tended to take himself seriously and lacked Celtic wit, Doddy, while he avoided the jester's image off-stage, could be funny in the company of fellow comedians as Frank Carson could verify. They each viewed the world through different lenses, and today in the studio the difference was marked, prompting the question of whether the comic was wise to accept producer Michael Ember's invitation to come on the programme.

Doddy was better acquainted with the exciting show business world, which though a jungle, thrilled him beyond words. It was a world he cherished and for him was filled with memories. There was the occasion, for instance, when he performed for the royal household's private Christmas party at Windsor Castle. The Queen and all the Royal Family sat round in a semi-circle, less than five or six feet away, and as he sang *Happiness* Her Majesty tapped the arm of her chair in time with the song.

'I chose my material to suit the occasion,' Doddy recalls. 'I looked around in this big hall where we were doing the show, and I saw these big oil paintings. "This is very nice," I joked, "but wouldn't you have thought with a photographer in the family that they would have had real snaps?"'

Looking at the comic now, seated at the studio table and talking cautiously into the 'mike', it was hard to associate him with glittering Royal Variety Show occasions. On his own admission, they usually made him very nervous. There was the occasion when the Town Clerk in Liverpool sent for him and said could he give him some advice because the Queen was going to open the Mersey Tunnel and the Corporation wished to put on a show in the Philharmonic Hall. Doddy told the man that in his opinion the Philharmonic Hall wasn't the place for it because it didn't lend itself to a variety show.

'At the gaffer's request,' he says,' on behalf of Liverpool I got in touch with Bernard Delfont and asked him if he would lend us the Empire Theatre and if they'd buy the rights of the show for television, thereby giving the Corporation some money to put the thing on. Delfont agreed and it went off very well. But I think I was more nervous in that Royal Variety Show, being in my home town, than I was in the others.'

Despite the impression that Doddy did not socialise

249

with show business people, and wasn't a gregarious person, the comic denied this was the case. 'I am a fan of showbiz people,' he said, 'and when I meet people I've always wanted to meet I get all excited and tattiphilarious.' Although some radio and TV producers felt that the comedian suffered from an inferiority complex in the company of top stars, Doddy was quick to point out that he was quite at home entertaining Bing Crosby, Bob Hope, Jack Benny and Sir Michael Redgrave in his dressing-room. He was at a loss to know how such an impression had got abroad.

Today in the studio, Dr Clare treated him as an entertainer and made no fuss about him. This was as Doddy wanted it. The psychiatrist always tried to put his subjects on the programme at their ease. From his research he knew that from an early age Ken Dodd's ambition was to be an entertainer, and now he heard him say, 'I wanted to be a star, I love being a star. I love being a comedian. I love being Ken Dodd.'

It was obvious by now that it was not going to be an amusing interview with Doddy retailing vintage Knotty Ash gags. The comic liked to remind people that it was not his job to be funny off-stage. As he said, 'I remind them about a Music Hall comedian who summed up the whole situation. He told one fan, "Hey, sir, if I were a brickie would you expect me to lay a brick?" '

Dr Clare would say that he had nothing against the comic being funny on the programme, yet at no stage did he encourage this; instead, he hoped to take Doddy along avenues new to radio listeners, to ascertain his attitude towards money, family life, marriage, comedy and success. The comedian, he noted, had a curious outlook on holidays. It was true, in the early days, Doddy proclaimed that the Costa Brava did not interest him. As he joked, 'I prefer standing on the banks of the Costa Mersey, listening to the dockers knocking off – knocking off rolls of lino and tins of paint.' Now he admitted he took more holidays in the sun and went to places like Venice and Majorca and when the weather was bad spent most of the time eating. In his view there were two kinds of holiday: one where you relaxed and tried to recharge your batteries, and the other where you needed a holiday for the mind and so visited cities such as Vienna, or Berlin, or Paris and worked your way around them.

It was no secret that Doddy regarded his work as a therapeutic exercise, and he rarely, if ever, turned down engagements, particularly when they presented fresh challenges. There was his role in *Doctor Who* . . . of which he said he was 'discomknockerated' when they asked him to appear in the TV series. 'I had always been an avid sci-fan, and the Doctor was one of my idols. Like all ham actors I was trying to build up the part. I had even offered to dust the Tardis if it meant a bigger part. And my death scene promised to be one of the longest ever.'

Playing the friendly clock repairer cum-detective in the 'death' scene was actor Don Henderson, who quipped,' I will be known as the man who killed Ken Dodd rather than Bulman.' Doddy reflected, 'It was my big acting break. I was thrilled.'

In conversation with Dr Clare, the comic got no opportunity to recall his big stage and radio successes, nor the stars he met. Listeners must have felt cheated. The psychiatrist was more determined to present the man behind the mask – and he was succeeding. He suggested to Doddy that he could be stubborn and that this affected his relations with show business directors. Doddy replied, 'In TV, and on stage, you find that the trouble with producers is that they will produce, they can't leave it alone. And the trouble with producers of a light entertainment show, whether it's on stage or TV, they have to get their four pen'orth, even nine pen'orth; they want the feathers and the spangles and they won't let the people who've been booked to juggle and be funny get on with it; they obscure it with lights and mirrors and smoke bombs and. . . .'

Dr Clare did not accept everything he was told. When Doddy talked of his own 'ordinariness' he was not impressed. With a wry smile, he said, 'You're not *that* ordinary . . . I mean, your hair, your teeth, your flow of comic language . . . they are unusual and out of the ordinary, aren't they?' It was the cue for the comedian to reveal the truth about his bushy hair: 'I was too busy to have my hair cut, to be honest with you.'

Plainly the psychiatrist was intrigued by the simplicity of the answer; he was sceptical too. 'You know that is the second time you've used *too busy* as an explanation for why you didn't do something,' he reminded Doddy. 'What it really means to me is that if you're too busy to do something, it really is relatively low on your list of priorities.'

This seemed to answer Dr Clare's earlier question as to why the comedian had not married. He could only assume that marriage to Anita Boutin was not a top priority with him, Doddy though was quick to reply, 'Oh, no, I don't think that's correct. No, it wasn't necessary for me to have my hair cut and it wasn't necessary for me to marry.'

Dr Clare was somewhat relieved. He had been warned by people in the BBC and elsewhere that Ken Dodd could be very unforthcoming and 'not to expect too much from the interview'. Nevertheless, the psychiatrist felt confident that he could get answers to most of the questions he asked. The comic, in his view, was reasonably co-operative, although he did get the impression occasionally that perhaps Doddy would be happier talking about pantomime or famous comics of the Music Hall than about his own private life. In this respect, he was no different from other entertainers who seemed reassured discussing their stage or television successes.

However, as he listened carefully today to what the comic had to say about his life and his problems, he decided the interview was worthwhile. 'I wouldn't have considered him for the programme if I didn't believe he was worth having,' said the psychiatrist.

It was true that the comedian had never spoken to anyone so frankly before. The direct and persuasive Dr Clare had succeeded where others had failed, probably because they were put off by Doddy's reputation of being reluctant to discuss his private life. The broadcaster admitted subsequently that people had written to the BBC about his questioning of the comic as to why he had not married. As he recalled, 'They wondered why I kept on about it and if it was really necessary to do so. Of course I thought it was worth pursuing in the context of Ken Dodd's life and career and I'm satisfied that I found the answer as to why he didn't marry. I had also heard how unpunctual he could be, so that was worth raising. I had been told also that he was thrifty and I accepted this to be true.'

They had, by now, been talking for almost an hour, but the tape was later edited down to thirty-five minutes. Dr Clare felt he had covered most of the ground and he did not doubt the comedian when he told him, 'I have a lady now whom I love very much.' He was referring to Sybie Jones, who was now sharing the same stage in all of his theatre shows. But he was guarded about their relationship and did not wish to elaborate.

A few lighter moments arose in their conversation, as when the psychiatrist remarked with a smile, 'Are you difficult to live with?' Doddy replied without hesitation, 'I don't think so, no. Like most people, I have my funny little ways (laugh). I'm very untidy. I'm a hoarder of things . . . newspapers, magazines.' When asked if he had any regrets about life, Doddy laughed and said, 'I've regretted there's not more of it, yes. I'm looking forward to (laugh) . . . I want to be shot by a jealous husband at the age of a hundred and twenty.'

Eighteen months later Dr Clare, who had returned to

Dublin to take up an important new hospital post, recalled the interview with Doddy and claimed he found it as enjoyable as any of the others in the series. He has a loyalty towards the people he interviews. During the conversation with the comic he concluded that he was very close to his mother, who was evidently a formidable influence in his life, in fact, *the* most formidable influence.

He thought that the interview had got 'bogged down' early on when he raised the question with the comedian as to why he did not marry. However, when he returned to the subject, he saw the issue more clearly. It was undeniably a question of priorities. As he said now, 'I think we find time for the things we want to do. When Ken Dodd stated that he couldn't find the time to marry Anita, to me it was just another way of saying that marriage wasn't high in his priorities. It's a situation I have met before and one can appreciate why it can happen.'

Prior to the interview, he had been told that the comic was not only a private person but a very secretive man. This he now believed to be true.

'I also got the impression,' he says 'that while Doddy lays great emphasis on communication with his audience, one aspect of his humour works against this, for it is quick-fire humour that keeps people at bay; it overwhelms them; if anything, the audience laughs in astonishment and not in the same way as they would react to Hancock comedy. Hancock used his own internal suffering to forge a relationship with an audience and was what I call psychological humour. In contrast, the audience doesn't enter into a relationship with Doddy; it is distanced from him and it's his way of ensuring that it is under his control.'

The BBC chiefs, it was claimed, were pleased by the listeners' response to *In the Psychiatrist's Chair* and regarded Dr Clare as a searching interviewer who pulled no punches no matter who his subject happened to be. For the psychiatrist, Doddy did not match up to some of his previous subjects. As he said, 'Occasionally he was wary and inclined to dodge certain questions. Looking back, I feel the interview fell into a pattern; I was pursuing and he was keeping me at bay. Other interviews in the series were more mutual events where we were examining material together. Every one of us has something to hide and this is true of Ken Dodd. He is thrifty and this is because money loomed large in his early life; you find that people rarely admit they are thrifty, but in Dodd's case it is a recurring theme. Thriftiness of course can be an indicator of insecurity. Lack of money in early life can frighten you later on with the result that you never take a spending view of life. If anything, you over-value money.'

When he was asked if he would mind going on a long train journey with Doddy, Dr Clare said, 'This is not the type of question I'd care to answer. I will say, though, that in my forty interviews for *In the Psychiatrist's Chair* I never found any of the subjects boring. We choose these people very carefully. Yes, I think I would be prepared to go on a long train journey with any of them, including Ken Dodd.'

Doddy, for his part, confided in friends that he regarded the programme as somewhat of an ordeal, and nobody cared to ask the amiable comic if he would be prepared to share a train compartment with the psychiatrist. Generally the interview attracted a good deal of newspaper attention and was regarded as a 'telling insight into the comedian's life'. Some colleagues found the whole thing 'too solemn and serious' and wished that Doddy had been allowed to retail some of his best Knotty Ash gags.

The interview with Dr Clare had another curious effect on Doddy. After years of silence on more private aspects of his life, he began to agree to interviews with magazines, as though his confession with the psychiatrist had opened his mind. In May, 1988, when he was interviewed for a woman's magazine, he commented, 'I would still like to have children, it would be absolutely marvellous. It's one of my regrets that having put so much into show business I look back now and wonder where all those years went, and I never had kids.'

At this time he was described as a 'cheerful and a happy sort of person and blessed with a sense of optimism' and sometimes in the course of an interview his humour surfaced, as when he stated, 'Someone once asked me if I was gay, but there's no chance of that. After all, I lived with a lady called Anita Boutin until she died tragically eleven years ago.' However, that was all in the past; he wanted now to get on with his life. He was sixty years of age and to some writers and friends he had lost none of his charm, although Doddy quipped, 'Make me fifty-seven, or better still, put me in my mid-forties, will you? Oh, I wish I were twenty-five again. It was a marvellous age sexually. I had such energy. It was wonderful having all those women buzzing around me.'

It sounded like a proud boast, yet there were people who could not confirm whether the zany comic was ever considered a Romeo in Knotty Ash, nor did they dare hazard a guess at the number of his conquests. But Doddy, on his own admission, liked having women around him. As he said joyfully, 'I love women. I always have, I think they're absolutely marvellous. I particularly like the company of clever and articulate women; I like women who are so clever they let you think that you're clever. That's one of the reasons why I couldn't bear to live on my own. I love having them around.'

To most women, at that time, he exuded an unmistakable warmth. 'There have always been women in my life,' he said in a way which left no room for debate. In restaurants, he loved chatting up women, signing autographs, and telling them how smashing they were. Paradoxically, as Britain's unlikeliest sex symbol, he had his admirers and the women certainly loved him. Even now, after years in the business, he always carried a photograph of himself ready to sign for a pretty woman. At his shows women clamoured at the front of the stage, and later jostled around the stage door. And Doddy adored it. He lived for the adulation that show business afforded him, not that his ego matched that of other more arrogant stars.

It was the laughter – he made them laugh, he made them happy. To most people, Doddy was a cheerful, happy sort of person, and an intelligent conversationalist, and yet he rarely dropped his guard completely. In the middle of his main course he might backcomb his hair with his fingers, so he looked like an irate hedgehog, and with a broad grin on his face, remark, 'My family life is a very personal world, it's something that I treasure and keep to myself. The public are entitled to know I sleep in bed with my socks on, which I do when the weather's cold, but otherwise I'm not obliged to tell them what's in my bank account!'

However, unknown to his admirers, a problem was looming for the Squire of Knotty Ash. Soon he would be facing a court hearing about alleged tax arrears. When the story eventually broke in the newspapers it created much the same sensation as the case involving Lester Piggott. For the Prince of Comedy, it was no laughing matter. But as the months passed he looked as though he was bearing up well to the trauma. As Cyril Critchlow, his magician friend in Blackpool, sadly remarked, 'The waiting is the worst.'

CHAPTER 23

'I've Done Every Panto Known To Man'

Early in December 1988, Doddy arrived in Halifax accompanied by his poodle – Doodle – but without his friendly cat which he had left behind in Doddy Towers. He was due to star in the pantomime, *Puss In Boots*, at the town's Civic Theatre and after rehearsals each day made the arduous road journey back to Liverpool. His decision to choose Halifax for his big Christmas engagement was regarded with surprise in the business, and in Halifax his presence sparked off some quiet discussion about his tax dilemma, although the locals were discreet and did not bother either Doddy or his girlfriend, Sybie Jones.

If he had wanted an ideal place to get away from the glare of publicity that his impending court appearance was attracting, he could not have made a better choice. Halifax is a friendly town tucked away snugly in the shadow of the towering Pennine mountain range with a reputation for producing sturdy Rugby league players. Although it has a diminishing number of theatres, the older generation can recall famous variety artistes topping the bill, and Halifax is the birthplace of Wilfred Pickles.

It was however too much to expect that one of the best-loved entertainers in the country could entirely escape the spotlight. In fact, he never really tried. Occasionally on stage he joked about the Inland Revenue and he was aware that his fellow comedians used him as the butt of their tax gags. But Doddy quickly made it clear on arrival that there would be 'no tears for souvenirs' during the four-week run of the pantomime.

One particular journalist decided to raise the question because, as he said later, it was impossible to ignore it. Doddy was obviously expecting it, and snapped, 'That's next year . . . meanwhile this is a happy show and I've got a job to do. I'm an entertainer who deals in happiness and the main thing is I'm here. Here to do the best panto-mime of my life. And that's what I'm going to do.'

The journalist did not refer again to the tax case. It was closed with an assurance from Doddy that there would be no Inland Revenue jokes in *Puss In Boots*, just as there would be no blue material. He said this with unusual conviction, as though anxious that it should be conveyed to the people of Halifax. As he said, 'It was a matter of pride in my school of comedy – and my idols were Sandy Powell, Jimmy James and Rob Wilton – that you don't have to go for cheap laughs. If you are a professional and proud of what you do on stage, as I am, you do the best you can for the people who pay the great compliment of coming to see you perform.'

Doddy went out of his way to make himself available to the show business columnists from Halifax and Leeds. He preferred to keep Sybie Jones in the background, though they were seen constantly together. He never pre-tended to be a sex symbol, but he has the ability to make people like him and he quickly became liked by the press. He was in irrepressible mood as he regaled them in the bar of the Civic Theatre, reminding them about the advice his father gave him. 'He said to me that if I was going to go on stage I had to have an act that was original.' Doddy talked proudly about his childhood in Knotty Ash. 'I'd clown around, burlesquing songs people knew. Clowning was all I thought I could do. Later, I became utterly obsessed with comedy. I totally love it. Comedy is a beautiful thing, a beautiful spirit. It's like a beautiful woman.'

To the press corps, Doddy seemed indestructible. He laughed as he said he felt half his age and how he enormously enjoyed the day-to-day challenge of being alive. They found his style personable, his smile warm and in their eyes he was a likeable bloke. As always, he enjoyed an audience, but at no time was he trying to put across a dual personality. The image that people saw was basically the man himself. He retailed a few funny stories, yet he was not deliberately trying to be funny. Physically, except for the odd wrinkle on his face, he looked in fairly good shape, despite the shadow of an impending court case. The mole was still conspicuous on his upper lip but he had no intention of having it removed.

It was hard to believe that a comic so full of vitality and enthusiasm was by now thirty-five years in the business. In that time, his name had become synonymous with the meaning of comedy. Not everyone by any means found his humour wildly funny, but almost without exception he was admired as one of the most professional and durable comedians. As he says, 'When you have been practising for thirty-five years, and a few more years before that around working-men's clubs, you should have a certain degree of skill. I'm still in the business of tickling people's chuckle-muscles.'

He was talking during a break in rehearsals and as usual was not reluctant to express some strong personal views about comedy. He felt that in modern times it was often misused. 'Cynicism has crept in far too much. Satire can be a skilful, subtle thing but too often people employ the aggressive cudgel instead.' He agreed that a show like *Spitting Image* fell into his bad books. And it wasn't only because the show lampooned him about his tax problem.

'It didn't bother me personally,' he said, 'but it's just part of that violent, hurtful comedy. Comedy and laughter should be a joyful thing.' To those people who were meeting him for the first time, the star's bushy hair and protruding teeth were unmissable hallmarks, yet they tended to be puzzled by his ordinariness. He was extremely good company and columnists could not complain that he did not go out of his way to provide them with adequate material. No one ventured to ask him about his love-life and the attractive Sybie Jones, who was rehearsing in the pantomime with him. To the more experienced newsmen, Doddy only wanted to talk about the things he cared to talk about. He did not suggest to them that they might like to chat with Sybie about her role in the show. But they were prepared to pass it over. Even if he wanted, Doddy could not disguise his affection for his native Liverpool: 'I do love Liverpool, it's a great city. So many of my favourite comics come from there – Arthur Askey and Rob Wilton and more – and I'm proud of it although I'm not sure I go much for series like *Bread*. The only funny thing about them is that they speak with a Scouse accent.' He admitted he liked *Fawlty Towers* and could watch the series over and over, but he didn't see anything particularly funny about so-called alternative comedy.

It was a sentiment also expressed by Frank Carson who failed to find it funny. In Doddy's case there never had been any such thing as alternative comedy. The only comedy there was, was the comedy which made people laugh. That was what it came down to after all. He claimed that British comedy had hit rock-bottom because the young blue brigade had arrived. 'They would like the public to believe it is a new style of humour, but it isn't. It is just infantile and silly. Comedy today is going through a bit of trauma because it has lost its way. There is a trend towards performers who go in for shock and outrage. They are unskilled and totally non-creative. Their jokes have been around for years. If I couldn't entertain people without shocking them I would be very sad.'

Was his criticism a sign perhaps that he was growing a little older and could not accept modern comedy trends?

Or perhaps a hint of envy at their success? The alternative comedians would argue that it was precisely the vagaries of human behaviour that point up our weaknesses and they deserve to be laughed at, just as mothers-in-law made legitimate targets because laughing at them defused their power. Undeniably, Doddy was sincere in his criticism and he was joined by an increasing number of comics who saw alternative comedy not only as a threat but ultimately bad for the business.

But he was never too serious for long. He regaled the *Halifax Evening Courier* with more stories. Someone mentioned that he was standing on a spot where once there had been a lavatory. The star quipped, 'It reminds me of a story from the Liverpool docks . . . A chap asks a docker where the urinal is. "How many funnels has it got?" says the docker.' He then said he was an animal lover and actually owned a horse. 'I'm a member of a couple of syndicates so I suppose I own a leg!' He convinced more than one young sceptic that he was Squire of Knotty Ash and loved every blade of grass in the district. He was in joyous mood and was intent on giving the columnists enough for five columns.

Soon he was back to the business on hand – pantomime. The smile vanished, as he defended panto against snipers who peppered the genre with gibes about its validity in modern entertainment. As he stressed, 'At one time it got to be quite a cliché for some people to say that pantomime was old hat. But every year panto continues to break records and provide the financial security of a theatre for the rest of the year. It is the one period when business booms for everyone, the bread and butter of a theatre's year.

'Cynics like to have a go at anything that is sentimental, warm and typically British. I see it as a marvellous Christmas pudding mixture comprising all branches of show business. You might feel strange the first couple of days, but by the end of the season you are like a family, borrowing cups of sugar from each other.'

Doddy was determined not to stay aloof in the town. He forgot about his tax problems as he met local people and pledged his support to a fund-raising campaign for a hospital scanner. In a second-hand book shop the owner presented him with a vintage copy about music-hall. To the local people the star was devoid of pretension and arrogance. They found him sometimes rather shy and serious and different from the funny-man image they had come to expect. No one had told them that the comedian did not try to be funny off-stage.

Despite counter-attractions in Leeds and surrounding towns, Doddy was confident of bringing in the crowds to the Civic Theatre. He was pleased with rehearsals. As he said, 'It's been marvellous – the cast have been great. It's nice for me as a solo comic to get away from that gladiatorial thing and share the stage with other people.' Among the individuals he would be sharing the limelight with were his Diddymen, the band of perky gagsters who had followed him around like Snow White's Seven Dwarfs.

He had no intention of upsetting the rest of the cast, although he did agree that there would be a degree of ad libbing in his Idle Jack. 'If you think of a good 'un you whop it in. If there is something topical in the paper, for instance. I would think that eggs and toy-boys will be coming in for a bit of stick this year. There's enough in your average daily paper to keep you going for twelve months.'

Traditional pantomime appealed to him. He saw it as good triumphing over evil and rooted in the medieval mystery plays. No matter how big the star, the principal boy and girl always came down last for the finale. And irrespective of how many space-ships, robot cops and Speilberg creations and the kinds children had seen during the year, in Doddy's view they always booed the villain and cheered the winner of the sword fight.

The star surprised some people in Halifax when he said he had but one remaining ambition: to play every live theatre in the British Isles. It was a vow he had made in 1982 and he was still committed. He had played a theatre built into the side of a hill in Bacup where you could go downstairs to the circle, a theatre in a mill, at Wigan Pier, the beautiful Georgian theatre at Richmond, N. Yorkshire. There seemed to be more theatres today than there had been twenty-five years earlier, which was excellent because they are the hub of a city's life.

While Doddy agreed that the old days were great, it was now 1988 and they had to accept the challenges and benefits, which were considerable. 'When I started, for instance, you couldn't pick up a phone and book a seat by credit card. One thing that doesn't change is the warmth of a Yorkshire audience. Some of the happiest times I've had were in Yorkshire. That explains how tickled I am to be in Halifax.'

Halifax Civic Theatre is situated at the corner of Commercial Street and is reputed to be ninety years old. It has an attractive foyer and spacious auditorium, with an excellent view of the stage from every side. The décor is easy on the eye. On the opening night of *Puss In Boots* there were cassettes on sale of Doddy's most popular songs, and the programme for the show carried a background piece about the star, in which he was quoted as saying, 'I've done every pantomime known to man, but *Puss In Boots* is my favourite, and the lovely Civic Theatre is the best possible setting for this fun-filled family panto that is designed to exercise your chuckle-muscles and send you out of the theatre feeling tattifelarious and full of plumptiousness.

'Anyone who doesn't laugh will be kept in the theatre afterwards and given the once-over with my ticklin' stick! Just remember folks: you don't just come to Doddy's pantomimes – you're in them!'

With many of the townspeople busy with their Chri-

stmas shopping, it seemed very unwise to open the pantomime on the evening of 23 December and unfortunately
this was reflected in in the disappointing house. Furthermore, it was soon evident that technically some more
work needed to be done before the curtain rose. The critic
of the *Halifax Evening Courier* stated:

> There is nothing much wrong with Halifax Civic Thea-
> tre's Christmas pantomime *Puss In Boots*, which opened
> last night, that some serious trimming will not put right.
> The truth was that the production overran by not less
> than an hour – and that takes into account that the
> opening show was delayed by twenty minutes after
> technical problems. That inauspicious start,
> accompanied by the fact that the first night house was
> somewhat disappointing, was soon forgotten as the
> cast, led by the exuberant Ken Dodd, gave us a show
> that was brimming with enthusiasm, just lacking a little
> polish at times. Dodd, though, is a splendid trouper of
> the old school, ad libbing his way out of several dead-
> ends quite brilliantly, and proving that for all his current
> problems, he remains one of Britain's premier
> entertainers.

Despite the show's rough edges, the critic thought that
this would be the Civic's best professional panto since the
theatre took up the idea in 1984. And he advised, 'It needs
a hint of more finesse, a cut here and there, and this
production will go with a real swing. The laughter quo-
tient is massive – now we need audiences to match up to
it.'

The Stage sent along Geoff Mellor to cover the show and
he, too, commented on the 'first night mishaps', but
added that Doddy had a gag to suit every occasion. At
one hold-up, the star quipped, 'What happened to the
script?' and at another, 'Are we really at the Crossroads?'

Mellor began, 'Ken Dodd begins his 35th year in show

business by starring in *Puss In Boots*. The Clown Prince of
Comedy plays Idle Jack – a misnomer if ever there was
one, for he is seldom off the stage, with or without the
Diddymen, tickling stick always at the ready. In fact
Doddy really had his pantomime sewn up with the audi-
ence in stitches of laughter. He works well with Puss
played by Sybie Jones, whom he introduces as My Magic
Moggy, or The Cat from the Chemists! Playing Queen
Gertrude is that master of dame parts Joe Black, who is
well remembered from the Laidler days.'

By Friday evening, 6 January *Puss In Boots* had been
trimmed and the show looked as though it might even
end on time at 10.30. There was a special ovation for
Doddy's first appearance. Armed with a tickling stick,
and wearing a full-length yellow spotted dress, he
skipped gaily on stage and exclaimed, 'Any accountants
in tonight?' He made no attempt to upstage his colleagues,
relying on teamwork to make an impact. As Idle Jack he
was always in character, but when he began to ad lib the
audience loved it.

As Queen Gertrude talked of two thousand ducats,
Doddy quipped, 'I owe some of that!' In another scene
he picked up an egg and aimed it at the stalls, 'Is Edwina
in tonight?' It was noticeable that he was appealing as
much to the adults as to the children. His voice at times
seemed husky and somewhat tired, but by the interval he
was in full spate, waving his tickling stick as if it were a
conductor's baton.

In Joe Black he had a perfect foil. Their kitchen scene
together, with the lines expertly timed, suggested that
perhaps Doddy should after all have devised a double-act
for television and maybe achieved the same success as
Morecambe and Wise. He worked well with Black, a born
funny man. The children loved it. Later, Doddy
exclaimed, 'Would you like to see the Diddymen?' This
was greeted by a spontaneous roar of 'Yes, 'Yes.' There

was applause as the Diddymen trouped on to the stage singing, *We Are the Diddymen from Knotty Ash*. Each child in turn sang, or impersonated a celebrity. There was little trouble in recognising the Prince of Wales, John Wayne and Cilla Black.

Doddy worked superbly with the supporting cast, the Cox Twins, as Fred and Frank, a lisping Fairy Sparkle from their partner Pauline Miles, and Sybie Jones. Directing the show was Peter Alexander ('Nasty Norman' in the panto) who is Phil Pearse in Yorkshire's TV's *Emmerdale Farm*. As Doddy predicted, there was no shade of blue in the show and before the curtain came down he led the audience in a singalong. Everyone agreed that it had been a most plumptious performance.

It is a tribute to Doddy's enduring artistry that no one, it seems, has ever asked if he intended to retire. Perhaps if he were, he would echo Ernie Wise's answer to the same question, 'If I retired, what would I do? Performing has been my life since I was eight.'

Bob Hope, one of Doddy's favourite comics, has worked on into his eighties. The secret of his longevity in the business may be found in his own words: 'In our business it's a great thing when audiences can keep you so exhilarated that they fool you – they make you think you're young; it's just a wonderful thing.'

There was never any danger of Doddy going stale as he scurried round the country on one-night stands, yet ensuring that he was free at Christmas for pantomime. It is a gruelling schedule but the Squire of Knotty Ash loves every minute. The truth is he needs an audience. As Bob Monkhouse says, 'There's an engine inside every great performer which is usually a need to satisfy, a need to please, a need to hear applause – in terms of either clapping hands or cheques through the post. It keeps them young.'

Even if at times Doddy has been dogged by ill-health, he has on his own admission been able to keep going and fulfil his engagements. Audiences have seldom noticed his off-moments, but the more perceptive can recognise when his 'chest is playing up'. Nevertheless, he will sing his romantic ballads and tell his gags as though he is in the full bloom of health. 'Doddy's a fighter,' his friends say. Behind his smile is a steely edge. This toughness and strength of character have stood him in good stead over the years. He has worked hard to ensure that his *persona* has been projected in the right manner. Apart from his tax problems, his reputation has remained untarnished and he has been untouched by scandal.

By now one of his old friends, Barney Colehan, had retired as producer of *The Good Old Days* but they have managed to keep in touch. Recognised as a star-maker in his day, Colehan bemoans the passing of the star system. As he explained, 'The stars are getting old . . . Harry Secombe . . . even Ken Dodd. But where are the new ones coming from? Many theatres have closed. There is no longer anywhere for them to learn. Talent is like an uncut diamond. And it could take three years on the rounds to polish an act.'

Like Doddy, he was unhappy to see the end of *The Good Old Days*. 'I would have liked somebody else to have taken it over,' he says, 'and carried it on in the same tradition. They would have achieved what people are asking for. People were sorry to see it end. You don't break up a winning team.'

During its phenomenal run it presented 2,000 artistes and was watched by 2,000 million viewers. Significantly, in his office in BBC Leeds, Barney Colehan had a large photograph of Doddy on the wall, a reminder perhaps of one of his best discoveries. He had but one regret. 'I would have loved to have Bing Crosby on the show. And he agreed to come. I talked to him in the Palladium dressing-room and he asked what he had to do. I said,

"Just come on and sing a number." He said, "OK, I'll do it, Barney." Three weeks later he was dead.'

Doddy himself liked to recall the fun he derived from his appearances on *The Good Old Days* and the pleasure he got when invited back. 'I always wanted my own discoveries back on my show,' recalls Colehan. 'And Doddy was one of my finest discoveries. I remained loyal to many of them and none refused to come on the show.'

To Doddy, the show provided a valuable platform for aspiring stars and young entertainers. Today there were fewer such shows which made it harder for entertainers to make it to the top. As Barney Colehan would say, 'Artistes liked the show with a reputation for friendliness and told other artistes.'

Doddy remains a crusader on behalf of live British theatre. It is an uphill battle as satellite television encircles the globe. But he will keep on trying to save the old theatres in Liverpool, Manchester and Blackpool, even if only to ensure that he will have an audience in the future.

CHAPTER 24

'I've Always Given Full Value'

For Doddy, the waiting was the worst. Five weeks had passed since he played pantomime in Halifax, and it seemed an interminable time since the Liverpool court proceedings the previous August. The strain began to show and it was obvious to his friends that he was undergoing psychological stress. None the less, he was resilient, he had survived the pressure of an unbelievably busy career and now looked for no sympathy. Just as he eschewed any hint of pathos in the theatre, he avoided sentiment outside it like the plague.

In his attitude, he remained intensely professional. As ever, his mission was to promote happiness and he strove to maintain a high public profile, eager to pursue his normal routine, which was not easy in the circumstances. He accepted invitations to attend civic functions and fulfilled one-night theatrical engagements. 'Doddy seems to be out and about more than ever,' remarked Philip Key, showbiz editor of the *Liverpool Post*. 'I met him a few weeks ago and he hadn't changed.'

He had opened a new style Jobclub in the city, aimed at making job-hunting easier. As he left the opening ceremony he laughed off a joke by a club member who indiscreetly told the comic, 'I know why you're here – you're getting a tax rebate!' And he was applauded by fans when he opened a local gala. As he joked about his court trial for alleged tax evasion his face showed signs of strain. He looked tired and worried but he had a smile and a joke for everyone.

Liverpudlians had by now got over the initial shock. Many had been shattered when the story first broke in the newspapers. To them, it was unthinkable that their favourite entertainer could face a prison sentence. But the memory of Lester Piggott was still fresh in their minds. The law must take its course. At the outset, they were vaguely reassured by the comedian's own words from the stage of the Arcadia in Llandudno: 'I've never hurt anybody or done anything wrong. Time will tell and the full story will come out. I've been an entertainer since 1954 and I've always given full value. I've not stolen anything.'

It was an emotional moment and he was cheered by the audience as he concluded, 'Thank you for being so supportive to me. You're like a family. Thanking God, I'll be here every Tuesday until November.' And a few months later a packed Liverpool Cathedral heard him read a poem – John Betjeman's *Christmas*. The comic was dressed in a light grey suit and appeared in good humour as he sang carols with enthusiasm, occasionally addressing a remark to those with him in the front pew.

Like Doddy, the people in the business thought the waiting was the most traumatic part of the case. If the comic had been a drinking man, which he wasn't, the wait might well have destroyed him. Now, ten months after the news had rocked show business, he had so far survived the ordeal. However, what his friends and colleagues dreaded most was a prison sentence, however short. All his life they knew he had been waited on. There was always someone there to do this and that for him. They couldn't see him coping on his own in prison.

They tried to forget such a likelihood. But the shadow over the comedian's career was ever present. To the majority of people in Liverpool, it was an ominous shadow. How could it be otherwise? However, Doddy continued to make trips outside the city and draw full houses for one-night stands. In Ipswich he renewed acquaintance with Antony Tuckey who had directed him in the early Seventies in *Twelfth Night* at the Liverpool Playhouse.

'I went to talk to Ken at the Corn Exchange here and despite a few troubles hanging around him, he was the same as ever,' Tuckey recalls, 'and a delight to talk to. Not, I think, quite as fast and neat on stage as he used to be, but still hugely amusing, and still with that delightful way of never milking a joke if it didn't quite work.'

They reminisced about the days in the Seventies in Liverpool when they worked together in *Twelfth Night*. The director's memory was vivid: 'I remember Ken took an extraordinary time to unwind after his performance as Malvolio, and would sit in the dressing-room for an hour or more enjoying a kind of "high" every evening. This is exactly the same when he does his variety show. He takes a long time to wind down. He very much wanted to make a first-night speech, but I told him he must not, as we never did that, and again it was exactly the sort of "You see, he couldn't resist it," idea that people were waiting for. Again, people could hardly believe that he really stood in line with the other actors and took his bow.'

Tuckey could scarcely resist a smile when he remembered that third night: 'I am afraid by the third night it all got too much for Ken, and he did start to enjoy a curtain speech, but I think by that time he was accepted as a success in the role. I remember that it certainly seemed to me at the time that the local press were building him for the fall of his life, and everyone was looking forward with glee to see this big-head fall straight on his face. Again, he is a genius, and had no intention of providing people with that pleasure.'

Today Antony Tuckey is Artistic Director of Wolsey Theatre in Ipswich. Looking back on Doddy's performance as Malvolio he said he was unable to make an objective judgement of its merits. 'Ken has charisma on stage, but whether it was a better or even different performance than another good actor would have given I cannot say. What was extraordinary was that it was Ken Dodd giving it, under control and word-perfect, and without any tendency to mess about. It belongs in a tradition, although not, I think, a particularly extensive one, i.e. George Robey once played Falstaff and one or two other comedians have essayed classical comedy in the past.'

Whenever Tuckey met Doddy the conversation invariably came round to Molière, for the director was anxious for the comic to play the title role in *The Miser*. 'Maybe one day it will happen,' says Tuckey. Sometimes he had been asked how much he paid the comic to play Malvolio at the Liverpool Playhouse. Now he was able to say, 'We paid Ken a substantial salary by Playhouse standards, but it was not talked about by Ken himself, only with his agent Dave Forrester. It was still chicken-feed as far as Ken was concerned, and I suspect that, having agreed to do it, money would not have been an important consideration. Off-stage, I found Ken charming and always interested in what was going on. Everybody enjoyed his company and it is, of course, an extraordinary bonus to have so talented a comedian in your midst talking very amusingly about his business in an uninhibited way!'

Tuckey felt he had got to know the comedian. 'Ken seemed in some ways a lonely man,' he recalls, 'but the main memory I have is of a feeling that there was real anarchy and perhaps genuine madness in the eyes, and in the man. I occasionally look into what I feel are the cold and rather calculating eyes of the so-called would-be anarchic alternative comedian, and I realise that Ken is the real thing.'

Before he left Ipswich, Doddy said to the director, 'By Jove, I may do *The Miser*. I always wanted to tackle Molière.' To Tuckey, it was a hopeful sign; the comedian was thinking ahead and beyond his current tax problems. Although he had failed to get Jimmy Edwards to play Falstaff in *The Merry Wives of Windsor*, somehow he felt confident that one day Doddy would keep his promise.

He had always been amazed, for instance, at how easily Doddy got audiences to accept quite surreal propositions. The conversation between two legs under the bed-clothes was one he remembered well: 'Legs I think being described as friendly things and lovely to have there with you.'

Tuckey's opinion of the comic had not changed since he left Liverpool. 'He is, without doubt, a genius and a wonderful craftsman. He has also I imagine many faults but I never came across them.'

Radio producer Bobby Jaye had not met Doddy for some years, but followed his successful career and later the court charges with a tinge of sadness. Although their offstage friendship had cooled, he still regarded Doddy as a comic genius. At his attractive home in Bromley he still had scripts and tapes to remind him of *The Ken Dodd Show* and sometimes he would take out a script that he considered particularly funny, or put on a cassette to hear again the voices of Doddy, Talfryn Thomas, Jo Manning Wilson, Michael McClain and Gretchin Franklin. One particular script he regarded as clever and included Doddy and Talfryn Thomas.

Ken: 'My wife is away on three months' holiday.'
Talf: 'Ooh, that's good.'
Ken: 'No, bad – today's the last day.'
Talf: 'That's bad.'
Ken: 'No, good. I've found meself a girlfriend.'
Talf: 'That's good.'
Ken: 'No, bad – she's an Eskimo.'
Talf: 'That's bad.'
Ken: 'No, good. Her name's Nell.'

Talf: 'That's good.'

Ken: 'No, bad, she's married.'

Talf: 'That's bad.'

Ken: 'No, good. Her husband's away and she's invited me back to her place.'

Talf: 'That's good.'

Ken: 'No, bad. Her place is in Greenland.'

Talf: 'That's bad.'

Ken: 'No, good. Because none of the neighbours will find out and tell me missus.'

Talf: 'That's good.'

Ken: 'No, bad. When we got back to her igloo, she invited all her friends in for a traditional Eskimo evening.'

Talf: 'That's bad.'

Ken: 'No, good. The tradition was wife-swapping.'

Talf: 'That's good.'

Ken: 'No, bad – the wife I got was me own. That's where she went for her holidays.'

Came the programme's closing announcement by Michael McClain: 'You have been listening to Ken Dodd in the Great Harvest of Comedy Show. Talfryn Thomas did squirrel impressions and showed us his nuts. Nice one Squirrel. Gretchen Franklin came along and said she was game and was later shot by the farmer played by John Grahan. Jo Manning Wilson brought along her melons and this surprised farmer Michael McClain so much he fell into the combine harvester and rotated the crops. The corn was picked by writers David McKeller, Norman Beadle, Dave Dutton and Philip. And the show was harvested and produced by Bobby "Farmer Giles" Jaye.'

Curiously, as the court hearing against Doddy drew nearer, Jaye did not find much sympathy for the comic in London. Perhaps they reserved all their affection for Southern comics? Those people who remembered his triumphs at the Palladium hoped he could stand up to the stress. Bobby Jaye felt confident he would, as he always saw a tough and durable side to the man. However, a jail sentence was another matter. He put the thought from his mind.

To Frank Carson, Doddy was a very funny man and the public loved him. He had been around the variety scene a long time and everybody in the business knew him. His genius sprang from his undoubted presence. The moment Doddy stepped on stage the audience felt this presence, and when he opened his mouth they laughed at his quick-fire gags and funny ad libbing. Carson was encouraged by the manner in which he had stood up to the pressure of the court charges. 'Ken will survive,' he told himself.

Doddy had confided his worries to Carson, a big, exuberant and friendly Belfast comedian who can be just as funny off-stage. They had known each other for twenty years and in recent years worked in radio together. 'Doddy always tries to make me laugh,' Carson says. 'He's gifted. Funny thing, though, they accepted Doddy in a Shakespearean part but they wouldn't accept me – I'm too big. I don't like Shakespeare's clowns anyway. I feel sorry now for Ken and I know what he's going through. The world of comedy can't afford for anything to happen to him. That's the way I feel about him.'

Eddie Braben had fallen out with Doddy in the late Sixties but the two men had made it up in the Eighties. The script-writer, who had once been very successful scripting for Doddy and later for Morecambe and Wise, had by now moved to Wales, but one morning he telephoned radio producer Jim Casey in Liverpool and asked him if he was interested in doing a new radio series with Doddy. 'I'd like to write the series,' Braben confided. 'Will you produce it, Jim?'

'It's up to the BBC,' said a surprised Casey. 'If they are agreed, I'll think about it.'

Braben: 'Good, I'll tell Ken.'

Casey suspected that Braben was doing it as a morale-booster for Doddy. It was, in his opinion, a fine gesture on Eddie's part.

In February 1989, Dick Condon was dividing his time between the Theatre Royal in Norwich and the revived D'Oyly Carte Company in London, to which he acted as manager. He was already thinking of booking Doddy for summer seaside dates and with that in mind he hoped there would be a successful outcome to his court hearing. As the trial drew closer, he knew that the pressure on the comedian was enormous. As he said, 'Ken is very sensitive and must be feeling the anxiety. It's no way to treat a star. How can one begin to measure his contribution to comedy – and the theatre? He could never be paid for the time he has given to his art.'

Jimmy Tarbuck reminisced on a radio programme about Doddy and recalled how nervous he could be before a Royal Command Performance. He retailed a few amusing stories about him and life in Liverpool. Liverpool Playhouse director, Henry Cotton, said his theatre would like to engage Doddy for a new production, probably a Molière play. The only question was whether they could afford him.

Everyone, it seemed, was anxious to see the future with Doddy around. No one – at least in Liverpool and the North – dared to contemplate a future without the king of comedy. It was a fine reflection of the affection in which he was held by the majority of people. They liked to remember him as the man who made them laugh. This goodwill was conveyed by friends to the star himself. He expressed his gratitude.

John Fisher, meanwhile, had become head of Light Entertainment at Thames Television and was keenly aware of Doddy's plight. He prided himself in being a friend of the comedian. 'Ken has always been a brilliant stand-up comic,' he reflected. He remembers producing two of Doddy's appearances on Michael Parkinson's chat show and he found conversations with him stimulating, particularly his study of comedy. Now he privately sympathised with his dilemma and hoped it would leave him unscathed.

Earlier, researching his book on comedians, Fisher watched a number of Doddy's stage performances and was quickly won over. He wrote: 'Ken's most relevant song is the infectious calypso-rhythmed *Happiness*.' When the curtain comes down the laughter must subside, but the exhilaration and joy of his performance as a whole remains embedded in us all. As with Bygraves and Secombe, it is a case of happiness first and foremost and it has really nothing to do with making people laugh, which is only the first hurdle.'

To Fisher, Doddy remained the one great Liverpool comedian of his day who actually clung to his native roots. In return he maintained an objective view of life as lived by the people he had entertained, namely the masses. It was a view not a little responsible for his prominence. His unique air of impish tenderness also played a part. He was a one-man situation.

Jim Casey was by now living in retirement in Crosby in the outskirts of Liverpool. However, he was still working on a contract basis for BBC Manchester and considering writing a biography of his father, Jimmy James, who had been described as 'that incomparable comedian'. Although he had known Doddy for thirty years, Casey was surprised that he had received no telephone call from the star in recent times, in particular since the news of his tax problem became public.

Months before, when he had first heard the news, he was, on his own admission, shocked. Having worked on radio series with the comedian, he felt close to him and hoped everything would eventually come right. 'I like Ken,' he would say. 'Like my father Jimmy, he is a great stand-up comedian. I know what he is going through. I remember Dad going on stage when he was ill and it was terrible. But he still managed to make them laugh. Despite his problems, Ken has been making them laugh in Liverpool and Blackpool and up and down the country.'

To Casey, the comic was right to stay in Knotty Ash. As he reasoned, 'I don't think Ken could have done anything else. I think he would have been totally lost in London, a fish out of water. His Liverpool roots are important to him and they are so strong that he has got to be here. Although he doesn't work as hard as he used to, he can still pack 'em in at shows in Blackpool and elsewhere.'

He thought that Doddy and Eddie Braben had a few characteristics in common. 'I regard Ken as a loner as I do Eddie. Ken survives through an audience. He really only comes alive on stage. And to my mind, he never really wanted to be Ken Dodd the Star, but rather Ken Dodd the Comic. His simple life-style has demonstrated this. I think it is important to him to have the respect of his showbiz colleagues and he has always had that. I've yet to meet a performer who didn't think Ken was a great comic. He has endured very well; I mean he has been on top for a long time, the best part of twenty-five years.'

They occasionally discussed Northern humour and Northern comics. So intriguing had Jim Casey found these discussions that he decided to do a radio programme devoted entirely to the subject. He invited Doddy to be the main spokesman and the opening sequence was broadcast in the theatre.

Doddy: 'We know how to enjoy ourselves up North, don't we? A Northern man likes nothing more than sinking down a pint of decent ale . . . and he doesn't care whose it is either . . . Northern pubs are great for relaxing in, in fact some blokes get so relaxed they have to be carried home at the end of the night . . . A lot of Northern nightclubs offer a variety of *haute cuisine;* you get something in this club you can't get at any other club – food poisoning . . . We love entertainment in the North. I mean we are great connoisseurs of the opera, we love to join in the choruses; some Northern men are fond of ballet, some go for dancing, some go for the music, and some go to make comparisons . . . We are a hardy bunch, a right bunch of hardies we are, a rough-faced lot with weather-beaten faces, fat hands and chilblains throbbing inside our hobnailed boots – and that's only the women . . . The North has always produced, spawned the finest comedians and entertainers in the world; if you don't believe me, then ask Harold Wilson in Huddersfield.'

Casey asked Doddy what, in his opinion, made people laugh in the North. 'You have to talk about things that Northerners have traditionally found comical, which is family life, domestic scenes, for instance, bath-night; that is always funny for some reason or other. I've told jokes about bath-night. There are jokes about dogs and cats; in Kirby if you see a cat with a tail it's a tourist. I make jokes about politicians as well. I am not terribly impressed by pomp and ceremony whereas Southerners are impressed by it and I think their jokes have more to do with the quality of life. For instance, in London they love their comedians, they regard them as totems. If you make it in London and if you behave yourself, you are made for life. Max Miller was beloved, so was Tommy Trinder. If you go further South they like character comedians.

Casey: 'Why have so many comedians come from Liverpool?'

Doddy: 'What a happy place! Actually it isn't Liverpool, it is Merseyside . . . where all ladies are on the mirth pill. It is a very exuberant and merry city. Look at the comics it has produced: Arthur Askey, Ted Ray, Tommy Handley, Rob Wilton, Jimmy Tarbuck, Norman Vaughan, Billy Bennett, Mike Burton, Tom O'Connor. There is a rainbow of laughter in the North and it goes right across the Pennines.'

By now Doddy had performed at seven Royal Variety

Performances and had, in Frank Carson's view, been a success in the lot. He had been impersonated by Mike Yarwood in typical style, with Yarwood looking plumptious: front teeth protruding, hair standing upright, eyes starting from their sockets. The impersonator used to stand in the wings and study the comic at work. Doddy knew it but didn't mind. After they appeared together in variety in Liverpool, Yarwood said mischievously, 'Naturally I remember it warmly, because I stole the reviews. One critic wrote, "The lad from Knotty Ash was not at his best. Brightest spot was provided by Stockport boy Mike Yarwood." ' But Yarwood was careful to add, 'It didn't do the size of my head any good. At that time I went through a very cocky period.'

Unlike Bruce Forsyth, who had always dreamed of repeating in the United States the phenomenal success he has enjoyed in Britain, Doddy never really tried to do the same. As the years progressed, he was content to become a millionaire on the home front, entertaining the folks of Liverpool, Blackpool, Manchester and occasionally London. It can be said that Forsyth was disappointed by his American failures, yet Doddy never sought success overseas to any great degree. Promoting laughter has been his ambition and he has gloriously realised that ambition in Britain.

In the traumatic weeks leading to the court trial he was able to draw on the loyalty of numerous people in the business, friends in the media, and countless fans up and down the country. But a section of the tabloid press in Fleet Street went out of its way to be hurtful. One headline, 'TOO MEAN TO BUY HEADSTONE' was a direct reference to the death of Anita Boutin years previously and it was alleged that he had never honoured his promise to pay for Anita's headstone. Her sister, Sylvia Donovan, who lives in Liverpool, was quoted as saying, 'It's been so long now we have pretty well given up hope.'

Doddy maintained a dignified silence. He was at that

time being portrayed as 'the great eccentric'. His name was linked with those of Benny Hill, Mick Jagger and Rod Stewart as among the 'meanest' in the business. When one paper showed a photograph of his home in Knotty Ash the caption read: 'RICH MAN'S RETREAT: Dodd's home in the district he has made famous, Knotty Ash in Liverpool'.

Bill Boutin, brother of Anita, was angry at the slur on Doddy's reputation. 'I didn't like what the papers wrote,' he said from his home in Liverpool. 'Ken and I are still good friends.' Boutin had always admired the way the comedian treated his sister and consequently saw a lot of good in him. He expressed anger also that people should snipe at Ken at the most difficult time in his career. He refused to talk to callers on the phone and he gave no interviews.

Widow Mrs Mary Wright, who has lived opposite Doddy for thirty years, had never been inside Doddy Towers, but she was able to say, 'Ken's a lovely man but he keeps very much to himself. He only ever has time to say, "Hello" and "Goodbye", then he's dashing off again. I know he always opens the local St John Ambulance bazaar, but he usually arrives late. He'll be late for his own funeral.' To Mrs. Wright, the comedian was jokey and jolly. She laughed as she said, 'He'd never give you a tickling stick – but he'd sell you one!'

Nowadays Doddy's phone has an answering machine, obviously because of the attentions of the press. Friends meeting him were relieved to find no hint of self-pity in his voice, more a sense of optimism that one day he would be over the trial and able to live a more normal and carefree life. He still wanted to maintain his position if he could. As he said, 'I still want to be starring, to be up front. Anything else would be humiliation.'

Despite the pressure and the private agony of the impending trial, he was considering one-night stands in various towns and cities. 'By Jove, I'm still in demand,' he reminded media friends in Liverpool. At sixty, he felt he had lots of years left in the business. 'We mustn't let the killjoys win,' the great Max Miller had said in another context; Doddy was now in wholehearted agreement.

Sensibly he kept the sunny side up. 'I like being busy,' he confessed. 'I get nervous if I'm not. I want to get on with life.' As ever, he was aware of the shadow across his path. And, as self-styled Squire of Knotty Ash he had been asked to surrender his passport after it was claimed in court he might flee the country to avoid standing trial on tax fraud charges. That bizarre accusation deeply hurt his pride. The Squire of Knotty Ash had never deserted his subjects and was not likely to now when he needed their loyalty most.

He had been granted £50,000 bail as he was committed for Crown Court trial on twenty-seven charges, including nine new ones. Keeping himself busy with stage engagements had eased his anxiety. The waiting, he admitted, was the worst. To his colleagues and friends, it seemed unjust, inhuman and unnecessary. The law could be cruel. If Doddy was vulnerable he didn't show it. He steeled himself now for the biggest ordeal of his life.

CHAPTER 25

Drama in Court 5-I

The long wait was coming to an end.

The trial was fixed for Tuesday, June 6, at Liverpool Crown Court. Doddy admitted that the months had 'dragged' and he was keen to get the hearing over with. He had been busy, making regular appearances at cabaret venues, mostly outside Liverpool, and even joking about his tax dilemma.

Events had tended to keep the trial out of the news. Soon it was almost forgotten as Liverpool was plunged into deep mourning for the victims of the Hillsborough disaster, when 94 football fans died and 170 were injured in a crowd crush.

Earlier in April Doddy had given a lecture on Charlie Chaplin to the National Film Theatre; he had long admired Chaplin's comic genius. He was also pleased to be asked by Mike Craig of BBC Manchester to star in a holiday special, *Doddy's Green Radio Show*, for it re-united him with old friends, actor Peter Goodwright and scriptwriter Eddie Braben, who indicated he was keen to do a radio series with Dodd again.

Unknown to the press, Doddy underwent medical tests in Manchester and it was only after he withdrew from the gala stage show in aid of the Hillsborough victims that the newspapers got the first hint that something was wrong. The fixing of the date of the trial revived interest among Liverpudlians in the impending court case involving their favourite comic. The hearing was scheduled to take place in Court 5-I, situated on the fifth floor of the six-storey building known locally as the Queen Elizabeth II Law Courts, and Doddy would be the first star celebrity to stand trial there since it had been opened by the Queen in 1984.

Long before the 10.30 am starting time, reporters, cameramen and the public, had gathered in the expansive square in front of the law courts. As Doddy arrived, accompanied by his girlfriend Sybil Jones and his solicitor, he was greeted by a few faithful fans. 'Good old Doddy,' cried one. 'Good luck, Ken,' remarked another, trying to shake his hand. The comedian, in dark brown suit and red tie, looked haggard and worried as he hurried through the swing glass doors to the lifts, unsmiling and silent.

Court 5-I is one of the largest of the thirty courtrooms in the building, yet on this cool June morning it was not nearly big enough to accommodate all the media men from Liverpool, Manchester and London. The public had queued outside the courtroom on the fifth floor since after 9 o'clock and at 10.25 seemed relieved to be admitted.

Inside the modern courtroom there was an undeniable air of expectancy. Most of the pressmen believed the trial would be a lengthy one and not a few of them had already made hotel bookings. They were in for a surprise. At 10.30, Mr George Carman, QC, defending, told the judge, Mr Justice Waterhouse, that he was applying for an adjournment to enable Mr Dodd to undergo further medical tests.

'The report of the examination carried out in May,' said Mr Carman, 'contains something of a bombshell. It shows that Mr Dodd suffers from ventricular tachycardia – irregular and fast heart beats. Because this is a potentially life-threatening condition of the heart, medical advice is that it would be unsafe and unwise to expose my client to the strain and stress of a criminal trial.'

Consultant physician Dr Rhys Williams of North Manchester General Hospital told the crowded court that he first examined Mr Dodd on May 19. It became immediately apparent that he had a grossly irregular pulse. So abnormal was the rhythm that it became impossible to record satisfactory blood pressure. Three or more extra beats in succession without a normal beat meant a condition called ventricular tachycardia which could lead to collapse or cardiac arrest.

Mr Carman emphasised that Mr Dodd was keen to face the charges and was not trying to avoid the trial. The judge commented that it was 'inexcusable and inexplicable' that the adjournment development should have taken place at the start of the court proceedings. He said he was told of the application at 10.35 that morning. Mr Brian Leveson, QC, for the prosecution, said he first heard of the medical report the previous Thursday. It had been absolutely impossible to obtain any form of informed outside opinion.

It was clear that the dramatic opening to the hearing had taken the press gallery by surprise. By the time the lunch break arrived the *Liverpool Echo* was on sale in the streets and the first editions were quickly snapped up. The front page banner headline read, 'DODDY: TOO SICK TO STAND TRIAL', with the accompanying sub-heading, 'QC Calls For Tax Case Delay Over Illness Threat To Comedian's Life'. And the page one report began, 'Comedian Ken Dodd is suffering from a potentially life-threatening illness, it was revealed today . . .'

Later in the hearing, Mr Justice Waterhouse commented on the medical report submitted by Mr Carman, and said, 'I suspect this report could be written about an awful lot of people in this country in their sixties. It is inevitable that Mr Dodd has to face some stress because he faces criminal charges. Nothing can remove that stress except a trial.' Although obviously unhappy with the application for adjournment, he agreed to grant it until Monday, June 19.

It was a transformed Doddy who turned up for the resumed hearing. In the scorching sun outside the law courts he joked with pressmen and TV camera crews, and told his fans, 'I can't get in, there's not enough seats.' He wore a smart grey pin-striped suit, red and blue spotted tie and a white shirt and was accompanied by Sybil Jones and his brother Bill. The comedian looked relaxed and confident. Gone was the grey pallor and worried frown of a fortnight ago.

The courtroom quickly filled. Interest in the case had increased since the adjournment. Doddy sat alone on a long bench in direct view of the judge, while Sybil Jones took a seat at the back of the court and prepared to make notes in a small notebook. Wearing light, broad-rimmed glasses, she appeared anxious.

Mr Carman rose to explain that the electro-cardiograph tests showed Mr Dodd's condition could possibly be the cause of sudden and unexpected death. Further medical examination however had not revealed any gross cardiac or arterial disease, so there was no immediate threat to his client's health, and he was now fit to stand trial and had expressed a wish to do so.

The QC's words took some members of the press gallery by surprise. A number of the more experienced court reporters expected the case to be adjourned until the autumn in view of the earlier disclosures about the comedian's health. Now they prepared themselves for a trial which might last four or five weeks.

Doddy stood in the dock, his hands clasped in front of him, as the lengthy indictment was read out. After hearing each of the eleven counts he replied in a loud, firm voice, 'Not guilty, my Lord.' He denied seven charges of cheating the public revenue, dating from 1973 to 1986, and four counts of false accounting between 1982 and

1988. At 11 o'clock the jury of seven men and five women was sworn in and took their place on the benches on the extreme right of the judge and facing the lawyers for prosecution and defence.

Mr Leveson opened the case for the Inland Revenue in a calm, measured voice he rarely raised. Mr Dodd, he said, was one of the great entertainers of our generation and was a character and a national institution. But there was another side to him. One of the consequences of his ability and fame had been fabulous earnings. He earned more fees in a month than most people earned in a year. But for years his dealings with the Inland Revenue had been characterised by dishonesty. After the Inland Revenue began inquiring into his tax affairs Mr Dodd instructed an international firm of accountants, Thornton Baker, now called Grant Thornton, and in June 1984 told them to prepare a report and comply with the Revenue requirements. Over the next two-and-a-half years he provided the firm with the details they required.

Pausing to consult his notes, Mr Leveson continued, 'The Crown alleges that during that period of two-and-a-half years not only did Mr Dodd continue deceiving the Revenue, but in addition, he deceived his own accountants. After December 1986, he abandoned Grant Thornton and went to another firm of international accountants, Arthur Young, who on his instruction prepared another report showing a very different picture. During inquiries for this the accountants and the Revenue learned of more than £700,000 in Jersey and the Isle of Man, and Mr Dodd was interviewed by tax officers in October 1987. Further material then started to come to light, and it was learned how he was paid for some shows partly by cheque, which went through the books, and partly in cash, which did not.'

The QC admitted that as Mr Dodd's business involved his being a unique entertainer it would be no good comparing him with anyone else, even another entertainer.

In the 1960s, he said that Mr Dodd set up a company called Ken Dodd Enterprises through which he did all his work and which was a perfectly legitimate method of reducing very high income tax and what was called surtax. His own affairs and the company's should have been quite separate but Dodd tended to treat the company's money as his own. In reality, he had known perfectly well what money should have been in the company, whatever the source. 'If somebody does a "foreigner" and receives cash which he puts in his pocket, he knows well that he should declare that money to the Inland Revenue, and if he doesn't he is defrauding them. He may believe he will get away with it and he may believe that the claims of the taxman are immoral, but he certainly knows what he is doing.'

Mr Leveson's tone became more emphatic. 'Mr Dodd's activities are just such frauds, not a few pounds but on a grand scale.' He said that over the years the comedian had a number of different accountants, and in the early 1970s was with Reginald Hunter who ran a practice in Widnes. For many years he had not only audited Mr Dodd's company accounts but also dealt with his personal affairs. The inquiry into Mr Dodd's affairs began in 1984, after Mr Hunter was prosecuted for false accounting. There was no evidence however that the accountant had dealt fraudulently with the comedian's accounts.

The court was told that in that year Mr Dodd and two Revenue inspectors met and Dodd was asked if details of his financial affairs were correct. It was made clear to him that if he came clean, a criminal prosecution would be highly unlikely. He replied that if there was any inaccuracy it was either a genuine mistake or a error of accountancy. Over nineteen months his accountants, Grant Thornton, compiled a report of the comedian's finances from information he gave them. When they submitted it to the Inland Revenue in January 1986, they concluded 'no pattern of omitted income arises.'

In October 1986 Dodd signed certified statements of his assets and bank accounts which, claimed Mr Leveson, again failed to mention the accounts in the Isle of Man and Jersey. The prosecution asserted that neither the January nor October 1986 declarations was 'worth the paper they were written on'. At a subsequent meeting with Mr Dodd in December 1986, Revenue investigators asked for authority to speak to a bank in the Isle of Man. Mr Leveson claimed the comedian, who had never acknowledged the existence of bank accounts in the Isle of Man, signed the authority but then revoked it the next day after employing another firm of accountants, Arthur Young.

'That request,' said the QC, 'had been an absolute disaster, destroying the facade which he had so carefully erected about his financial affairs.'

Doddy, who listened intently to the evidence, scribbled a note and passed it down to his solicitor seated a row in front of him. At the same time, Sybil Jones was taking her own notes, and occasionally looked across at Doddy. There was a brief adjournment at 12 o'clock and the court resumed ten minutes later.

During the course of the afternoon's proceedings the secret life of the comedian was further revealed. Within a period of sixteen weeks he made numerous trips to the Isle of Man and Jersey and deposited a total of £298,720 in each account – nearly £200,000 of which was invested within three weeks. Mr Leveson asked, 'Where did all this money come from? Doubtless it was earned but how much of it was ever declared?'

By April 1967, Dodd had £777,453 in overseas bank accounts of which £371,079 had accrued in interest. It was also disclosed that the comedian had purchased a country house for just £26,500 but which was now estimated to be worth £250,000. He bought the six-bedroomed house, the court was told, fifteen years ago as a retreat from his home in Knotty Ash. He and his fiancée, Anita Boutin, chose it but Miss Boutin died eighteen months after the purchase. Haunted by memories, the comedian had never lived in the house at Whitchurch, Shropshire.

Arthur Young, his new accountants, had by now prepared a comprehensive report of his assets which they forwarded to the Inland Revenue. Attached to it was a reference to the comedian's charitable work (including fund-raising for cancer research) and also letters from Mrs Margaret Thatcher and two former Prime Ministers, Mr Edward Heath and Mr Harold Wilson, which Mr Leveson suggested sought to persuade the Inland Revenue the man they were investigating deserved special treatment.

In a letter dated October 31, 1980, Mrs Thatcher thanked the comedian for a wonderful stage performance the previous Thursday, and said, 'I hope you enjoyed doing it as much as we enjoyed seeing it.' In a second letter on October 21, 1980, she acknowledged his 'marvellous show' during a Tory party conference, and added, 'It was good to get away from serious politics for most of the evening. I was only sorry Denis wasn't there to share my enjoyment.'

A letter from Harold Wilson stated, 'Thank you for a wonderful evening at the Palladium. My family and I enjoyed ourselves and particularly the thrill of being able to see you in the dressing-room after the show. I do hope you and your friends will come to see us at No 10.' Drinks before Doddy's stage performance, or a weekend lunch were suggested.

When Edward Heath was Tory Prime Minister in October 1968, he wrote to Doddy, 'I was tickled by the blue feather duster you sent me just before my speech at Blackpool. The speech went so well I didn't have to tickle up anybody.'

As the letters were read to the court, Doddy sipped from a glass of water and a faint wistful smile indicated that the letters perhaps evoked a feeling of nostalgia in him. At that moment he wrote another note and slipped it to his solicitor.

On Tuesday, the hearing was resumed at 10.30 and Mr Leveson continued the case for the prosecution. It was to prove an intriguing day's proceedings and often in the course of the evidence reporters slipped quietly away to catch early deadlines. Strangely, the public gallery was not full; perhaps the heatwave outside was to blame.

The court was told that Mr Dodd had a secret nest egg amounting to more than his net earnings over a lifetime in show business. He had earned more than one million pounds during thirty years as one of Britain's greatest entertainers, and he *had* paid back more than half that sum in tax. But what the comedian failed to tell the taxman about was the massive hoard of over £700,000 – including interest – locked away in secret accounts in Jersey and the Isle of Man.

'Since Mr Dodd started in show business back in 1949,' elaborated Mr Leveson, 'his gross income, up to 1982, was £1,154,556. After tax total earnings over the thirty-three years were £575,783 – the "net income over his entire life available to spend." But in all that time he spent just £23,100 in cash.'

Turning directly to the jury, he took them through the detailed report drawn up by Mr Dodd's accountants, Arthur Young. They had suggested that Reginald Hunter must have put in the books of the comedian's own company, Ken Dodd Enterprises, any amount of money as having been spent on business when in fact it had been retained by the comedian in cash. 'We are not talking about small sums of money but thousands and thousands of pounds. The error being made by Mr Hunter could not have been made once but must have been made time and time again, year in year out. Why should Mr Hunter make this kind of mistake and how could Mr Dodd so frequently not make it clear to his accountant that there was money over which he was accumulating. If Mr Dodd knew what was going on, of course, he is deceiving deliberately the Revenue and the dishonesty which the Crown allege is made out.'

As the QC paused to check a document, Doddy remained upright in his seat, and gazed ahead. Originally he had denied seven charges of common law cheating and four of false accounting. Now, after legal discussions, three of the charges referring to common law cheating were dropped, but would remain on file.

The court was told of a series of manoeuvres, when 'Mr Dodd opened new bank accounts under his name and those of Artson and Jones. Artson came from the comedian's father's name, Arthur, and Jones was girlfriend Anne's surname.' The comedian claimed the name was to protect the privacy of the account after papers relating to it were stolen. Mr Leveson said it was not to confuse burglars, but the taxman.

'When the tax probe began,' added the QC, 'Mr Dodd told his accountants he had no deposits abroad, yet seventeen days later he went to the Isle of Man and withdrew £181,000 in cash and hid it in wardrobes, cupboards and under the stairs at his three Liverpool houses. At one time he had kept £336,000 because he liked having a lot of cash, and he used to carry £1,000 in cash with him in Liverpool but up to £5,000 if he travelled away from the city.'

The court heard how the comedian flew to the Isle of Man on April 21, 1980 to pay £110,300 cash into three Manx banks. The following day he flew to Jersey and deposited a total of £44,000 in two banks. Between March 28 and April 21 1980 he had deposited £196,800. Ten weeks later he again flew to the Isle of Man and paid £27,000 into the Royal Trust Bank. Mr Leveson went on to explain how the cash, or some of it, was accumulated by Mr Dodd. After the first tax probe, the comedian was said to have received £230 for an appearance in Lancashire

– but pocketed £600 more in cash. His fee was later increased to £287 by cheque and £750 in cash – and this was paid just four days after a second meeting with the Revenue investigators.

To the prosecution counsel, this 'demonstrated Mr Dodd's dishonesty and his defiance to the taxman'. Nobody liked paying tax, he summed up, but they were dealing with an individual who had 'fiddled' for years and when investigated had continually lied. 'This trial is not about how much tax Mr Dodd owes, it is about honesty. On any showing there is a vast amount of money upon which tax simply has never been paid.'

There were times during Wednesday's hearing, in the rather humid courtroom atmosphere, that Doddy's mood appeared to alternate between the anxious and relaxed; yet on leaving the room he invariably smiled and had a word with a friend. He looked confident.

It was time to call witnesses for the Inland Revenue. Mr Joseph Atkinson, seconded to the Revenue's inquiry branch at Liverpool for seven years, described how when he was carrying out an investigation into Reginald Hunter's accountancy affairs he discovered copies of letters to Mr Dodd. His suspicions were immediately aroused.

One letter in particular was jokey and referred to 'the Aladdin's Cave of Knotty Ash'. It read: 'Once again Ken Dodd Enterprises' balance sheet omits its greatest asset, i.e. the Great Drum, better known in Stock Exchange circles as the Aladdin's Cave of Knotty Ash. Long may that priceless possession remain secluded in the Merseyside mangrove swamps to be seen but rarely and by very few.'

There was an implication that there could be assets omitted from Ken Dodd Enterprises, added Mr Atkinson. Mr Dodd later claimed the Great Drum was something he used on stage.

The letters were discounted as meaningless jokes – but

not before they had triggered an exhaustive inquiry into the comedian's financial affairs and the discovery of off-shore bank accounts. Earlier Mr Carlton Baron, who for a period was also attached to the Liverpool inquiry branch, told of Mr Dodd's 'frugal existence'. He accepted the comedian lived an unusual lifestyle, not in keeping with his star status. He did not travel in chauffeur-driven Rolls-Royces, live in an exotic house with swimming-pool, or employ bodyguards.

'My client still lives in the same house in which he was born and raised by his parents,' said Mr Carman, QC. 'And in respect of the one million pounds he earned between 1949 and 1982, Mr Dodd paid more tax in a month than the average man does in a year. Yet he never put in expenses claims for helicopters, a chauffeur or bodyguard, or entertaining people.'

Cross-examining Mr Baron, the QC said, 'Apart from a funny man when you meet him, he is modest and pleasant.'

Mr Baron: 'I would not say he was displaying a particularly happy nature during our interview.'

The tempo of the hearing rose on Thursday, the fourth day of the trial, when Mr Carman cross-examined Mr Atkinson. The QC's approach was noticeably more assertive than Mr Leveson's as he recalled a meeting between Mr Dodd and tax inspectors Mr Atkinson and Mr Peter Williams, after which they pressed his client to allow them to visit his home in Knotty Ash in order to check his private and business cash. This led to a note of 'unpleasantness' between them. Mr Dodd pointed out that it was not convenient for him, but Mr Atkinson continued to press him and this made Mr Dodd angry and he accused Mr Atkinson of using 'Gestapo' tactics.

Mr Atkinson: 'I recall something that Mr Dodd said. It was more of an aside, rather than unpleasantness.'

Mr. Carman: 'You don't just march into someone's home. You visit by appointment.'

He asked Mr Williams why the reference to the use of 'Gestapo tactics' had not appeared on the official record.

Mr Williams: 'Basically, a lot of people call us names. I don't think it was relevant to the facts I was trying to put down.'

Eventually, a compromise had been reached whereby Mr Grant Thompson, the accountant who accompanied Doddy to the meeting, was asked to go with him to his home to be shown any money stored there. The comedian produced £4,000, insisting that was all the cash in the house.

Mrs Yvonne Rice, who was employed on a private basis to keep Doddy's accounts, said Dodd would call in in the early evening, usually on his way to an engagement, with a pile of invoices and receipts. She would have to sort the mess out. She was never asked to write-up the books in a certain way.

Mr Carman: 'Is he a little scatter-brained when it comes to accountancy and book-keeping?'

Mrs Rice: 'Yes, that is probably a good description.'

Monday, June 26, the first day of the second week of the trial, did not attract a full public gallery, or as many pressmen as before, probably due to the nature of the evidence which dealt with accountants' figures. Most of the next morning's Fleet Street dailies did not report the proceedings.

Mr Carman told the court of the falsification of Mr Dodd's expenses by his first firm of accountants and said that an 'Alice-in-Wonderland' imagination was used by Mr Hunter, or his staff, to boost these annual expenses to £37,000. 'Unknown to my client his general expenses were increased by 400 per cent from £1,000 to over £4,000, and a laundry and dry cleaning bill of just over £300 catapulted to £2,000.'

When chartered accountant Mr Paul Marshall of Grant Thornton was called to give evidence next day, he said they produced a £54,000 report on Mr Dodd's finances for the Inland Revenue. 'I wanted to know about every bank account Mr Dodd had in the 10-year period up to January 1986.'

Mr Leveson, QC: 'During your discussions with him did you ever receive any hint at all of overseas accounts?'

Mr Marshall: 'No.'

The court was told that Mr Dodd would make 'cash and carry' flights to Jersey and the Isle of Man to deposit cash personally. He had twenty bank accounts holding more than £777,000. Asked why he had mentioned the Isle of Man when asking Mr Dodd about overseas assets, Marshall replied, 'This was because a lay person may not realise that, for tax purposes, the Isle of Man is not part of the United Kingdom. It has its own tax laws and its residents pay a lower level of taxation. Before 1979 it was enormously lower, but is not much lower now. In 1980, when Mr Dodd took his cash to the island, people not living there paid no tax on deposits.'

As the comedian sat in the dock taking notes and leafing through documents, his fiancée Sybil Jones, who shared his Knotty Ash home, sat at the back of the court taking occasional notes.

The main interest in Thursday's proceedings was the evidence of Mr Roderick Mackinnon, the tax inspector who led the Inland Revenue inquiry into Ken Dodd's finances. He admitted he was 'very surprised' by the details the comedian provided of his lifestyle. Doddy claimed he never had a holiday until he was fifty-one and that was on cut-price tickets, and had not bought a new suit for two or three years. He paid out £7 a week on his daily lager and £50 a year on wine.

On Friday, the last day of the trial's second week, the

court was told of a six-hour interview at the Inland Revenue office in Liverpool between the comedian, who was accompanied by his accountants, and solicitor, Mr David Freeman, and two tax inspectors. When the latter referred to the £336,000 Mr Dodd had hoarded in his three houses in Liverpool, the comedian told them,' I like having a lot of cash. The cash you refer to was my savings from my taxed income. I feared a civil war in this country. The whole economy was going wrong.'

Speaking of 1979 and the so-called winter of discontent before the Conservatives came to power, he added, 'I would have been taxed at 98p in the pound. Banks were collapsing and the pound was collapsing.' During the meeting, Mr Freeman made a strong plea on his behalf. 'What we wish to do is to avoid prosecution,' he said. 'All our efforts have been towards a successful conclusion on this matter without prosecution. I would ask that you recommend that there be no prosecution. We have thrown ourselves completely at your mercy. Mr Dodd has apologised not only once but two or three times today for his misunderstanding and lack of appreciation of the Revenue laws affecting the Isle of Man. I would ask that any report carries a request that this matter be settled in monetary form.'

Mr David Hartnett, head of the Revenue's inquiry branch, the second taxman at the interview, replied, 'There are a number of matters to be considered. This will involve a report to our head office.'

Mr Freeman: 'Mr Dodd is entitled, in my view, to expect sympathy and mercy from the state as some recompense for what he as done for others.'

Doddy's appearance in the witness box promised to enliven the third week. Despite the absence of showbiz stars at the trial, it was reckoned the best was yet to come. Even Wimbledon had failed to push the case off the news columns of the Fleet Street dailies. Already it was a *cause célèbre*.

There was a touch of comic irony at the resumption of the hearing on Monday, July 3, when it was revealed that the chairman of the committee which organised the cabaret in aid of the Derby Phoenix Swimming Club was a tax inspector. Mr Peter Doleman described how he was called to Mr Dodd's dressing-room together with the event treasurer, Gordon Peach. After waiting outside, they were later called in and confronted by a lady who demanded the cash. Mr Peach methodically counted out £1,550 into the palm of this lady in the presence of Mr Dodd, who was completing his changing. Mr Doleman said he made a statement to the Inland Revenue in June 1986, after hearing that the comedian was being prosecuted.

The first hint of rancour surfaced on the next day, Tuesday. A letter written to Doddy by theatrical agent Jack Oatley was read to the court by Mr George Carman, QC, defending, in which Mr Oatley said, 'Dear Ken, I am sorry that our 15-year association must end on a sour note, but I can no longer tolerate the deceit and double-dealing that has crept in over the past few months. I have given loyal and conscientious service over the years and am certainly not going to join in with the rat-race sycophants and hungry fighters who seem to have taken over.

'Over the past fifteen years, I have introduced you to many new dates which, with your ruthless disregard for the ethics of the business, you will have no trouble booking through your new agent. However, these things have a strange habit of levelling out. And knowing you are a superstitious man, I believe you will ultimately find that Friday, February 13, was not a lucky day.'

Mr Oatley, of Shelley Road, Widnes, stated in evidence that he wrote the letter because he discovered other people were also acting as the comedian's agents. 'There were dates being booked which I knew nothing about.'

Questioned by Mr Carman, the agent denied the letter was spiteful, venomous and contained a threat or a warning.

There was an unexpected development on Wednesday. Mr Justice Waterhouse told the jury, 'Unfortunately, one of your number is unwell. This is much too important a case to proceed with only 11 jurors.' When the trial was resumed on Thursday morning, Mr Carman, opening the defence case, declared, 'To the allegations that Mr Dodd has lived in a world of fantasy – a world, on occasion, of folly and a world of insecurity – we say "yes". To the allegation that this man is devious, this man is deceitful, we say "no", and we shall continue to say no. His conduct, so obviously eccentric, was to be explained not by dishonesty but by the close-knit family upbringing of which he was so much a part for most of his adult life.

'It was an upbringing which stamped on him for the rest of his life the values almost of another age: thrift, relentless hard work, close family loyalty and great charity for others. Money is not the beginning and the end of Ken Dodd, far from it.'

To the courtroom audience, the star performer of the hearing so far was undeniably Mr Carman. The QC's virtues were obvious: a commanding court presence, sharp vocal delivery, and potent cross-examination. At times, he displayed a neat theatrical flair that appealed to the audience. How he would perform in the double act with Doddy was an aspect that intrigued more than a few pressmen in the gallery.

That afternoon, came the moment the audience – particularly the press – had eagerly awaited. Doddy was summoned to the witness box. As he rose from his seat in the body of the court, he looked tense and nervous, but after taking the oath he seemed more relaxed. On his right, only a few yards away, sat the judge, and opposite was the jury. There are elements of the tragi-comic about a comedian in the dock, and on this occasion they were in abundance. The courtroom audience saw the paradoxical side, the media undoubtedly regarded the case as more tragic than comic.

Doddy proceeded to give his evidence standing upright with his hands resting on the witness box. In a firm voice he traced his happy childhood in Knotty Ash. 'I was aware when I was a child, and when I saw my father in the local coal business and admired him, that I knew that one day I would be a coalman like him. Then all of a sudden when I was twelve or fourteen something very wonderful happened.' At that moment he paused and his voice dropped. 'I found that I had been given . . . blessed with . . . a magical gift, the gift of making people laugh. It is a gift. Over the years I have tried to develop it and looked after it and shared that gift with everyone.'

Unsurprisingly, there was a queue early next morning outside Court 5–1 to hear the comedian continue his evidence. At last, it seemed, the case had gripped the public's imagination. Those fans who had laughed at Doddy's performances at the Empire in Liverpool or the Opera House in Blackpool now wondered how he would face up to the court ordeal. Would he try to be funny in the witness box?

That morning, he looked dressed for the most unusual role of his career as he climbed by lift to the fifth floor and was greeted outside the courtroom by old friends who would see his performance free of charge, as though it was a recording of one of his radio shows. He wore a grey pinstripe suit and red tie and looked neat – even his hair was in place. As the zany Ken Dodd, who brandished his tickling stick in the Palladium, he was unrecognisable, though the mole on his upper lip still stood out. As the pressmen took their seats near the witness box, Philip Sherwell of the *Daily Telegraph* remarked, 'Doddy will have to give the best performance of his career.'

Soon the audience was given a rare insight into the lifestyle of the comedian. Two television sets were pro-

vided to show a six-minute video of his house in Knotty
Ash. To the amusement of the crowded public gallery,
Doddy proceeded to give a rapid-style commentary as
different scenes appeared. The first scene was of the
exterior of the house, which was described as Georgian
and two hundred years old. The scene then switched
to dilapidated adjoining buildings which could be seen
nestling in overgrown, weed-infested gardens. Doddy
commented, 'The outbuildings are unsafe and have to be
held up by timber props.' Describing the rear of the brick-
built house, he pointed out, 'You can see the burglar
alarm box.' And almost excitedly, he added, 'There's the
lean-to kitchen built by my father in 1935.'

Fascinated, the courtroom audience eyed the screens.
They were told that three generations of Dodds had lived
in the historic house since it was bought by the comedian's
grandfather. As the camera panned over the rear of the
building, Doddy pointed out the security arrangements.
He said the house was built in either 1778 or 1789. As the
scene switched to the colourful interior, Doddy
announced, 'Here you see the Aladdin's Cave of Knotty
Ash. It is a double garage containing all sorts of props
and instruments. There's a Diddy man's body and costumes from various shows. And there is one of the great
drums of Knotty Ash together with instruments.'

If the primary aim of the video was to highlight the
comedian's eccentric lifestyle, then it succeeded admirably. Mr Carman, QC, who sat together in the body of
the court, looked as inscrutable as ever and gave no indication of what they thought of Doddy's commentary.

At that moment, Doddy gave the impression he was on
stage, so engrossed had he become in his own commentary. Afterwards, he stood in the witness box, arms
folded, waiting to be led by Mr Carman who proceeded
to ask him how he had handled fame and wealth compared with other stars of the era. 'It is a strange thing that
happens to you when you get paid a lot of money,' began

the comedian with enthusiasm. 'Some people go crazy and go in for all sorts of things and some people don't. Most entertainers suffer from fear of not getting any more work – the basis of stage fright, when you wonder what the audience will be like and whether they will like you – but the big fear that maybe next week or next year you might not get a summer season or a panto season. Show business is littered with people who have gone bankrupt.'

It seemed that his words underlined more than anything else his own basic insecurity, which was inexplicable in view of his remarkable success since the late fifties. He referred to P. J. Proby and Kathy Kirby, whose plight had been featured in a Sunday newspaper, and of Terry Thomas whom he described as a 'megastar multi-millionaire' now living in a one room flat in London suffering from Parkinson's Disease.

There was a wistful note to Doddy's voice as he went on. 'I know hundreds of people who have earned very big wages. I wanted to save my money partly because I wanted a nest egg, partly because I didn't want to go into the old folk's home, and partly because other people had things to show how they were successful, such as a Rolls-Royce, or a villa or a big house with a swimming pool. I didn't do any of these things. The one thing I wanted most in life was to be a star and get to the Palladium and prove to my family that I could be someone. It was positive proof that I was a star – to have that nest egg.'

As the comedian became emotional, Mr Justice Waterhouse cautioned him that his evidence must progress more quickly, and then ordered a short adjournment.

Doddy resumed his evidence in a more controlled voice. He confirmed that he opened his first account with the Isle of Man Bank Ltd with a deposit of £600 on December 20, 1979, and by the end of that year the total deposit was £3,000. He agreed that he opened his first Jersey account on February 22, 1980. During the year 1980 he split £256,000 between five banks in the Isle of Man and £57,000 between three banks in Jersey. Folding his arms, he looked across at the judge as he said, 'I never took a holiday before 1980. I was always too busy. I liked show business. I had a day now and again, or a week off if it was convenient.'

As a double act, the Carman-Dodd performance was working well, though on occasions the courtroom audience was amused when the comedian pre-empted the QC's questions and almost threw him off balance. Mr Carman led him skilfully, though, and next asked why he had a number of accounts overseas rather than just one.

'There was nothing secret about it,' said Doddy, growing in confidence. 'I opened so many because its an old adage, "never put all your eggs in one basket". I enjoyed going to the banks. The bank manager would say, "Oh, it's you Ken Dodd." They would bring all the staff out. I would sign autographs and they would take photographs. We would have morning coffee in the bank. Each bank had a different character and it was nice to go shopping in different banks.'

Mr Carman: 'With your appearance, your smile, your hair and your teeth, and all your television appearances, would you expect to be recognised?'

Doddy: 'One of the penalties of being a well-known person is sometimes the intruding attention the press give you, particularly in times of tragedy. One of the bonuses is to walk down the street and people say, "Hello, Doddy" and want to talk to you and strike up conversation.'

He smiled as he said this would happen every time he went on the aircraft to go to the Isle of Man or Jersey and that he would chat to people and the air hostesses and that when he went to the banks a whisper would go round. It was quite a carnival spirit.

Mr Carman asked if he had been ushered privately into offices at the banks or if efforts had been made to keep him concealed from other bank staff or customers.

Doddy: 'Quite the reverse.'

When questioned why he hadn't put the money in UK banks, the comedian replied unhesitatingly, 'My father died in 1979 and a little later I realised that the house was falling down. It was riddled with dry rot and I decided it would have to be emptied to allow workmen access. I realised I would have to move the cash savings. Around the same time I had read these adverts and I decided to put the money away. The adverts said that the interest in the Isle of Man and Jersey was tax free. I was paying 83%, the top rate of tax plus 15% on top of that. I would get £2 out of every £100 I earned in interest.'

Mr Carman: 'Did you realise that the actual law of this country was that if you lived in England but invested money abroad whatever the law of that country you still had to pay tax on the interest earned in that country?'

Doddy: 'That isn't what the adverts said. I didn't realise that.'

Mr Carman: 'Now that you know the true position, do you think you were misled by the advertisement you looked at?'

Doddy: 'Yes, I was misled. As soon as I found out that I had made a mistake I told the Revenue about every one of the bank accounts. I didn't wait for a moment – as soon as I found out I told right away.'

The third week's proceedings had ended. So far there was a feeling of predictability about the trial, which was reflected in the rather limited newspaper coverage. People in the public gallery expected perhaps more from their favourite comic. Even his one-liners lacked sparkle. Could they expect more when he was cross-examined by Mr Leveson?

Shortly before 10 a.m. on Monday, July 10, Doddy walked briskly to the witness box. Immediately he opened his briefcase and began to examine a number of documents. He looked drawn and under strain, but then it had been noticeable since the opening day that he never looked his best before lunch. By the time Mr Justice Waterhouse took his seat on the bench, the press and the public galleries were crowded. The fourth week promised to be the most eventful yet of the trial.

Anxious to demonstrate the enormous amount of charitable work undertaken by his client, Mr Carman dealt with the years 1985–86 in which he said that Mr Dodd gave his time freely to raise funds for a variety of causes, including cancer research. The comedian replied, 'I have never let a charity down nor did I ever take a penny myself. I counted it a privilege to do this work.'

In the relaxed courtroom atmosphere, Doddy sometimes coughed or sipped from a glass of water. The courtroom audience seemed amused when he was asked about the M registration Jaguar he bought and left in the garage for years.

Mr Carman: 'Was that a normal thing to do?'

Doddy: 'I'm not abnormal. I'm eccentric, yes. The most precious thing in the world is time. You cannot do 400 shows a year and go floating around in Jags.'

Eventually he was asked to take the car from the display rooms and he parked it in the backyard of his home in Knotty Ash. He preferred to use an estate model to carry his stage props around to theatre venues. An unusual note of bitterness was introduced when he was asked by Mr Carman to talk about the accounting firm of Grant Thornton. He said that some people in the firm had a 'superior air' about them which he found offensive. One member of the staff put embarrassing questions to him. 'He was always making facetious remarks and told me I would need every bus ticket if my accounts were to be handled properly. He said it was like a Chinese laundrette: No tickee, no laundry. The man I was dealing with was a cross between Brian Rix and Bertie Wooster.'

The judge, Mr Justice Waterhouse, rebuked the comedian and directed him to stick to the relevant points. He said he did not want a character sketch. But Doddy replied in a slightly arrogant air that he thought it was relevant. He said he was first introduced to Grant Thornton in 1984. 'They were not friendly,' he recalled. 'They were certainly not very patient, and they did not explain things very well to me.'

Mr Carman: 'Did you trust them?'

Doddy: 'At first, yes. But eventually I began to doubt their ability.'

Occasionally the comedian ran his fingers through his hair or folded his arms. He was attentive as Mr Carman led him on to what he described as a 'vital meeting' with his accountants Grant Thornton in 1986, when he was asked to sign statements of assets and certificates of disclosure on bank accounts which were to be passed on to the Inland Revenue.

Raising his voice, the QC added, 'I must now come to a personal matter, and it is essential that we deal with it. You and Miss Jones, who was then forty-five, had been trying to have a child? Had you both wished to have a child for years?' The comedian hung his head before he quietly replied, 'Yes.' Some people in the public gallery leaned forward at that moment to try to catch his words. Obviously the intimacy of the question took them by surprise.

Mr Carman: 'Had she been placed under a consultant with a view to taking medical techniques to improve the chances of her becoming pregnant?'

Doddy whispered: 'Yes.'

The QC went on: 'At this stage, she being forty-five years of age, was she at this very time at Hunstanton in Norfolk?'

Doddy said that Miss Jones had been with him. They had travelled down on October 2, 1986, to the Princess Theatre in the town. He was to perform two shows and then give a radio interview before travelling back to Liverpool to meet Grant Thornton to sign documents declaring his assets to the Inland Revenue.

Mr Carman: 'To increase Miss Jones' chances of becoming pregnant she had been having a course of injections, and it was necessary sexual relations should occur within 24 or 30 hours of the last injection. Was that the position that arose at Hunstanton, when you were there?'

Doddy: 'Yes.'

Mr Carman: 'Did you, Mr Dodd, after Hunstanton and that matter to do with Miss Jones, did you drive back to Liverpool yourself with Miss Jones?'

Doddy: 'I drove back all the way because she wasn't too good.'

He had driven back through the night and the seven hours' journey left him shattered. He grabbed four hours' sleep before arriving at the offices of Grant Thornton to sign the statement of his assets. Feeling under extreme pressure, he failed to study the papers and have them explained to him.

Mr Carman said that the first allegation against Mr Dodd was that he had deliberately omitted bank accounts in the Isle of Man and in Jersey.

'I did not think I had to put them on the list,' stated the comedian.

The QC said the second allegation was that his client omitted them with dishonest intent. To this Doddy quickly replied, 'No, I did not. I was not being dishonest at all. It was my life savings and money that I had already paid tax on, so I put it into the Isle of Man and Jersey.'

People in the public gallery tried to catch the comedian's words in reply to Mr Carman, who had asked him, 'Did you take the Inland Revenue investigation lightly?' Clutching his forehead and with his voice breaking with emotion, Doddy whispered, 'I have had five years during which I have not had one happy day. I've had eighteen months of torture.'

To his fans in the gallery, it was the most painful

moment of the trial. Looking at their favourite comic in such obvious distress cannot have been easy for them. It put a new slant on their concept of the comedian in the dock.

After a pause, Doddy stood upright as he told the jury he only realised he was in a 'bit of bother' after tax inspectors grinned when he gave them permission to talk to one of his banks in the Isle of Man. Then he phoned the manager to confirm that the interest was tax free. 'He said I had misunderstood and that it was not the case. I said he had given me to understand the interest was tax free and that I had also read it in adverts. He said he thought I was in a spot of bother and ought to get good advice. Within days I disclosed the details to the Inland Revenue.'

When Mr Carman asked about the unrecorded cash payments for cabaret engagements, the comedian explained that the cash was used to pay the artists and as far as he was concerned it was expenses. Organisers of these events understood this was the way he operated. He was not trying to cheat the taxman.

During the lunch break, the early editions of the *Liverpool Echo* were snapped up in the scorching city streets. Splashed across the front page was the heading, 'HEARTBREAK OF MY FIGHT TO BE A DAD', with the subheading, 'Doddy Whispers Secret Agony He Shared with Girlfriend Anne'. The revelation would come as a shock to most Liverpudlians who thought they knew most things about the comic from Knotty Ash.

At exactly 3.35 that afternoon, Mr Brian Leveson, QC, rose to begin his examination of Doddy. In a forceful voice, he said, 'You don't believe you are scatter-brained, do you Mr Dodd?'

Doddy: 'I am a comedian. I know about comedy and jokes.'

Mr Leveson: 'What you are earning, is it important to you?'

Doddy: 'In my early days as a comic it was a measurement of my success.'

Mr Leveson: 'So you had a good memory for money?'

Doddy: 'I would say not different from anyone else.'

The QC, whose mild manner was deceptive when it came to cross-examination, now concentrated on the comedian's savings and put it to him that he had made a conscious decision not to tell the Inland Revenue officials about his overseas accounts.

Doddy replied that for a long time he believed it was not their business what money he had outside the UK. When the court was then told that he went to the Isle of Man, where he picked up £181,000 in cash and returned to Liverpool with it in a briefcase, some people in the public gallery laughed at the judge's question, 'What does it look like – all this money in a briefcase?'

Doddy: 'The notes are very light, my lord.'

It was the comedian's only funny one-liner of the hearing. In subsequent gruelling cross-examination, Mr Leveson suggested that he did not record the cash payments for cabaret engagements because he wanted to hoard it, or bank it overseas. Doddy, again displaying a hint of arrogance, said it was not true. 'I regarded them as expenses,' he stated. Once, when he interrupted the judge, he was rebuked. 'Don't interrupt me, Mr Dodd,' declared Mr Justice Waterhouse, 'you're being asked about your intentions and motives.'

Chairs were provided for those people who wished to queue next morning outside Court 5-I. An hour before the trial resumed every seat was occupied. Not all of them were Doddy fans; a few, judging by their comments, were somewhat critical of his performance. None the less, as the comedian passed them on his way into the courtroom, he greeted them with a faint smile.

Mr Leveson, QC, asked him about 'family money' and expressed regret that he would have to ask some 'personal questions'. Doddy replied that his mother had given him their savings because she was afraid that Arthur Dodd would blow the money. 'My father,' he pointed out, 'was fond of a flutter on the horses.' When he was questioned about Anita Boutin, he said she could draw money out of the 'family pool' as she required it. 'Anita loved show business. She was a remarkable lady.'

In a further reply to Mr Leveson, Doddy blurted, 'Since I've been stripped naked in this court I might as well tell you the lot. Early in show business I fell in love with comedy. The only thing left open to me was to discover the secret of humour and find out how it is created. For forty years I have read every possible book on humour and the psychology of humour. I have formulated formulas for the creation of jokes and comedy and I believe I have cracked it.'

To the evident surprise of the public gallery, he revealed he kept his precious collection of joke books in a bank safety deposit box, with his OBE, and love letters. He said that a sum of £19,000 Grant Thornton could not explain came from 'gifts' made to him by his father and Miss Boutin. Anita, he reflected, did not need to spend much. She would sometimes give him her money, and his father Arthur often handed over his winnings from the racetrack. 'It was like a family pool.'

When Mr Leveson accused him of misleading the tax inspectors, Doddy replied firmly, 'I thought they were nosey. You know how they want to know everything about your lifestyle. At the time I thought, "This is no business of theirs". I had already paid tax on the money I saved.'

Mr Leveson: 'Why not say, "It has nothing to do with you"?'

Doddy: 'I don't want to be flippant, but it is like talking to the KGB . . . you just answer what they ask you. I wasn't keeping anything hidden. As far as I knew there was nothing wrong. At that time I didn't know I had made a mistake.'

The QC asked him why he had not told tax officials about £180,000 in cash hidden in two of his homes.

Doddy: 'I didn't think it had anything to do with them. I had brought my savings from the Isle of Man. It was on its way to Jersey.'

Questioned about any other assets including jewellery, he told Mr Leveson, 'I don't wear jewellery unless you mean my watch. I don't have any diamonds.'

Another question put by the Inland Revenue inspector to the comedian at one interview had been whether anyone was holding his assets in safe-keeping, and he said no. Now Mr Leveson pressed him, 'But who was living at 66 Bankfield Road, Liverpool?'

Doddy: 'My fiancée's brother, but he was not looking after assets.'

Mr Leveson: 'But what was in the house?'

Doddy: 'Just over £100,00. The cash was kept in the roof.'

Although he appeared to be standing up well to the court ordeal, there were times when the comedian looked unhappy and frustrated. Watching him bare his soul and rake up the past saddened the many Doddy fans present. They decided however to see the trial through, joining the ever bigger queue next morning outside Court 5-I.

The comedian continued to look unwell in the mornings, and today Wednesday, July 13, was no exception. As he assembled his documents in the witness box he scarcely noticed anyone around him. If Mr Carman had stolen the limelight in the early days of the hearing, it was now clear that Mr Leveson was emerging as a very skilful and astute lawyer.

When he asked the comedian why he had kept £336,000 in cash at home, he could hardly have expected the answer he got. 'I know it is old-fashioned and eccentric,' Doddy replied calmly, 'but I liked having my savings there. It proved to me I have played the Palladium, that I was someone.'

Asked by the QC if he was aware that keeping money in his attic put him at risk, he said that after once being burgled he had had alarms and steel window grilles fitted to his home in Knotty Ash.

Mr Leveson: 'The question is, where it came from and how you managed to build it up, and are these savings out of taxed income?'

Doddy: 'That is correct.'

Mr Leveson: 'That is simply not correct. You could not in that space of time have built up cash savings out of taxed income to £336,000.'

Doddy: 'Well, I did. I had saved tremendous amounts of money out of my legal earnings, my taxed earnings. It gave me a feeling of accomplishment. I had nothing else in life to prove I was successful. I had no home, children, Rolls-Royce, villa or racehorse. Only these few quid.' He said he had paid every penny in tax he had been asked for.

Questioned why he took his money to the Isle of Man in person and in small amounts, rather than transferring it by cheque, the comedian replied, 'I wanted to do it personally. Being a cautious person, if I did it in small amounts it would be rather like putting your toe in the water.'

He gave vent to his frustration in an unexpected outburst after Mr Leveson charged that he had disclosed his accounts in Jersey and the Isle of Man only because he knew the Inland Revenue had been told of them.

Doddy: 'Rubbish. I opened every one of those accounts perfectly legitimately in my own name. I told them if I had made a mistake then everything must be disclosed.'

Mr Leveson: 'The reason for all this dealing in cash is because a large part of those accounts is money on which you knew you had never paid any tax.'

Doddy: 'Untrue, Mr Leveson. That is completely

untrue. Every penny of that money is legally earned and had tax paid on it. That was my savings from my wages from forty years of very hard work. I am an honest man and I realised I had made a mistake. I have done nothing dishonest. Mistaken, maybe, not dishonest.'

The judge asked if he understood why the Inland Revenue was interested in his capital. 'If you see a man driving around in a Rolls-Royce,' he said, 'and see him in a big house and the Inland Revenue know he has been declaring £10,000 a year, do you understand they will want to know where it came from and how he managed to pay for that house?'

Doddy: 'I don't want to be facetious, but I don't have a Rolls-Royce and I don't have a big house. As far as I was concerned I was trying to be honest and had nothing to hide whatsoever.'

Mr Leveson asked him if his view was that he had paid enough money to the Inland Revenue.

Doddy: 'I have paid every penny I have been asked for. No, I have never been dishonest.

The QC ended his cross-examination saying, 'Yes, you have – that is because lots of money you have earned has never gone to the Revenue.'

Doddy retorted, 'That is completely untrue. It is wrong on the evidence you have. Every job I have ever done has been reported to the Inland Revenue.'

Sybil Anne Jones (her stage name is Sybil) arrived in court on the following morning, Thursday, dressed in a mushroom-coloured suit. Since the trial began she had been busy making copious notes and was sometimes seen to hand slips of paper to Doddy or his solicitor. In the witness box she looked a little pale and nervous. When asked about the comedian's taste in clothes, she said she bought his suits at Marks and Spencer and Debenhams. The only tailored clothes were those for his stage appearance.

Mr George Carman, QC, asked her if her lifestyle compared with that of other stars as famous as Ken Dodd. Miss Jones replied, 'To be quite honest I'm uncomfortable with people who live a very flamboyant, exquisitely dressed life. I am not that way. We don't like clubs unless we go to see a specific act. We go to the theatre occasionally. We enjoy the simple sort of life.'

The QC asked her to explain about her efforts to have Doddy's child. As he did so, the comedian sat silently in the dock, a solitary figure, almost in tears it appeared from the press gallery.

'Having Ken's baby was the most important thing in my life at that time,' Miss Jones said. 'I am now forty-eight, and for five years from 1982 I took fertility drugs in an attempt to become pregnant. But the treatment, which required we made love on specific days, had placed stress on us both. I felt probably it put more on Ken. He disliked the clinical nature of it, which reduced what was an act of love to a clinical matter. It was a requirement for the end of what we were trying to achieve.'

It was noticeable that her voice wavered as she spoke. After a slight pause, she told of a night in October, 1986, when the comedian had played Hunstanton, Norfolk, and then left at 2 am for a seven-hour drive back to Liverpool because he had an important meeting with his accountants over his Inland Revenue affairs. They made love after arriving back in Knotty Ash because 'it was the only time it would be successful with the treatment.'

The QC asked her to talk about the comedian. Miss Jones replied in a soft voice, 'In his professional life, he has always been insecure. He was too severe on himself, too critical. He never put any store on what he had achieved and was always striving for something better.'

Asked by Mr Carman if the comedian was also insecure in his personal life, she said after a long pause, 'I always felt very protective to him.' She moved in with him three years after his previous fiancée Anita Boutin died from a brain tumour in 1977. The house was overflowing with theatrical odds-and-ends. It was clean enough, but untidy.

'When he finished a season,' she recalled, 'he would bring a vanload of stuff back and that would be off-loaded into a room. That would happen every time until the room was full. Then the door would be shut and another room would be used. There were four attics, a double drawing room and an office completely full. There were masses and masses of scripts and notebooks. His father, Arthur, had been a very, very nice man but he didn't like anything being done to the house.' It had been rewired after the lighting exploded with a bang and builders spent years renewing rotting timber and plaster. She said she had to take over his finances because he was so hopeless.

It had been a busy morning for TV cameramen and press photographers as show business personalities arrived to pay tribute to Doddy. Eric Sykes was easily recognisable as the star of *The 19th Hole*, ITV's popular series, and comedian Roy Hudd, chairman of the Entertainment Artists Benevolent Fund, had a word with the waiting pressmen outside the law courts. John Fisher, a friend of Doddy's, and head of variety at Thames Television, was, he said, determined to be in court. Someone asked where were the Liverpool comics. Belatedly, the trial was taking on a showbiz dimension, even if the glamour was decidedly missing.

Long before 10am the biggest queue of the hearing waited to be admitted to Court 5-I. It was to prove another traumatic day for Doddy. As he listened to the tributes, he sat slumped in the dock with his head bowed, wiping away tears. Earlier, he had finished giving evidence after spending a total of 21 hours in the witness box over six days.

The tension was broken when Mr Carman, QC, defending, asked Eric Sykes, 'May I ask how old you are, or is that impertinent?'

The comedian, who is deaf, held his hand to his ear, paused and looked a tiny bit confused in the manner familiar to millions of his TV viewers. 'I am past my sell-by date,' he replied. 'No, I'm 66.' He told the court he had known Ken Dodd for the best part of thirty years. As he said, 'I would not say we are close. But I don't think I have ever been in a gathering of our people and not heard Doddy's name mentioned without reverence. I have seen him on stage.'

Mr Carman: 'Can we hear your judgment of his professional abilities and performances?'

Sykes: 'He is the King now. There was Tommy Cooper, Eric Morecambe . . . and Ken Dodd. He is held in high esteem. There are many jokes about Ken Dodd, but none which are derogatory. His comedy creations, such as the Diddy men and Jam Butty Mines, are simply wonderful. I have wholehearted admiration for him. I know what it takes to create these things. If happiness is the best medicine, this country owes Ken Dodd a great debt for what he has done.'

Movingly, he described going to a Doddy show at Blackpool and seeing people with tears streaming down their faces. 'I had never seen such a wonderful performance in my life. I thought: "This is the way an entertainer should be". There were people who had to leave for the last bus home, but they were not walking up the aisle. They were backing up the aisle so they would not miss anything.' After the show he visited his dressing-room and saw Dodd surrounded by forty people, the sweat falling off him. He had allowed all these people in. To me, he is the greatest contributor to comedy in this country. I volunteered to come up here. I thought it was the least I could do to pay my homage.'

As Doddy, head bowed, wiped the tears from his eyes, Miss Jones sometimes glanced anxiously in his direction.

By now the trial was no longer a tragi-comedy; it had clearly sunk to the realms of pure tragedy. One of the greatest stand-up comics of his generation looked an anguished and helpless figure. At that moment a few of the comedian's most faithful fans in the public gallery had tears in their eyes.

Roy Hudd described the comedian as one of the most admired in the country. 'As a professional entertainer Ken Dodd is an eccentric and a terrible time-keeper who always arrives late for shows. The obsession of his life is the perfection of his art as a comic. And he has always been a great supporter of Cinderella charities.'

John Fisher, who produced some of Doddy's television series, counted himself a friend. Now he told the crowded court, 'In my opinion, he is the greatest stand-up comedian in my lifetime. He may well be the greatest stand-up comedian this country has produced. Such comedians are the loneliest men in the world. It is the hardest sphere of comedy to conquer. That Mr Dodd has done.'

On Doddy as a man, he said, 'He has provided me with great moral support. My wife was in hospital with cancer. I still treasure a 10-page letter that he wrote to me which got me through the blackest moment of my life. He is the most life-enhancing personality I have ever met in show business.'

The tributes continued next day. Critic Michael Billington, who, in the seventies, had made a special study of Doddy's comic art, now told the court, 'He is a comic genius with a superabundance of energy on stage and an exuberant joy at performing. He is completely a man of the theatre. But he can also be unpunctual. He always ran into jams of appointments and his life was often very hectic and frenetic. He once told me that he often went on stage to get a rest.'

As the fourth week of the trial concluded it was obvious that Liverpudlians were divided on the possible outcome. In the bars and hotels it remained a popular topic for discussion and it was accepted that the lawyers on both sides had argued their cases vigorously to the jury. Doddy's loyal fans appeared more hopeful now than at any stage of the hearing. Everyone awaited the verdict in the city's most celebrated trial for years. It was expected within days.

Plainly there was not enough room in court on Monday morning, July 17 to accommodate all the people who wanted to be present for the drama of the closing stages. By the time Mr Leveson, QC, rose to begin his summing up for the prosecution not an empty seat was available in either the public or press gallery. This, the fifth week of the trial, was regarded as decision week.

In a smooth, authoritative voice, Mr Leveson said, 'If this trial was about Mr Dodd's rating as a comedian and entertainer it would not have lasted very long. My words about four weeks ago were that Mr Dodd is one of the great entertainers of our generation. If this trial had been about the extent of his charitable activities it would not have lasted very long. I described them as undoubted. If it had been about his love of the theatre, the assistance he has given to younger artists or his relations with his fellowmen, it would have been over very quickly.'

Doddy sat listening, his head on one side and his hands crossed over his chest. Wearing the same grey suit and the same red and blue tie he had worn throughout the hearing, he directed his gaze at either Mr Justice Waterhouse or at his notes in front of him. At times, he appeared anxious.

He listened attentively as Mr Leveson continued: 'What you the jury are concerned with are not the issues I outlined but whether Mr Dodd had a very different attitude towards a very different institution which affects us all, the Inland Revenue. The trial is about Mr Dodd's honesty and in particular the false, deliberately false, answers that he gave over the years to his accountants and the Inland Revenue.'

The court had heard how Mr Dodd hid £336,000 in cash around three homes at one time. He later made 'cash and carry' flights to the Isle of Man and Jersey to deposit money in twenty accounts without telling the taxman. Mr Leveson said undeclared income or unclaimed expenses both produced cash which was not in the books. Even assuming a very low level of expenses put forward by one of Mr Dodd's accountants, the sum came close to £250,000 before any allocations. He considered that Mr Dodd's behaviour had been devious and deceitful throughout his dealings with the Inland Revenue, and he now told the jury, 'Irrespective of your view of Mr Dodd as an enter-tainer or supporter of charity, on this account your verdict can only be guilty.'

The main interest for the courtroom audience on the next day, Tuesday, was in Mr Carman's closing address to the jury. A number of people had failed to gain admit-tance to the public gallery. Every press seat was occupied before 10 a.m. The QC was in forceful mood as he accused the Inland Revenue of failing to produce a key witness, Mr Reg Hunter, who was Mr Dodd's accountant from 1972 to 1982.

He was the one man, the QC said, who might have helped to throw light on the case, yet he was never called. He argued this was because he might put at risk a pros-ecution where the stakes were high. The idea that Mr Hunter could not help was nonsense. It was an affront to commonsense and an insult to the jury. Hunter had ple-aded guilty to eleven charges of false accounting at Mold Crown Court, north Wales, and the 'disgraceful way' he kept the accounts was the reason Mr Dodd was now in a mess.

'Can you not see the frustration we feel for the defence that this prosecution has brought?' Mr Carman asked the jury, turning round once more to face them directly. 'Mr

Dodd is accused of false accounting and they do not interview the accountant who himself had behaved falsely.
Does this appeal to your sense of fair play?'

The QC paused and switched his gaze towards the
judge as he said sharply, 'It is a disgraceful avoidance of
the truth. One thing we have learned from this trial is that
comedians are not chartered accountants but sometimes
chartered accountants are comedians.'

Mr Carman's remark amused members of the public,
but Doddy remained tight-lipped. The longer the trial
went on, the deeper his involvement became, as though
he was playing Malvolio all over again.

Mr Carman said it was the jury's job to draw up Mr
Dodd's balance sheet, in which the asset of goodwill was
immeasurable. 'The prosecution say he is some sort of
miser or Scrooge, but the flaw in that attack is that Scrooge
was a man with no friends, no laughter, a man who
suffered from a meanness of spirit. In the case of Ken
Dodd, you have a man of most generous free spirit.'

He went on to accuse the Inland Revenue of 'moving
the goalposts' during the hearing by switching the evidence from a question of cash received to inflated
expenses. This would have involved the comedian being
paid for public performances in cash on hundreds of
occasions by reputable clubs and promoters. The Inland
Revenue had failed to produce any evidence that this
practice had happened up to 1980, even though they had
investigated the books of companies such as Apollo and
Mecca. 'They did their homework and they checked up,'
stressed the small bespectacled QC. 'The answer was a
raspberry. Were all these clubs breaking the law? Was
it all some giant Diddyland conspiracy? What a load of
nonsense, what a load of rubbish.'

He contended that while most criminals did not leave
'visiting cards', Mr Dodd deposited money in the Isle of
Man and Jersey under his own name and in person. Mr
Carman also claimed that the prosecution had been hasty

to dismiss the relevance of evidence from Mr Dodd's fellow comedians, Roy Hudd and Eric Sykes. Their testimonies of his support for 'Cinderella charities' were not designed to excite sympathy, but to reveal the true nature of the man.'

Mr Dodd, he said, was a man of strange and eccentric behaviour with a considerable mistrust of people he did not know. The paradox was that on stage he was the most outgoing, fun-loving creator of happiness in the country. 'But inwardly, privately do you not think that he is a reserved and insecure person?'

It was regarded as a telling closing speech by Mr Carman, who must have managed to plant considerable seeds of doubt in the Liverpool jurors' minds, particularly on the vital question of Doddy's expenses from gigs or one-night performances. The QC had rarely examined his own copious legal notes written out in an immaculate copperplate hand, and he had used his formidable wit and the experience of thirty-five years to demolish, it appeared, a few key aspects of the Inland Revenue case.

At this point in the trial, a number of the more experienced pressmen, including Philip Sherwell, expressed the view that Doddy stood a good chance of escaping a jail sentence. Much would now depend on the judge's summing up to the jury. This began on Tuesday afternoon when Mr Justice Waterhouse said it was for the prosecution to prove that the comedian had deliberately acted dishonestly.

Next morning the courtroom was again packed with members of the public, some of whom started queueing before the court buildings opened. Many were unable to get in when the hearing started and formed a queue in the lobby area outside the courtroom. Doddy sat looking towards the judge or making occasional notes. Sybil Anne Jones, who had not missed a day of the trial, was also preparing to make notes.

The red-robed judge described the comedian as 'as star who has stayed at the top'. All the witnesses agreed, he said, that the defendant was a very hard-working man and a dedicated performer. It was obviously necessary for the jury to discuss the role of Mr Dodd's former accountant, Reginald Hunter, and here he mentioned the strong attack made by Mr Carman on the prosecution for failing to call Mr Hunter to give evidence.

'You will give appropriate weight, according to your assessment, to that comment,' said the judge, directing his words to the jurors seated on his right.

On Thursday, Doddy arrived at Court 5-I still wearing a grey suit while Miss Jones wore an orange blouse and floral skirt. There was by now a noticeable increase in the squads of photographers and camera crews in the square outside the court buildings. Inside the court, Inland Revenue officials involved in the two year inquiry sipped water and prepared for a long sitting. There were thirty reporters present.

In a clear voice, Mr Justice Waterhouse referred to the false accountancy charges, and told the jury, 'I am sure you will record what was said by the prosecution.' The court heard that Doddy would take a cheque – which went through the books – and also cash payment which was not recorded. The judge said the prosecution agreed that 'no doubt' some cash was paid to assistants and for equipment – but not on the scale alleged by the defence witnesses.

'The prosecution alleged that the defendant was involved in personal bargaining in arranging the fee and mode of payment,' he added. 'They say that it is remarkable that no proper record was kept of who helped. But the defence claim the cash payments were to cover expenses incurred on the gigs.'

Turning his head to the jury, Mr Waterhouse said, 'Remember that the essence of these charges, as indeed of all the counts before you, is the allegation of deliberate dishonesty on the part of the defendant. You must be sure that all the ingredients of each separate count are proved before you can convict on that count. If you are left in any little doubt about an essential ingredient of the count you are considering, then it is your duty to acquit the defendant on that count.' He said that he would give the jury a separate direction if the question of majority verdicts arose.

'You should try to reach a unanimous verdict in respect of each of these counts,' he told the jurors. 'It is important that you should not feel under any stress or pressure.'

He had just completed more than ten hours of summing up the evidence.' he said. 'I am afraid it has taken considerable time.' He had examined it in remarkable depth and clarity, leaving the jury in no doubt about the nature of the charges against the defendant.

In the dock, Doddy looked weary, his bright-blue eyes were dull and hooded, and even his bushy hair, so long a hallmark of his stage performances, was flat. The indignity of constant revelations about his private life showed on his drawn face. For days and days he had not smiled. Already the court ordeal had taken its toll. At times, he appeared older than his sixty-one years, and he knew the biggest moment in the courtroom drama was still to come.

The jury had been sent out to consider its verdicts. In the square outside, a large crowd waited to see the comic emerge and to hear him say, 'Hello Mrs tattifilarious. How are you diddling?'

Women laughed. It was a brief reminder of the old, irrepressible Doddy, the people's comedian, the hero of the working classes in Liverpool and Blackpool. And at Walton prison someone scrubbed off the graffiti where some wag had announced: 'Appearing here soon, Ken Dodd.'

For Doddy fans, it wasn't funny.

EPILOGUE

The Jury's Verdict

Only one question occupied the minds of most Merseysiders that Friday, July 21, and it was: 'Doddy – guilty or not guilty?'

Everywhere, in shops, offices, bars and hotels, they discussed the comedian's plight. The great majority of Liverpudlians would miss, of course, the final emotive courtroom scene and the jury's verdict. They saw Doddy as a sad and vulnerable figure who had already gone through hell; in Knotty Ash, though, they reckoned he was more durable and resilient than he was given credit for and there was no way they could see him going under in the final drama.

While he remained centre stage, a solitary figure in the dock, the one individual everyone saw as his saviour was Blackpool-born Mr George Carman, who through the lengthy trial had never allowed his eloquence to run away with him, and whose record as a defence barrister was impressive. In 1979, he saw former Liberal leader Jeremy Thorpe cleared on conspiracy to murder, and he successfully defended Dr Leonard Arthur, the paediatrician charged with murder after he prescribed 'nursing care only' for a Downs syndrome baby. He acted for Peter Adamson, the Coronation Street actor, when he was acquitted of indecent assault on two young girls. The QC's instinct for engaging the jury's sympathy, together with his northern roots, had made him an obvious champion of Ken Dodd.

Those who had followed his superb 45-minute opening speech, and his well argued closing speech to the jury, now believed his powerful pleas might yet save the comedian from the ultimate indignity of going to prison, a prospect which appalled Doddy from the very beginning of the trial. Court 5–1, a low ceilinged room, walled in light ash and hessian and carpeted in deep green, was crowded to hear the verdict. Before he entered the courtroom, Doddy smiled faintly as he received a kiss on the cheek from Sybil Anne Jones, then he walked quickly to take his place in the dock where he began to put his plastic pens and notebooks in front of him. He looked expressionless. The jury had stayed overnight in a Liverpool hotel to consider their verdicts.

The first of these came at 11.45 when the comedian was cleared of five charges, including four alleging false accounting over the way he was paid for one-off gigs. The verdicts meant the jury accepted his explanation about the way he was paid for one night performances at two hotels and a restaurant. Doddy had remained motionless as the court clerk asked the foreman whether the jury had reached an unanimous verdict on each of the counts on the indictment. He replied firmly, 'No.' He was then asked if he had reached in unanimous verdict on any of the counts and he replied, 'All counts bar one, two and seven.'

The jury retired to consider the remaining counts. The comedian's fans in the public gallery appeared more hopeful than before, but their ordeal was not over. Outside in the square, the crowds had swelled, with everyone waiting for the answer to the question, 'Doddy – guilty or not guilty?' It was the only thing that mattered to them. Agency reporters hurried to the pressroom in the court buildings to file their stories; others hung around the lobby on the fifth floor for fear of losing their seats in the packed press gallery. Everywhere there was an air of bustle as well as tension.

At 1.30 the court re-assembled. As Doddy sat in the dock he placed a green pencil on the ledge in front of him and balanced a pen across it. His hands shook but he concentrated on nudging the pen until it lay still. Then his right hand dived into his grey jacket pocket to produce two small jewellery boxes, thought to contain his OBE and the engagement ring belonging to his late fiancée Anita Boutin. But there was no time to open them as the jury filed in, led by the white-haired foreman. Doddy appeared to grow more nervous, as though suddenly aware that his life was at stake.

The jury had been deliberating for nine hours and six minutes in all. As the court waited for the foreman to speak, Doddy stood erect, gripped the rails of the dock and stared impassively at the floor. In a firm voice, the foreman said, 'Not guilty.' The comedian did not flinch. It seemed every eye in the public gallery was directed at him.

'Not guilty', the foreman repeated, and sighs of relief could be heard among the public.

There was a pause. The words 'Not guilty' were repeated once more.

From a position in the press gallery the comedian seemed to tremble and cast his eyes to the ceiling. Supporters clapped and cheered and leapt to their feet. In a daze, Doddy embraced his solicitor. He was in tears. The prison officer who stood behind him gave him a reassuring pat on the shoulder. He looked disoriented and his hands shook as he replaced the boxes in his pocket, the notebooks in the briefcase. Turning to the jury, he said, 'Thank you.'

In the public gallery they were trying to revive Sybil Anne Jones with water. She had collapsed after hearing the verdict and wept uncontrollably. At that moment, Doddy appeared to break down in the dock, struggling again to hold tears back. He repeatedly put his left hand to his mouth or eyes. Then, he stepped shakily from the dock and was congratulated by some of the public. It was taking a while for him to realise he had been cleared of all the charges, that he could walk free from the dock.

In the packed pressroom reporters were busy catching deadlines; a few were feverishly working on 'colour' stories of the dramatic climax to the trial. Stephen Guy, an agency man who had been there since day one, was filing his story. 'Comedian Ken Dodd came through the biggest crisis of his life today displaying emotions suitably summed up by two of his song hits – *Tears* and *Happiness*,' Guy began. 'The whacky Squire of Knotty Ash was at last able to don his clown's mask again after a 23-day courtroom ordeal with his being cleared of cheating the taxman.'

By now Doddy was being swept along in the excitement. He piled into the lift and arrived on the ground floor to be met by more well-wishers and friends. The familiar toothy smile broke through. He was happy again, even if at times he looked somewhat bewildered. Outside, in the sunshine, hundreds of people thronged the square, waiting to greet him. All that mattered to these men and women of his own generation was that Doddy was free. Rene Geddes, one of the elderly fans who queued for a seat in court every day, said, 'He's a splendid man, he's been a bit silly with the tax people, but he was always there when someone needed him for charity work. And let's face it, all he has ever done in his life is to make people laugh, make them happy. He can't be that bad, can he?'

Standing on the step of the court buildings, Doddy greeted the crowd. 'Thank God it's all over,' he told them, 'and thank you all the thousands of people in Liverpool and Merseyside and from all over the country who said prayers for me and sent me their good wishes.' Brushing his hands through his hair in typical Doddy-style, he added, 'All I want to do now is to put it all behind me and get back to work. Does anybody know where I can get a drink tonight?'

Someone produced a bottle of champagne. The crush outside the court was now so great that the comedian was pushed back inside the foyer before a phalanx of policemen cleared a space for him to talk to the crowd again. Sipping champagne from a paper cup handed to him, he added, 'We will be having a big celebration show for Merseyside charities in Liverpool.' He thanked his fiancée for her support, and gave a special thank you to his counsel, Mr George Carman. The silver-haired barrister stood beside him now, beaming.

Doddy made a calming gesture with his hands and everyone became quieter. It was the old performer putting the audience under his spell. He toasted them with champagne before being hustled by police to his waiting car and driven away. An exhausted Miss Jones sat in the seat beside him.

In a more relaxed interview for television that evening, Doddy said, 'When your life is at stake – that's what was at stake – I don't think if anything had gone terribly wrong I could have appeared in public again. I had to try to prove my honesty. I had to say, "All right, so I'm a human, but I'm not dishonest." I never tried to be dishonest.'

However, the biggest enigma remained unanswered. Why had the case proceeded at all? The Inland Revenue claimed that they would not have pursued him after June 1984 if he had revealed all the information about his bank accounts. The *Guardian* saw a possible parallel with Britain's last great show business trial, almost a century ago. Then, Oscar Wilde decided against the advice of many, to prosecute the Marquess of Queensberry for calling him names.

Perhaps like playwright Wilde, the comedian was determined to take on the Establishment. Did he, like Wilde, find irresistible the prospect of putting his enemies to flight in open court, the 'grandest theatre of all'? Kenneth Arthur Dodd is known to be an independent spirit, the champion of small men, innately suspicious of Establishment figures or institutions, a workaholic who has earned his money the hard way. The Inland Revenue took on the wrong man if they wanted to show other entertainers what they could expect.

The Revenue defended its decision to prosecute the comic. It was policy to 'prosecute people when, after they have made what they said was a full disclosure, it appears that they have in fact concealed further income and assets.' The spokesman added, 'It was only after extensive inquiries had been made that Mr Dodd had signed certificates of full disclosure, that he revealed his bank accounts in the Isle of Man and Jersey. These contained substantial sums of money. There had been a large scale loss of tax. The decision of the Board of Inland Revenue to prosecute was consistent with its policy on false certificates of full disclosure.'

To Doddy, the staggering cost of the trial meant little compared with proving his own innocence. A substantial amount of the £2 million bill he faced was an estimated £825,000 – the tax he promised to pay whatever the trial's outcome. Before his trial began, he paid the Inland Revenue £450,000. A further £375,000 was lodged in tax certificates and bonds pending the resolution of his total tax liability. The comedian's solicitor, Mr John Carden therefore claimed that his client had no outstanding tax to pay.

'When Ken Dodd found out he owed tax back in April last year he paid every penny in full,' said Mr Carden. 'As far as he knows he has at this moment no outstanding tax due.'

Among the other bills to be met were: an estimated £250,000 for defence counsel Mr Carman and his junior, plus two years' work by solicitors and 'expert witness' accountant and and enquiry agents; £51,000 for two previous solicitors; £54,000 for accounting firm Grant Thornton, and £25,000 for Arthur Young, the accountants who compiled a second report after the first was shown to be incomplete.

Doddy's known assets included his two homes in Knotty Ash, estimated to be worth £300,000, and an empty farmhouse in Shropshire said to be worth over £200,000. According to the evidence he possessed £600,000 in shares and building society accounts.

As Mr Justice Waterhouse made no order as to costs, both sides paid their own.

Although he had retained his freedom, it was reckoned that the trial had left the comedian a poorer man. And the legal process mercilessly laid bare his personal life and private feelings. Was it worth it? There are many Liverpudlians who feel the comedian should never have gone to court. Nothing compensated in their minds for Doddy being 'stripped naked' before the world.

The trial attracted enormous media attention. It was screened on European TV networks and newspapers carried lengthy reports. The *Guardian* thought it important enough to editorialise, and under the heading 'Tickled, or troubled?' observed:

> The verdict, in a sense, wraps things up. The taxmen were right to bring the case. The jury heard the evidence, and decided. End.
>
> Money was the heart and also the bemusement of the Dodd case. It was what it was all about. It was also beside the point. Had anyone suggested that the missing millions were financing three lush mansions in Guatemala, with hot and cold running Tiller Girls *en suite*, then the jury might have pricked up their ears. But not all. The ten pound notes were just bits of paper – dumped in cupboards, under beds, in

redundant off-short accounts where inflation simply
washed chunks of them into the sea year by year.
There was no rational point to the exercise . . .
  There are conclusions. Funny men after often funny
chaps. Taxes are there to be paid. But perhaps the
one with a little more resonance is the thought that
there's nowt so queer as folks . . .

'All I want to do now is to put it all behind me and get
back to work,' mused a relieved Doddy. As always, work
was as important to him as the music of laughter. He
never tired of telling friends, 'I've been blessed with the
gift to make people laugh'. He admitted he had missed
his work during the long trial. Yet it wasn't all gloom.
  The trial had increased his love for Sybil. Going back
together each evening to Knotty Ash had helped him to
keep sane during the worst moments. Doddy felt he
needed her more than ever before, not only because she
constantly reminded him of the tablets he must take for
his bronchitis and emphysema, but also as a lover and
stage entertainer. It would have been unbearable in court
without her support. It had helped him to cope. Now he
was aware that people were asking if he would marry
Sybil. It was inevitable after the publicity focused on them
during the trial. Although they were in love for nine
years, he had not given her an engagement ring. None
the less, he didn't rule out marriage at some future date.
It was a private matter between them and he refused to
talk in detail about the relationship.
  At times, Sybil worried about his health. It had come
as a shock to them both to learn from the medical special-
ists about his unusual heart beat, which indicated a heart
defect. He admitted there were times in the dock when
he found it hard to draw his breath due to his chronic
bronchitis. At other times, he feared that his health would
give out on him.
  Although tickled at being cleared, he wanted to put the

'terrible memory' of the trial behind him. He was grateful that it had shown his *real* friends and he was amazed at the number he could count on. He wasn't a criminal. As Squire of Knotty Ash he had nothing to hide. If they were alive, he knew his parents would be proud of the way he fought to clear his name. He sought stage success to please them in the first place.

Everyone in Knotty Ash expected Doddy and his fiancée to holiday abroad after their ordeal. Instead, they decided to stay. As the comedian said, 'This is where I'm happiest.' And on the Sunday after the court hearing he took his usual seat in church and thanked his friends for their prayers. In a brief address to the 200-strong congregation, he said solemnly, 'I would just like to say thank you for all your prayers. As you see, 'I'm still here. God bless you all.'

He had earlier sat with his head bowed as Miss Jones gave a solo rendition of a song about God's support during 'trials and tribulations' of life. Afterwards, Doddy chatted and joked with children during the annual Sunday School service at St. John and Evangelist, where he once sang as a schoolboy.

Turning to the comedian and Miss Jones, the Rev Michael Rooke, vicar of St. John's said, 'We are delighted that you are here. We are so joyful that the lord has lifted up his son of Knotty Ash.'

In the air of serenity in the churchyard the court nightmare seemed far away for Doddy. As he mingled with friends, he knew nothing had changed. Home for him was Knotty Ash. Neither fame nor riches could alter that.

It was the way he wanted it to be.